CLUMSY

A NOVEL

BY JEFFREY BROWN

For everyone who has ever
loved and lost.

THANKS TO: CHRIS WARE FOR GETTING
ME STARTED, MIKE AND CHRISTINE,
DANIEL FOR EVERYTHING, JAMES KOCHALKA
FOR HIS SUPPORT, THERESA FOR HAVING
LOVED ME, MY FAMILY AND FRIENDS,
AND TO PAUL HORNSCHEMEIER FOR
HIS ENDLESS HELP AND UNEXPECTED
FRIENDSHIP.

PUBLISHED BY
TOP SHELF PRODUCTIONS
PO BOX 1282
MARIETTA GA 30061-1282
www.topshelfcomix.com

4th printing

PRINTED IN CANADA.

CLUMSY

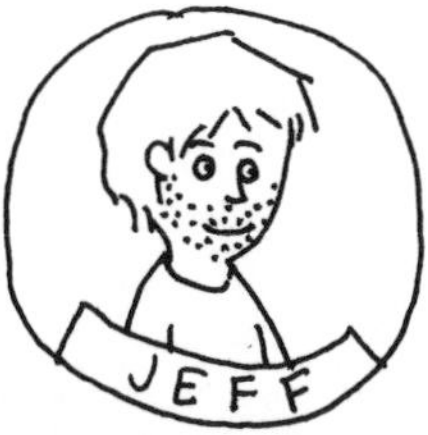
JEFF

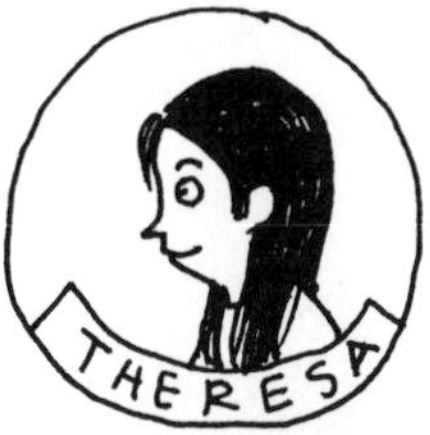
THERESA

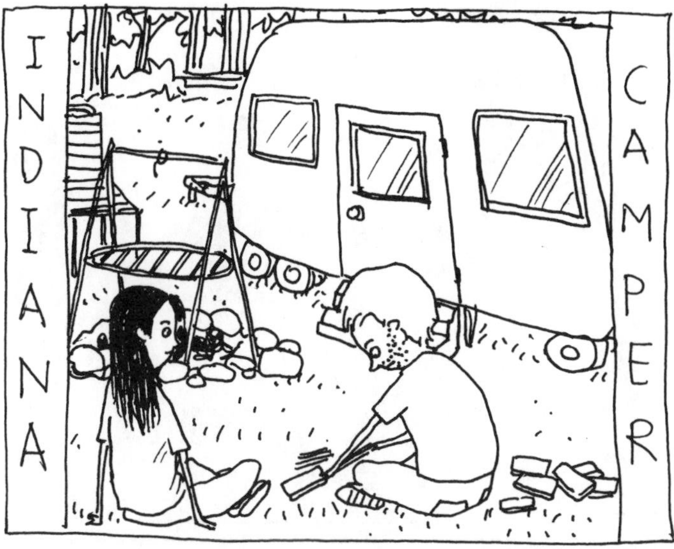
INDIANA
CAMPER

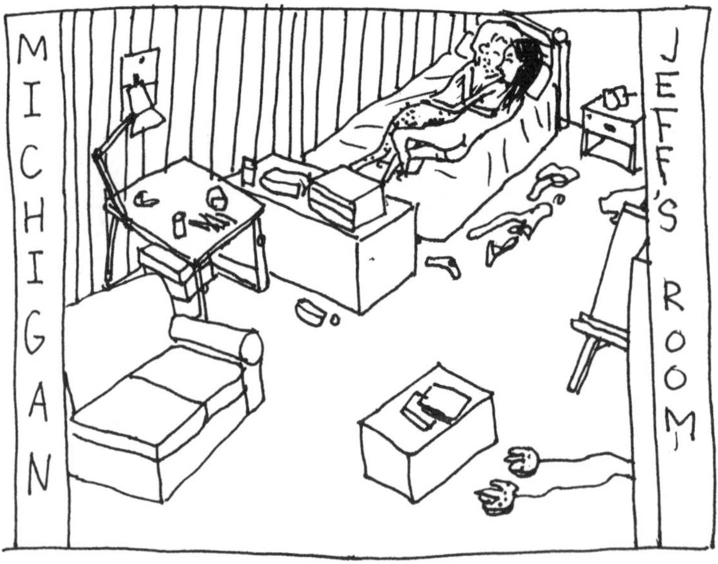
MICHIGAN
JEFF'S ROOM

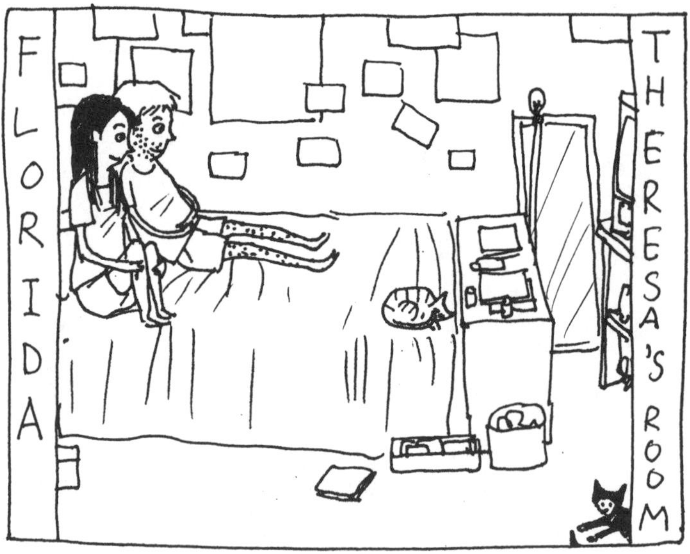
FLORIDA
THERESA'S ROOM

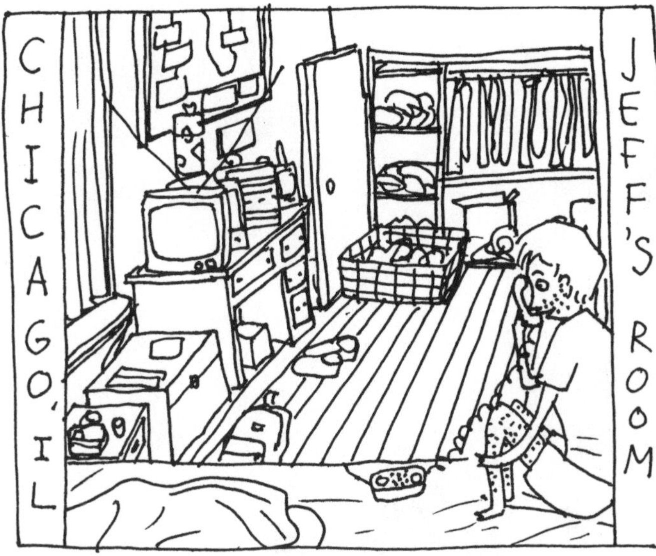
CHICAGO, IL
JEFF'S ROOM

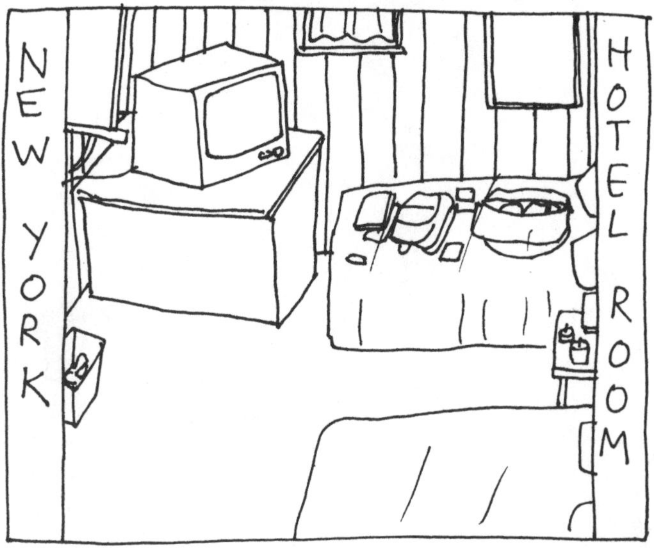
NEW YORK
HOTEL ROOM

MY FIRST NIGHT WITH THERESA

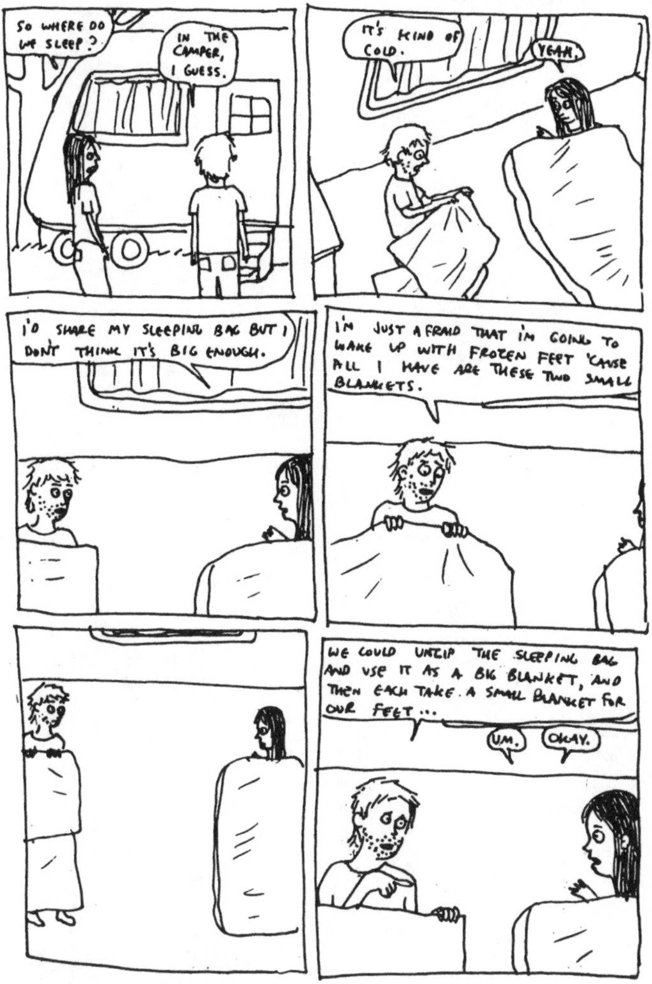
SO WHERE DO WE SLEEP?
IN THE CAMPER, I GUESS.
IT'S KIND OF COLD.
YEAH.
I'D SHARE MY SLEEPING BAG BUT I DON'T THINK IT'S BIG ENOUGH.
I'M JUST AFRAID THAT I'M GOING TO WAKE UP WITH FROZEN FEET 'CAUSE ALL I HAVE ARE THESE TWO SMALL BLANKETS.
WE COULD UNZIP THE SLEEPING BAG AND USE IT AS A BIG BLANKET, AND THEN EACH TAKE A SMALL BLANKET FOR OUR FEET...
UM.
OKAY.

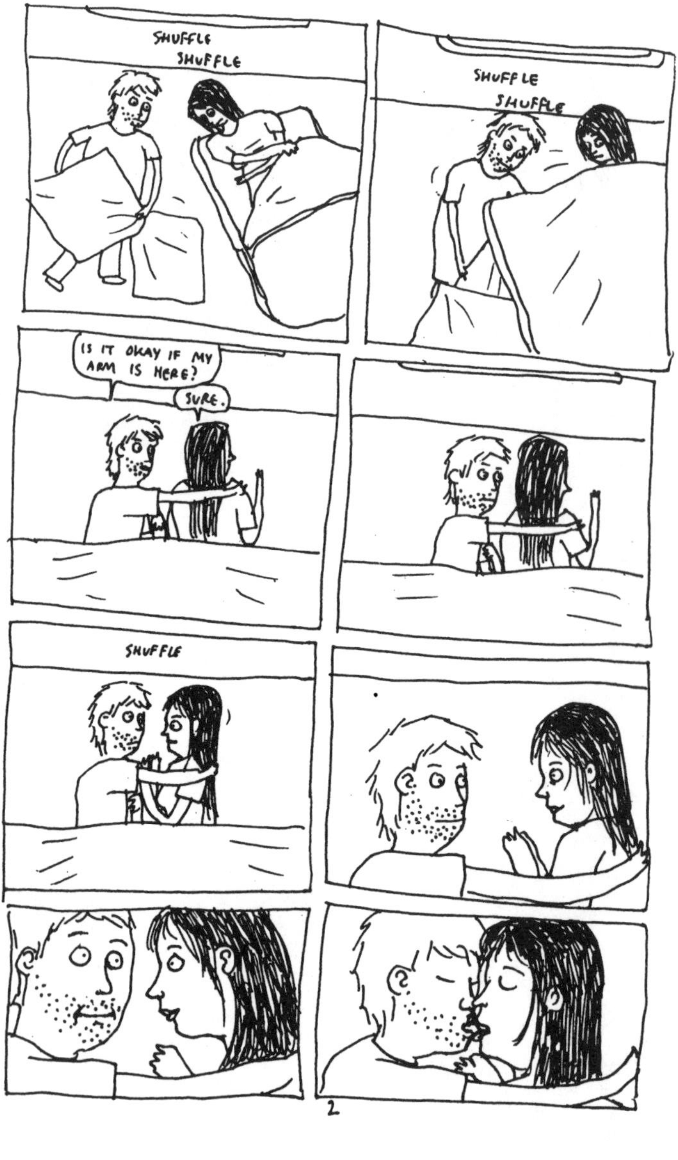
SHUFFLE
SHUFFLE
SHUFFLE
SHUFFLE
IS IT OKAY IF MY ARM IS HERE?
SURE.
SHUFFLE

MY LAST NIGHT WITH KRISTYN

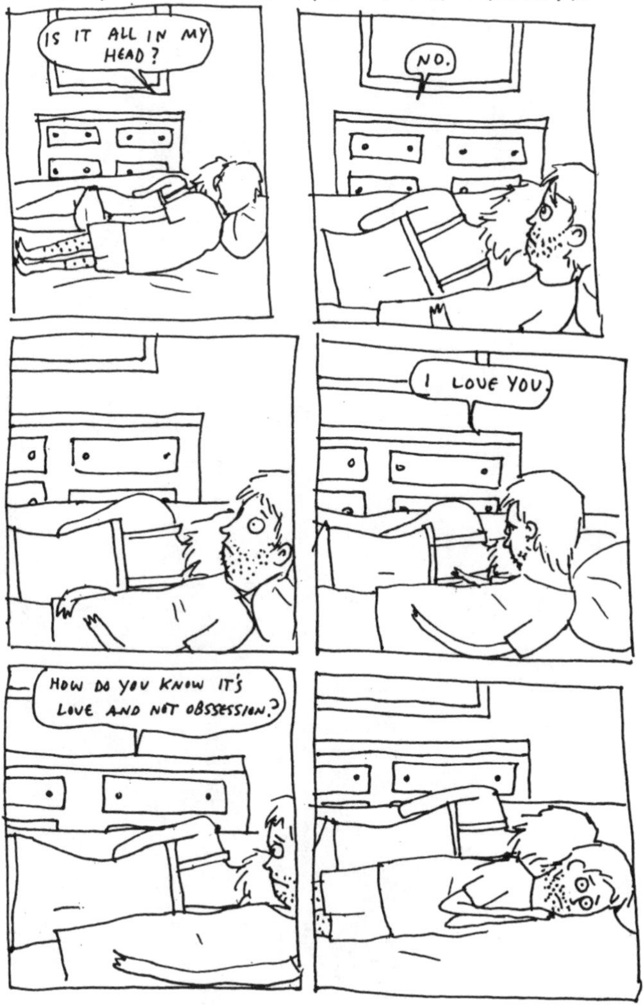
IS IT ALL IN MY HEAD?
NO.
I LOVE YOU.
HOW DO YOU KNOW IT'S LOVE AND NOT OBSSESSION?

MY DAY AT THE BEACH

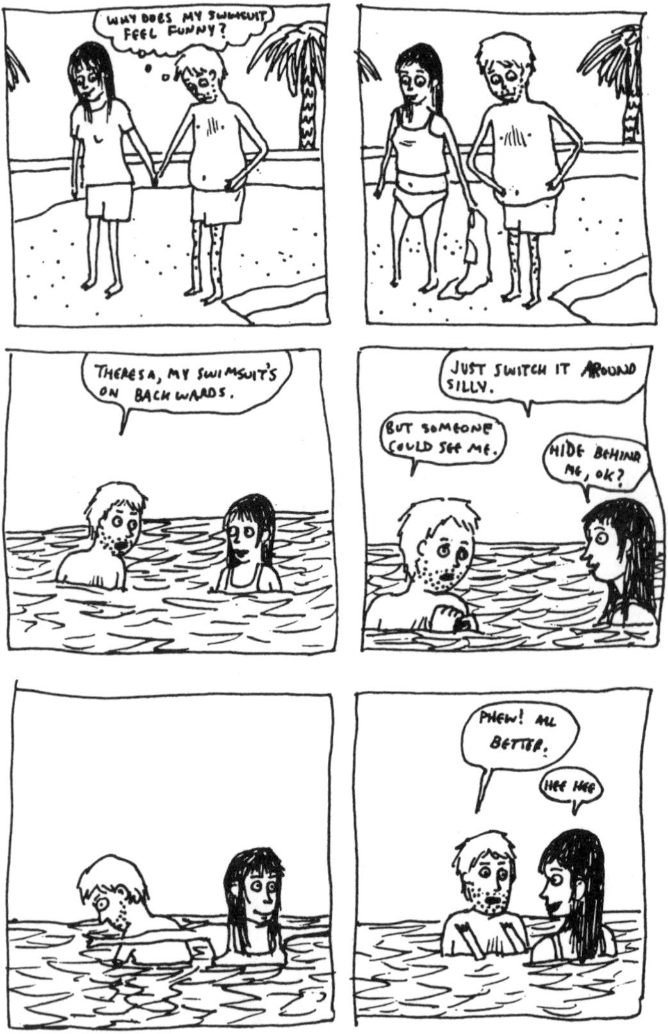
WHY DOES MY SWIMSUIT FEEL FUNNY?
THERESA, MY SWIMSUIT'S ON BACKWARDS.
JUST SWITCH IT AROUND SILLY.
BUT SOMEONE COULD SEE ME.
HIDE BEHIND ME, OK?
PHEW! ALL BETTER.
HEE HEE

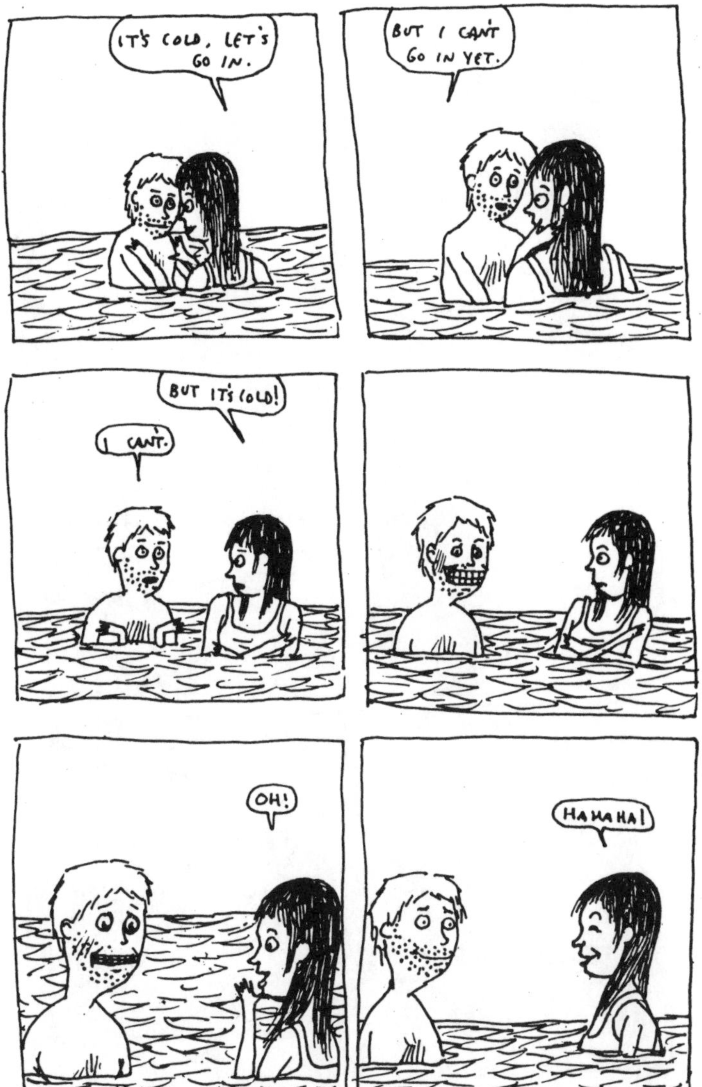
IT'S COLD, LET'S GO IN.
BUT I CAN'T GO IN YET.
BUT IT'S COLD!
I CAN'T.
OH!
HAHAHA!

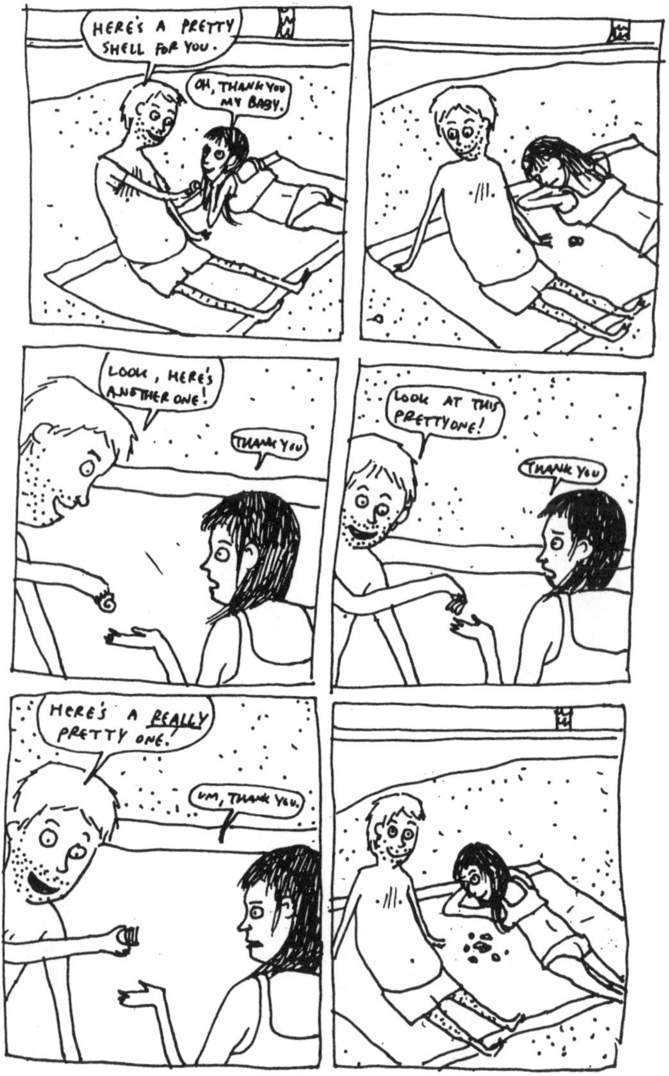
HERE'S A PRETTY SHELL FOR YOU.
OH, THANK YOU MY BABY.
LOOK, HERE'S ANOTHER ONE!
THANK YOU
LOOK AT THIS PRETTY ONE!
THANK YOU
HERE'S A REALLY PRETTY ONE.
UM, THANK YOU.

I DRAW HER NAKED

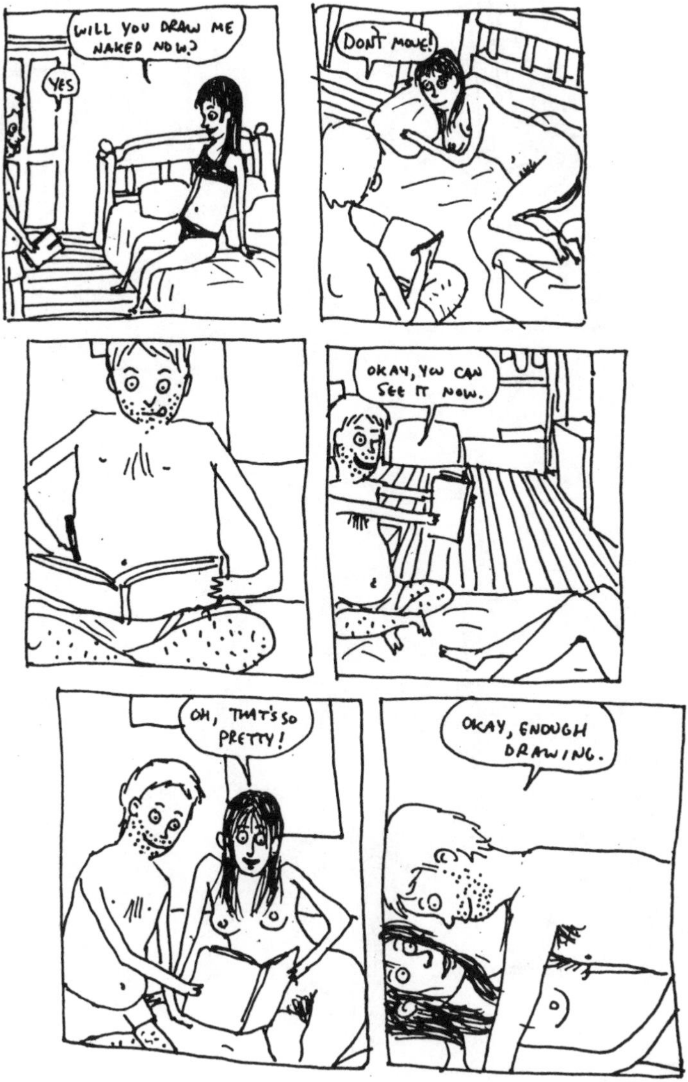
WILL YOU DRAW ME NAKED NOW?
YES
DON'T MOVE!
OKAY, YOU CAN SEE IT NOW.
OH, THAT'S SO PRETTY!
OKAY, ENOUGH DRAWING.

WAITING FOR HER TO CALL

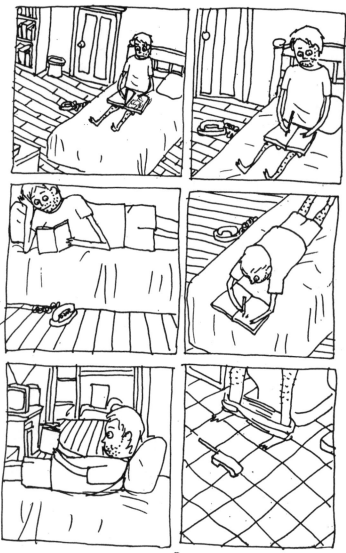

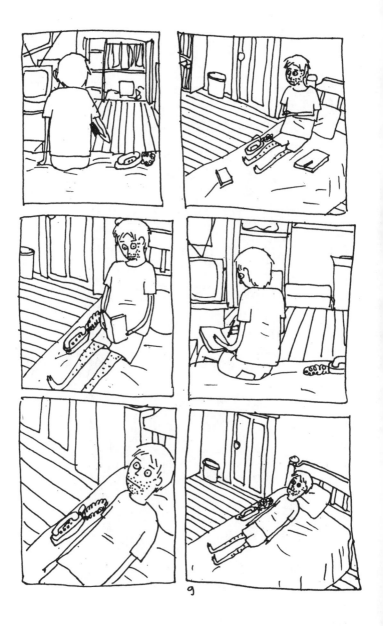

DO YOU LOVE ME?

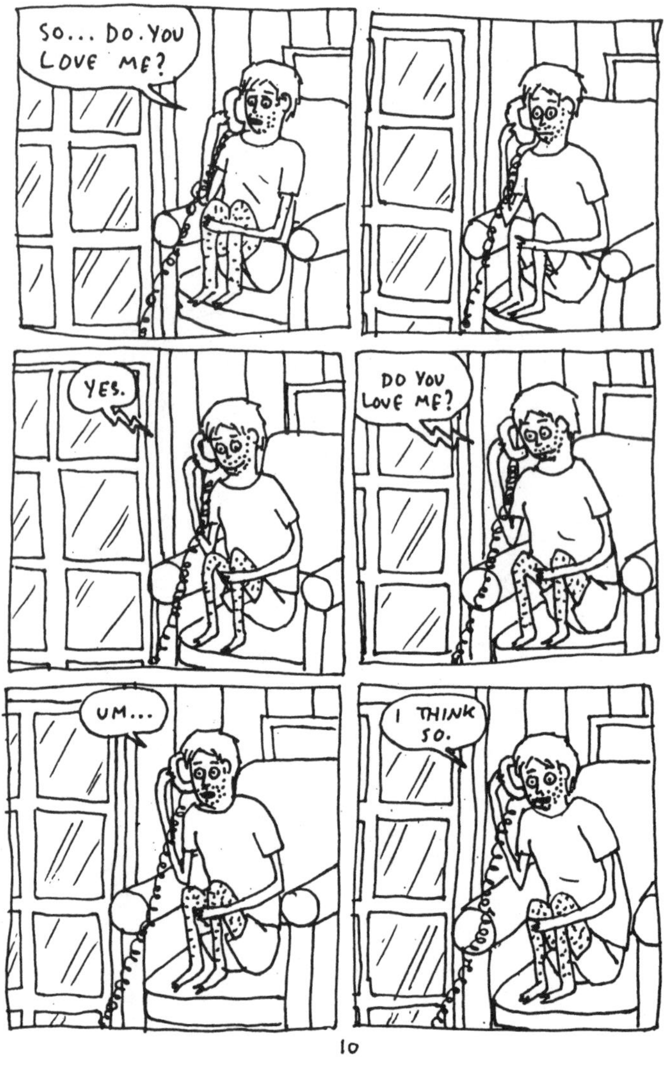
SO... DO. YOU LOVE ME?
YES.
DO YOU LOVE ME?
UM...
I THINK SO.

ONE LAST QUICK TIME

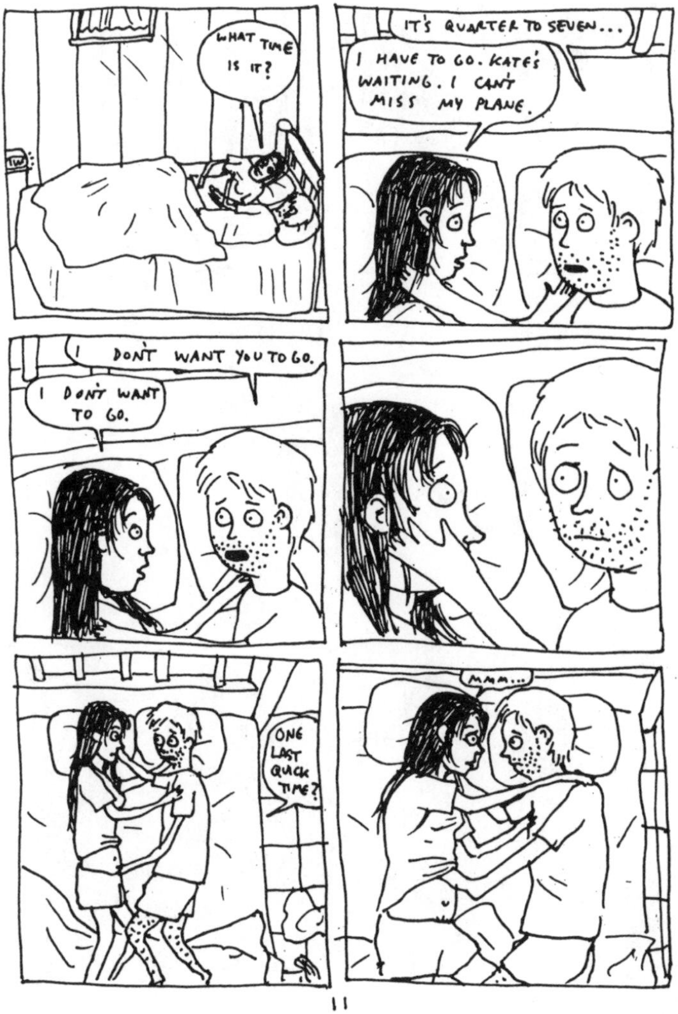
WHAT TIME IS IT?
IT'S QUARTER TO SEVEN...
I HAVE TO GO. KATE'S WAITING. I CAN'T MISS MY PLANE.
I DON'T WANT YOU TO GO.
I DON'T WANT TO GO.
ONE LAST QUICK TIME?
MMM...

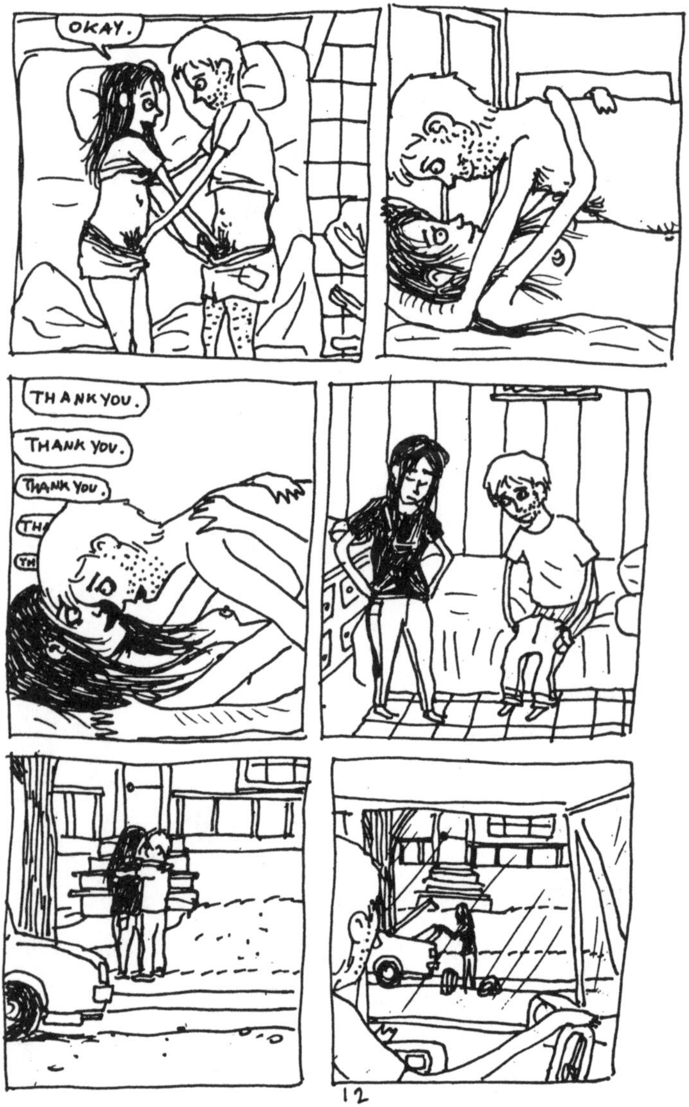
OKAY.
THANK YOU.
THANK YOU.
THANK YOU.

I DONT KNOW

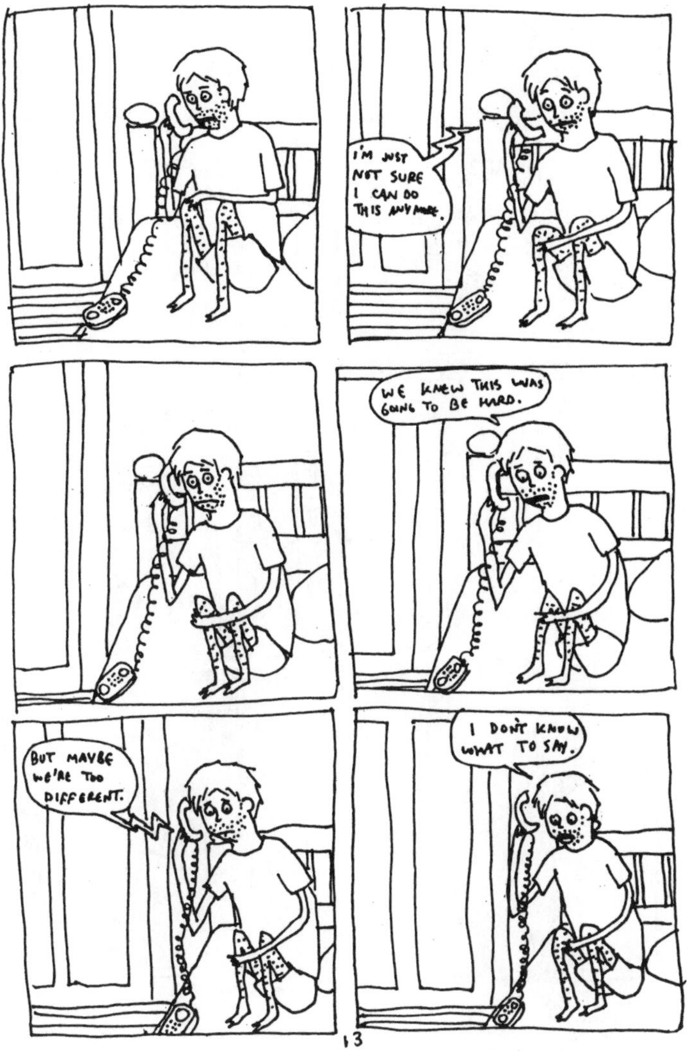
I'M JUST NOT SURE I CAN DO THIS ANYMORE.
WE KNEW THIS WAS GOING TO BE HARD.
BUT MAYBE WE'RE TOO DIFFERENT.
I DON'T KNOW WHAT TO SAY.

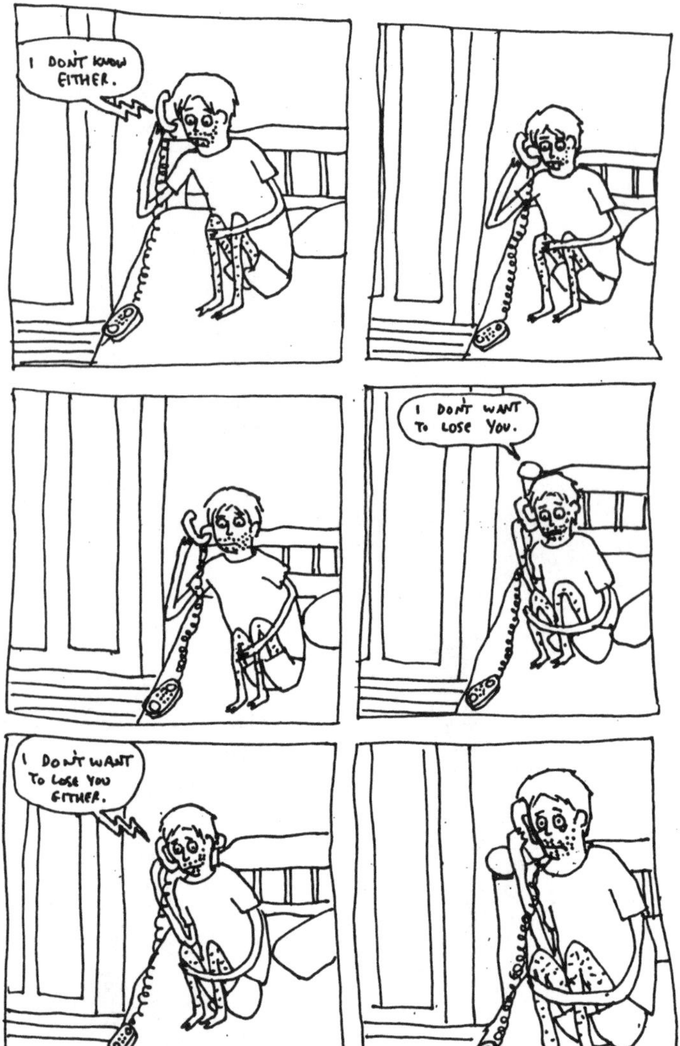
I DON'T KNOW EITHER.
I DON'T WANT TO LOSE YOU.
I DON'T WANT TO LOSE YOU EITHER.

SHE'S STRONG

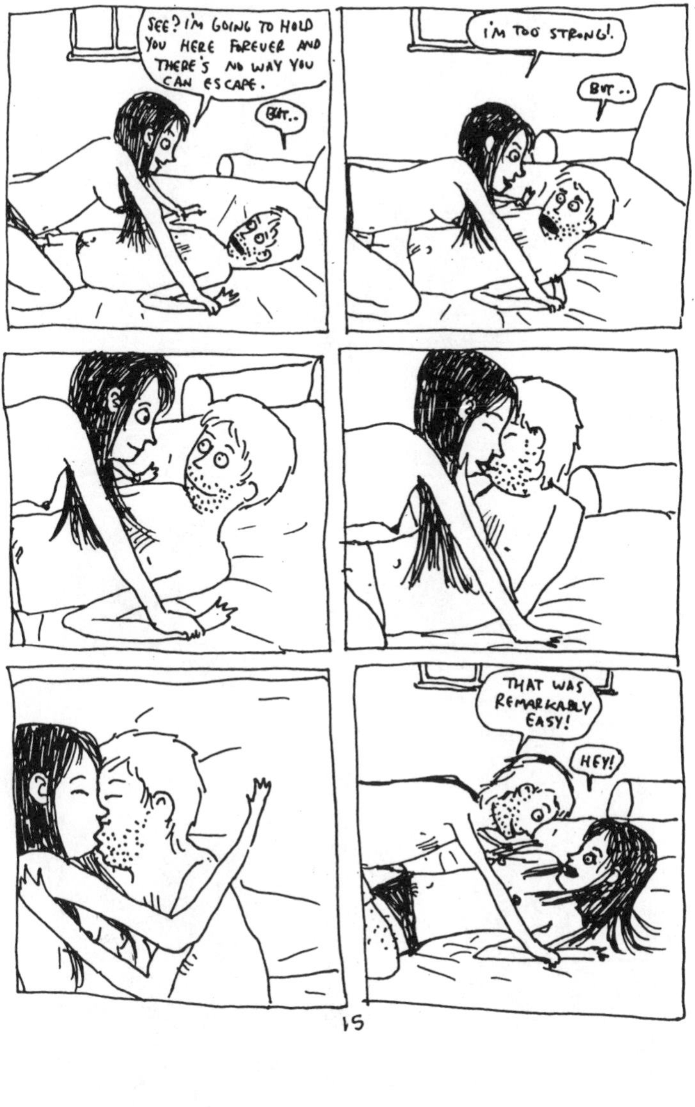
SEE? I'M GOING TO HOLD YOU HERE FOREVER AND THERE'S NO WAY YOU CAN ESCAPE.
BUT..
I'M TOO STRONG!.
BUT..
THAT WAS REMARKABLY EASY!
HEY!

WARM SPOT

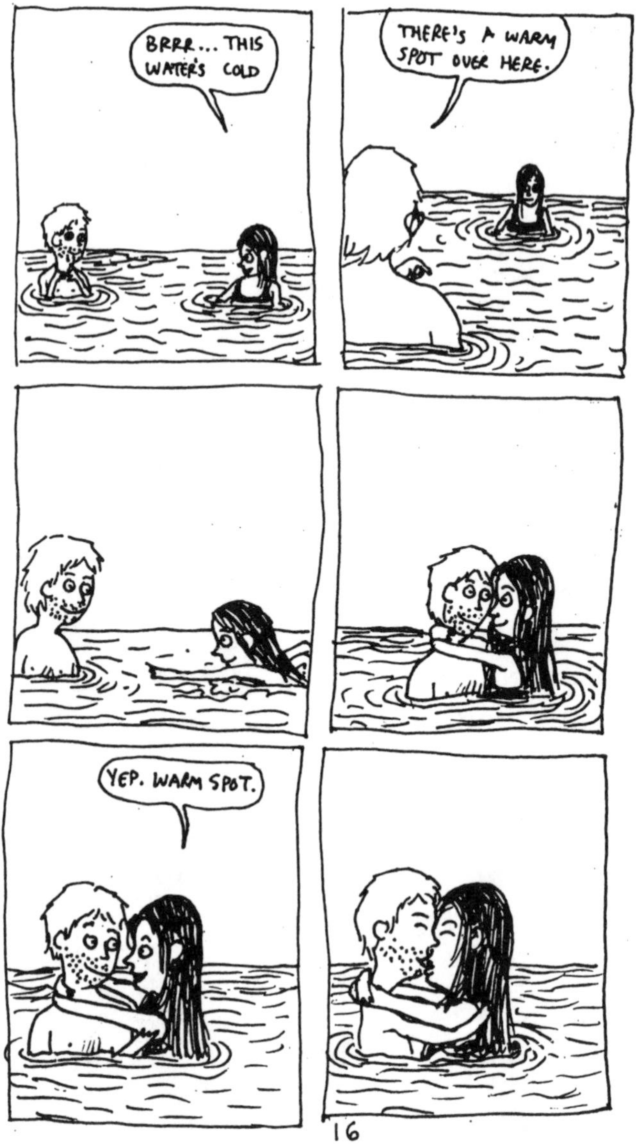
BRRR... THIS WATER'S COLD
THERE'S A WARM SPOT OVER HERE.
YEP. WARM SPOT.

PLANES LANDING

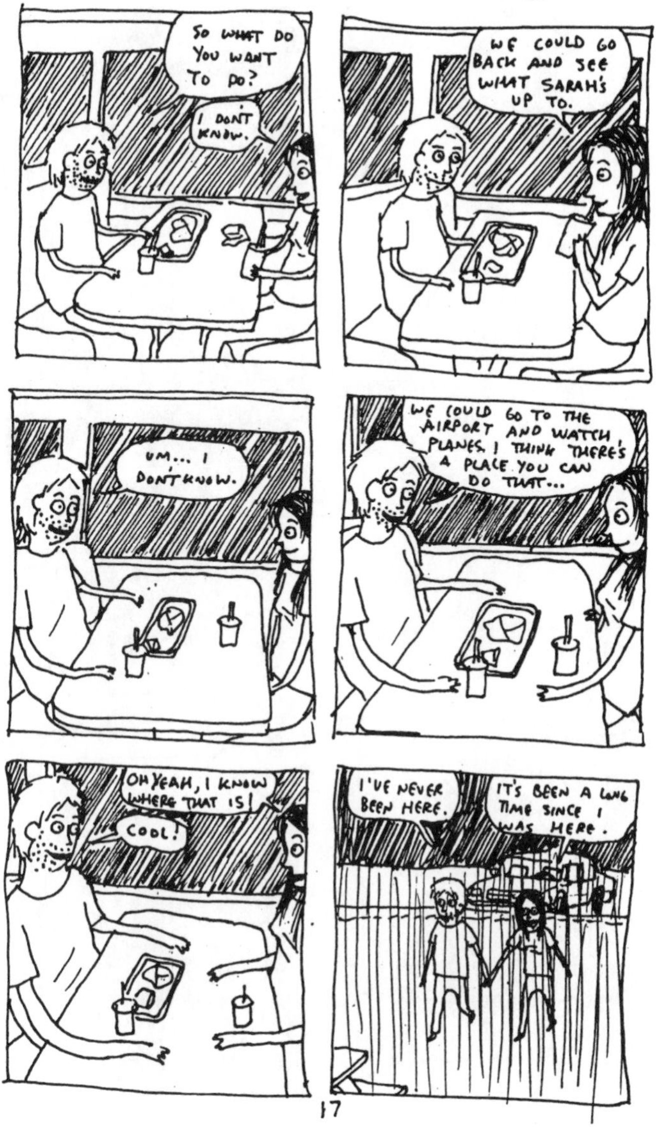
SO WHAT DO YOU WANT TO DO?
I DONT KNOW.
WE COULD GO BACK AND SEE WHAT SARAH'S UP TO.
UM... I DON'T KNOW.
WE COULD GO TO THE AIRPORT AND WATCH PLANES. I THINK THERE'S A PLACE YOU CAN DO THAT...
OH YEAH, I KNOW WHERE THAT IS!
COOL!
I'VE NEVER BEEN HERE.
IT'S BEEN A LONG TIME SINCE I WAS HERE.

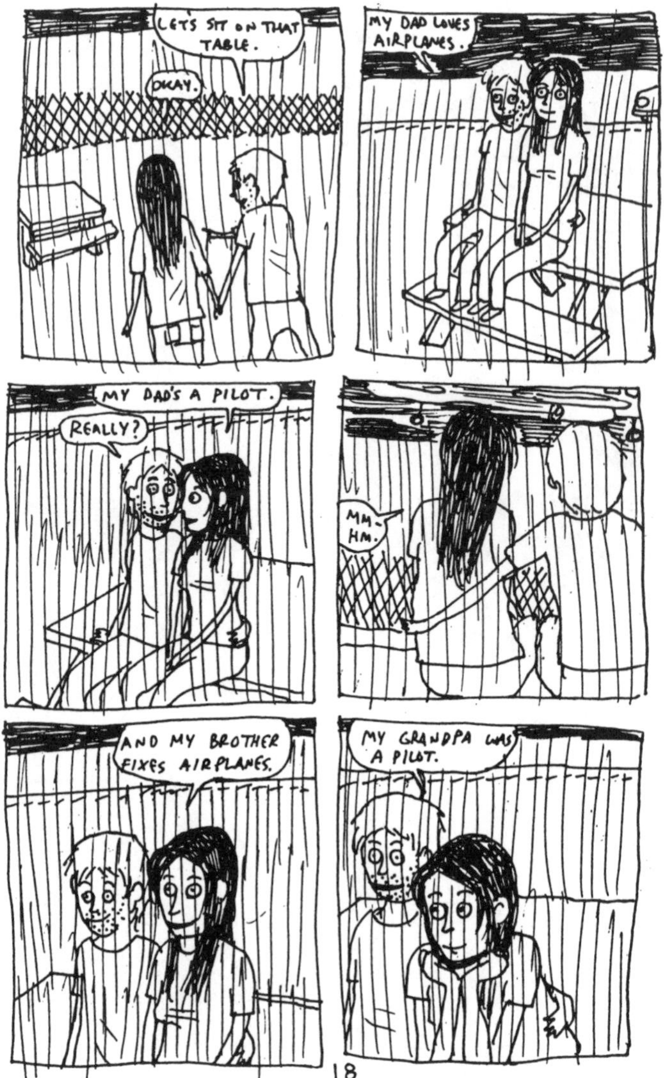
LET'S SIT ON THAT TABLE.
OKAY.
MY DAD LOVES AIRPLANES.
MY DAD'S A PILOT.
REALLY?
MM-HM.
AND MY BROTHER FIXES AIRPLANES.
MY GRANDPA WAS A PILOT.

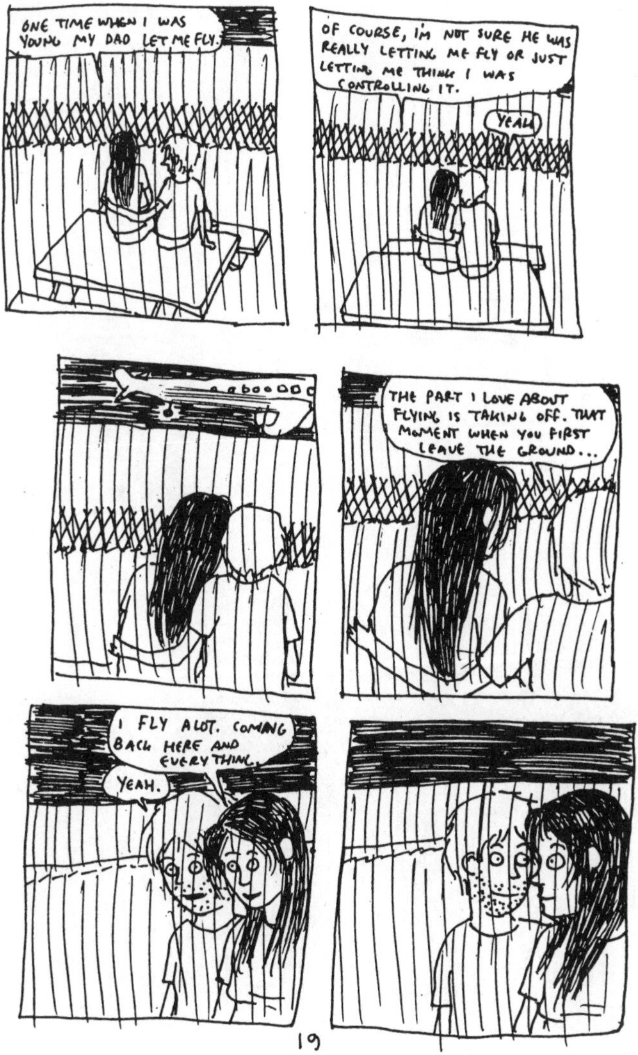
ONE TIME WHEN I WAS YOUNG MY DAD LET ME FLY.
OF COURSE, I'M NOT SURE HE WAS REALLY LETTING ME FLY OR JUST LETTING ME THINK I WAS CONTROLLING IT.
YEAH
THE PART I LOVE ABOUT FLYING IS TAKING OFF. THAT MOMENT WHEN YOU FIRST LEAVE THE GROUND...
I FLY ALOT. COMING BACK HERE AND EVERYTHING.
YEAH.

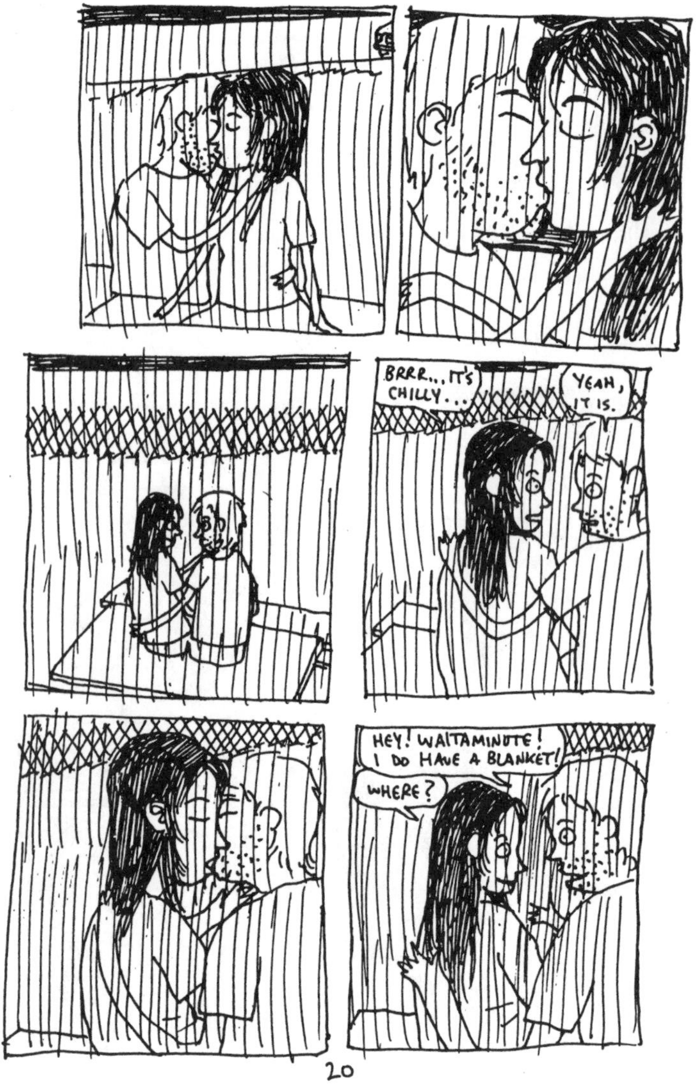
BRRR... IT'S CHILLY...
YEAH, IT IS.
HEY! WAITAMINUTE! I DO HAVE A BLANKET!
WHERE?

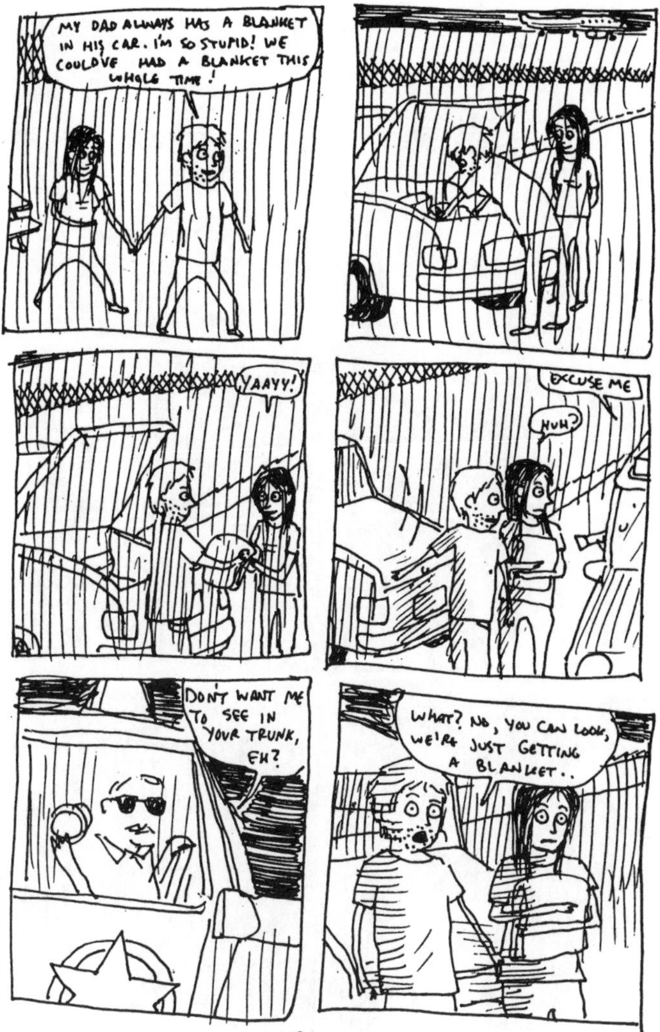
MY DAD ALWAYS HAS A BLANKET IN HIS CAR. I'M SO STUPID! WE COULDVE HAD A BLANKET THIS WHOLE TIME!
YAAYY!
EXCUSE ME
HUH?
DON'T WANT ME TO SEE IN YOUR TRUNK, EH?
WHAT? NO, YOU CAN LOOK, WE'RE JUST GETTING A BLANKET..

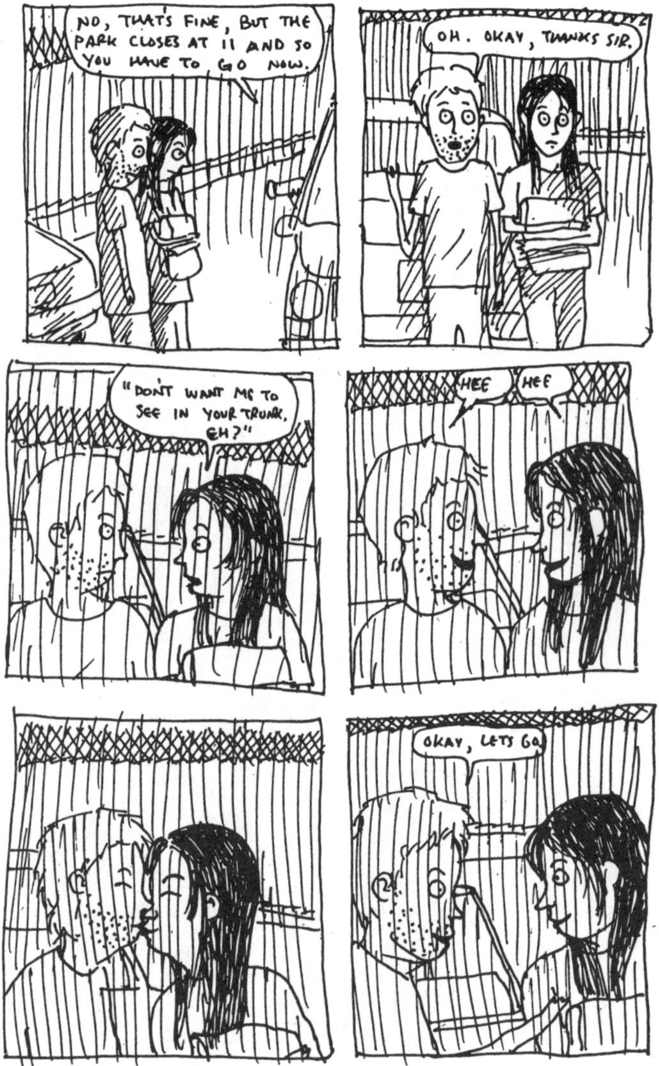
NO, THAT'S FINE, BUT THE PARK CLOSES AT 11 AND SO YOU HAVE TO GO NOW.
OH. OKAY, THANKS SIR.
"DON'T WANT ME TO SEE IN YOUR TRUNK, EH?"
HEE
HEE
OKAY, LETS GO

THE VERY FIRST TIME I SAW THERESA

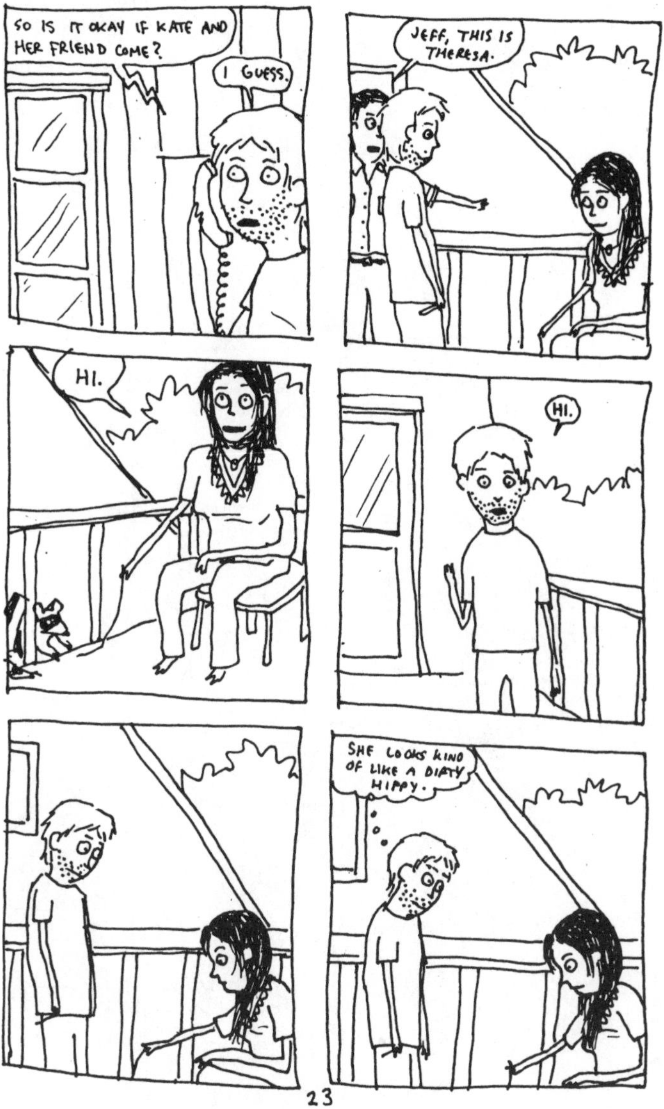
SO IS IT OKAY IF KATE AND HER FRIEND COME?
I GUESS.
JEFF, THIS IS THERESA.
HI.
HI.
SHE LOOKS KIND OF LIKE A DIRTY HIPPY.

DRIVING

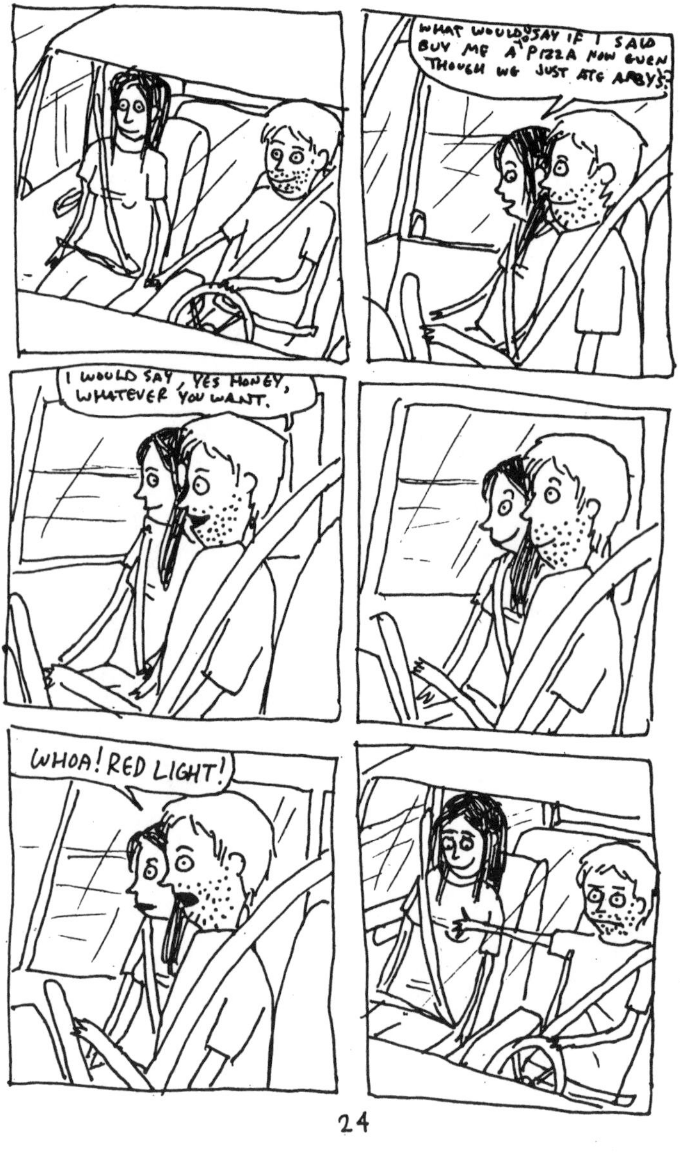
WHAT WOULD YOU SAY IF I SAID BUY ME A PIZZA NOW EVEN THOUGH WE JUST ATE ARBY'S?
I WOULD SAY, YES HONEY, WHATEVER YOU WANT.
WHOA! RED LIGHT!

HAPPY NEW YEAR

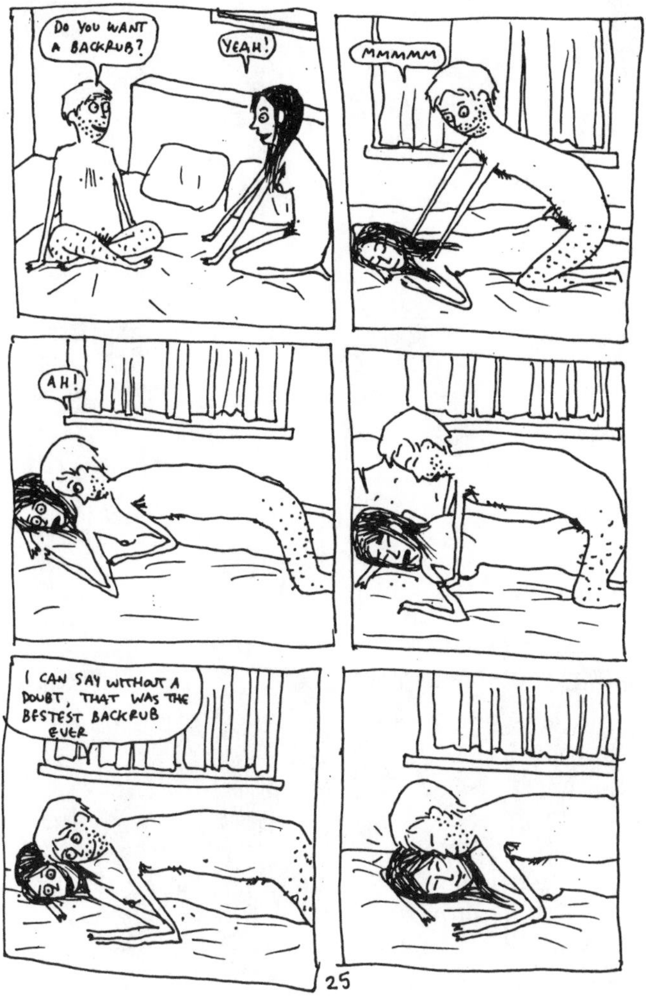
DO YOU WANT A BACKRUB?
YEAH!
MMMMM
AH!
I CAN SAY WITHOUT A DOUBT, THAT WAS THE BESTEST BACKRUB EVER

19 CENTS

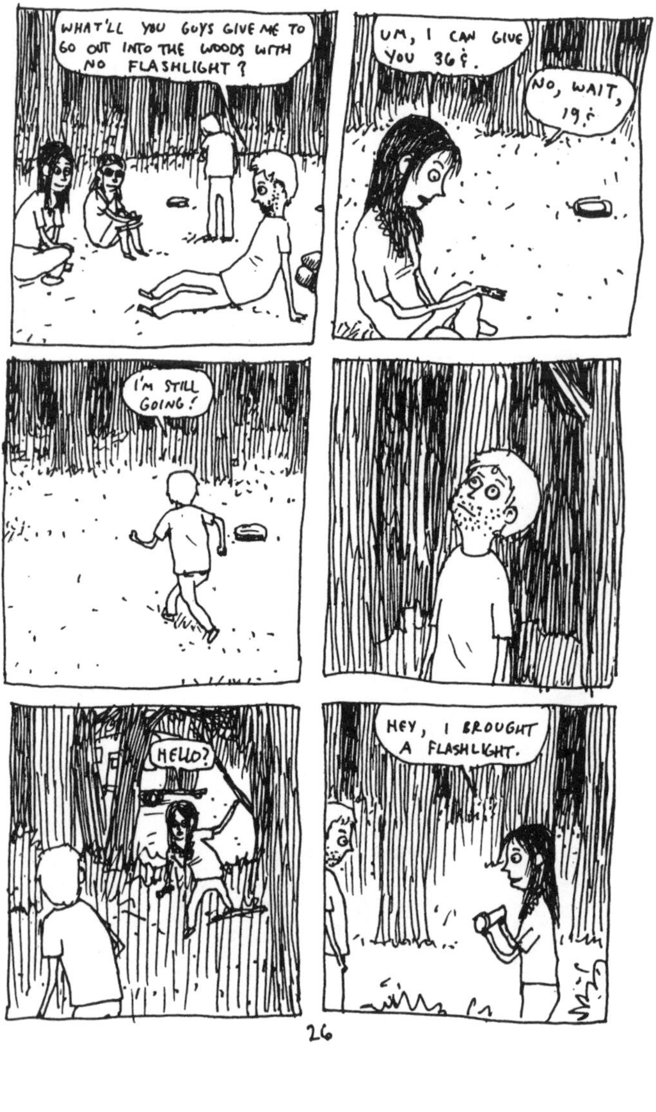
WHAT'LL YOU GUYS GIVE ME TO GO OUT INTO THE WOODS WITH NO FLASHLIGHT?
UM, I CAN GIVE YOU 36¢.
NO, WAIT, 19¢
I'M STILL GOING!
HELLO?
HEY, I BROUGHT A FLASHLIGHT.

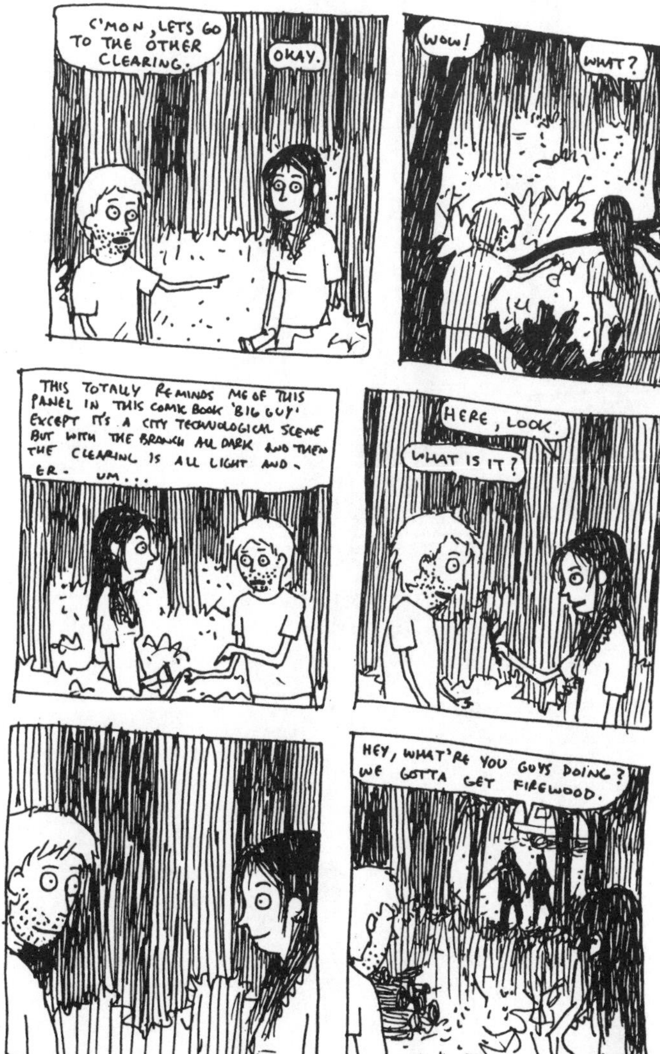
C'MON, LETS GO TO THE OTHER CLEARING.
OKAY.
WOW!
WHAT?
THIS TOTALLY REMINDS ME OF THIS PANEL IN THIS COMIC BOOK 'BIG GUY' EXCEPT IT'S A CITY TECHNOLOGICAL SCENE BUT WITH THE BRANCH ALL DARK AND THEN THE CLEARING IS ALL LIGHT AND - ER - UM...
HERE, LOOK.
WHAT IS IT?
HEY, WHAT'RE YOU GUYS DOING? WE GOTTA GET FIREWOOD.

PICTURES OF KRISTYN

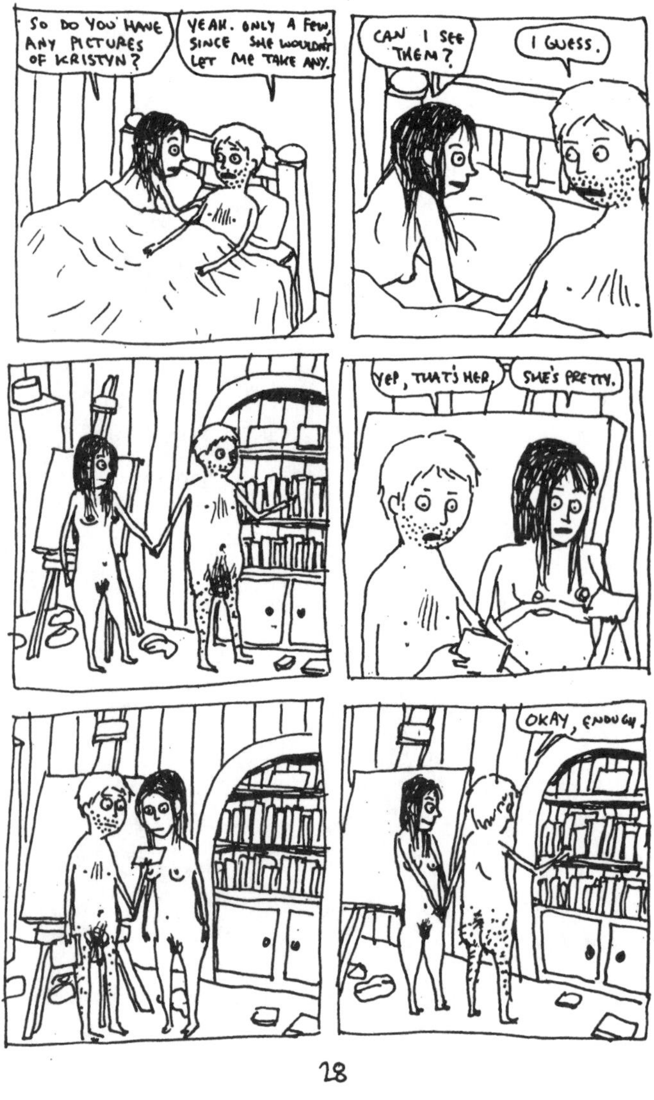
SO DO YOU HAVE ANY PICTURES OF KRISTYN?
YEAH. ONLY A FEW, SINCE SHE WOULDN'T LET ME TAKE ANY.
CAN I SEE THEM?
I GUESS.
YEP, THAT'S HER.
SHE'S PRETTY.
OKAY, ENOUGH.

WEIRD

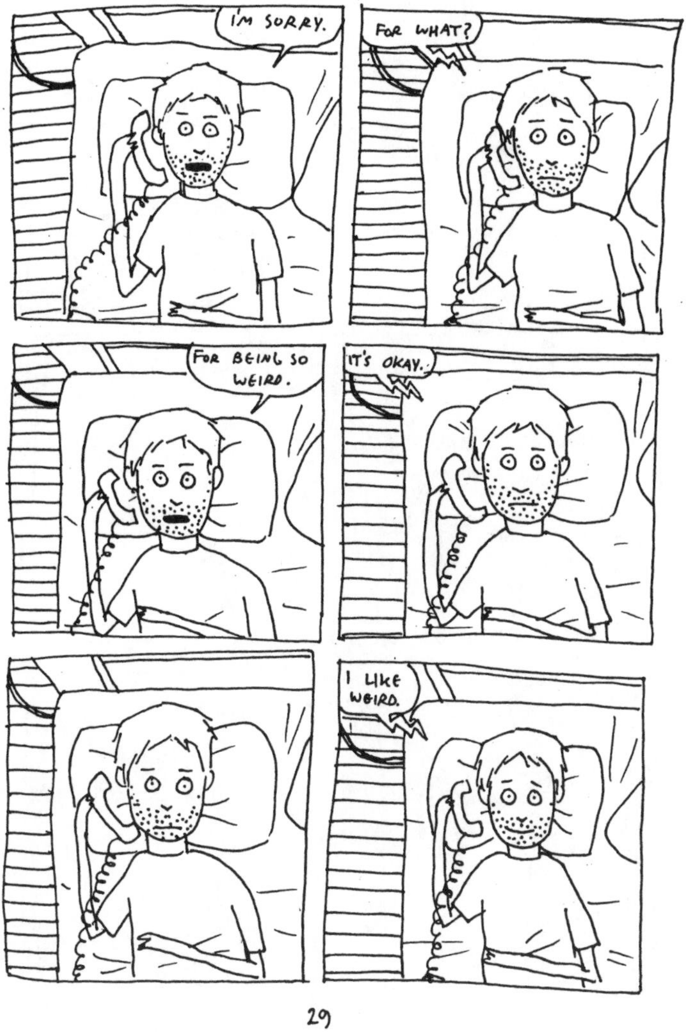
I'M SORRY.
FOR WHAT?
FOR BEING SO WEIRD.
IT'S OKAY.
I LIKE WEIRD.

FLOWERS

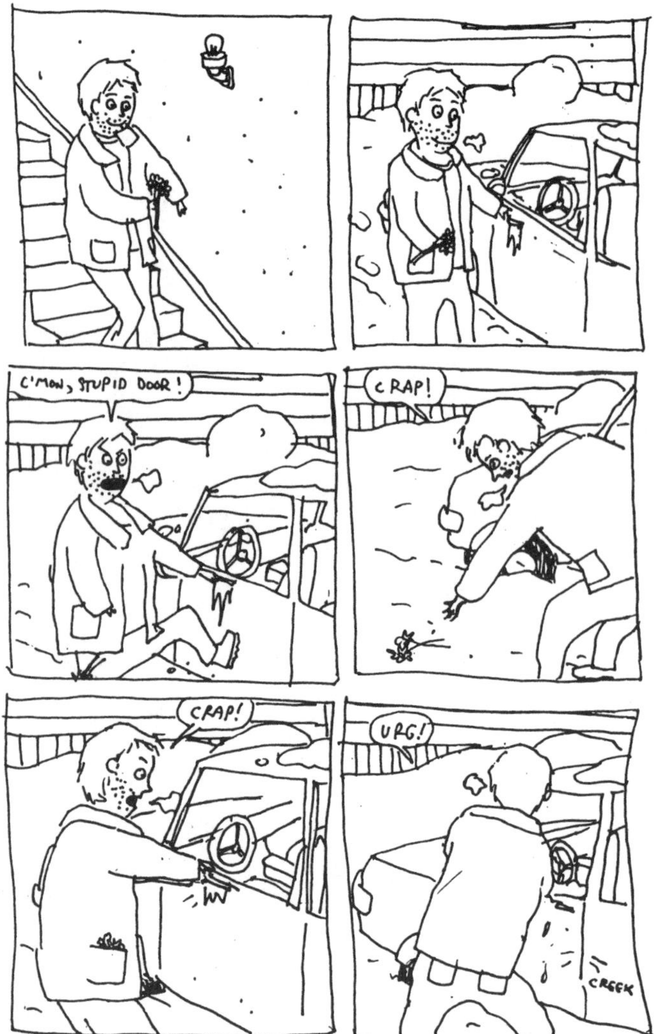
C'MON, STUPID DOOR!
CRAP!
CRAP!
URG!
CREEK

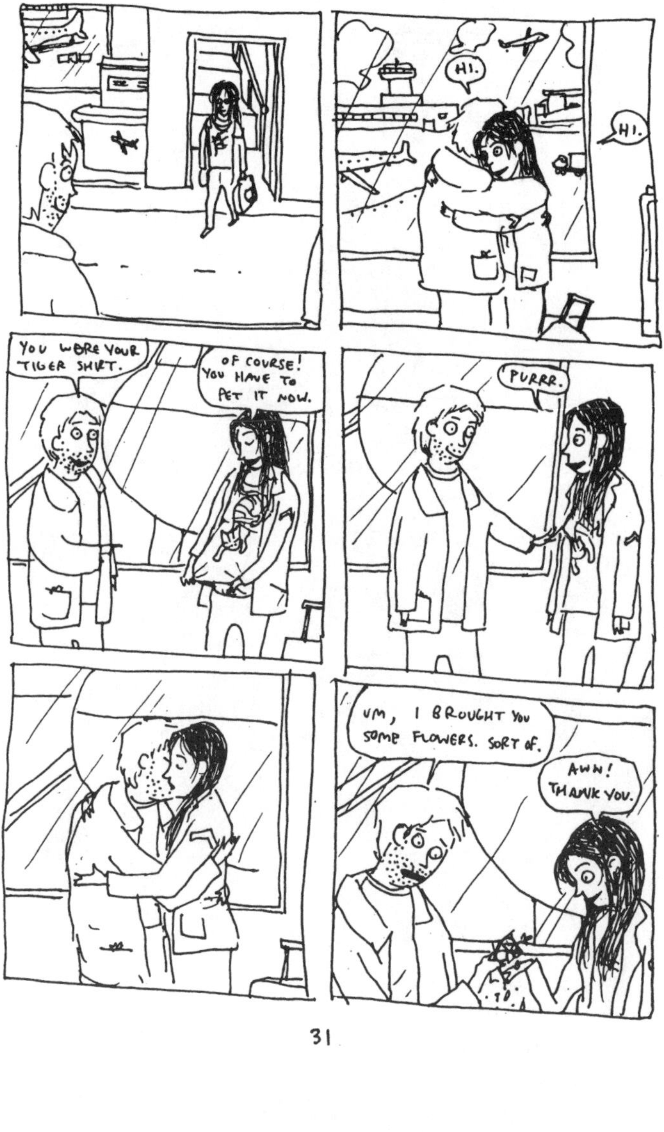
HI.
HI.
YOU WERE YOUR TIGER SHIRT.
OF COURSE! YOU HAVE TO PET IT NOW.
PURRR.
UM, I BROUGHT YOU SOME FLOWERS. SORT OF.
AWN! THANK YOU.

RUBY TUESDAY

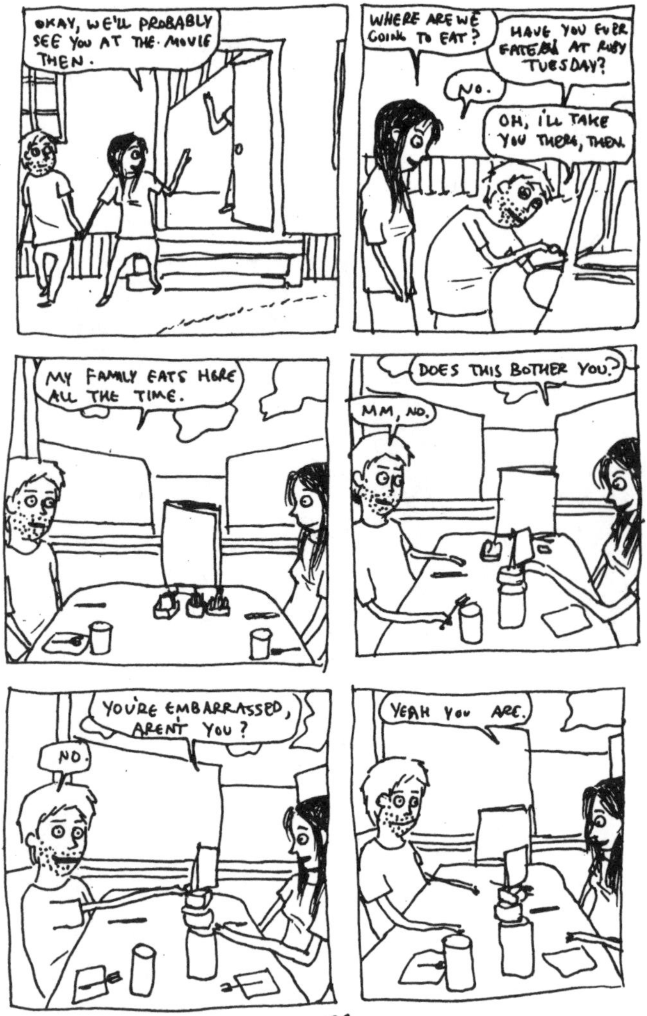
OKAY, WE'LL PROBABLY SEE YOU AT THE MOVIE THEN.
WHERE ARE WE GOING TO EAT?
HAVE YOU EVER EATEN AT RUBY TUESDAY?
NO.
OH, I'LL TAKE YOU THERE, THEN.
MY FAMILY EATS HERE ALL THE TIME.
DOES THIS BOTHER YOU?
MM, NO.
YOU'RE EMBARRASSED, AREN'T YOU?
NO.
YEAH YOU ARE.

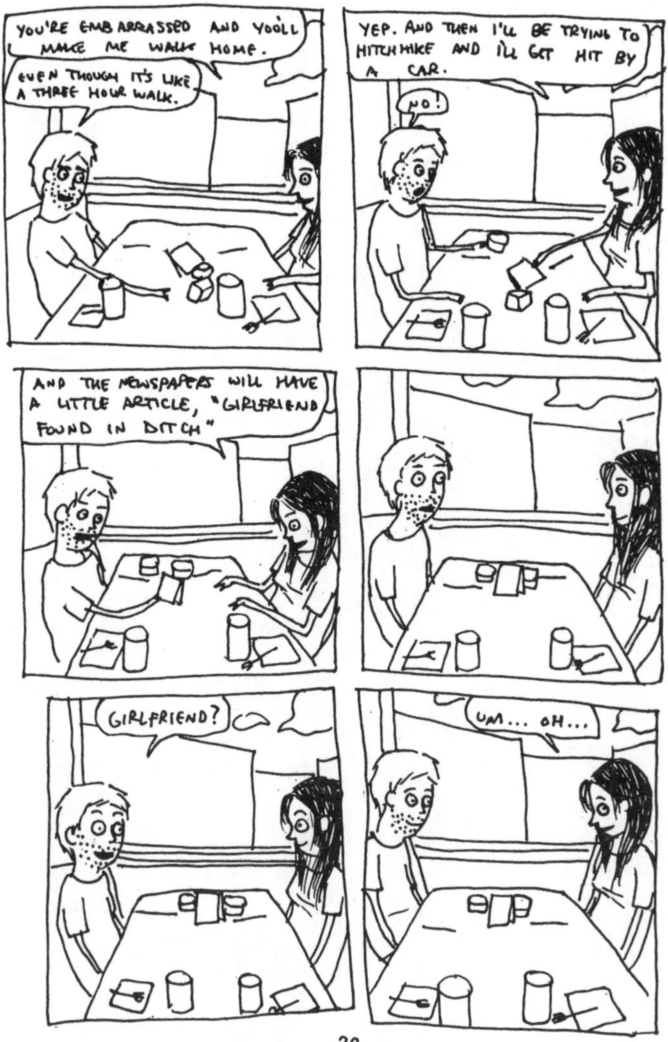
YOU'RE EMBARRASSED AND YOU'LL MAKE ME WALK HOME.
EVEN THOUGH IT'S LIKE A THREE HOUR WALK.
YEP. AND THEN I'LL BE TRYING TO HITCHHIKE AND I'LL GET HIT BY A CAR.
NO!
AND THE NEWSPAPERS WILL HAVE A LITTLE ARTICLE, "GIRLFRIEND FOUND IN DITCH"
GIRLFRIEND?
UM... OH...

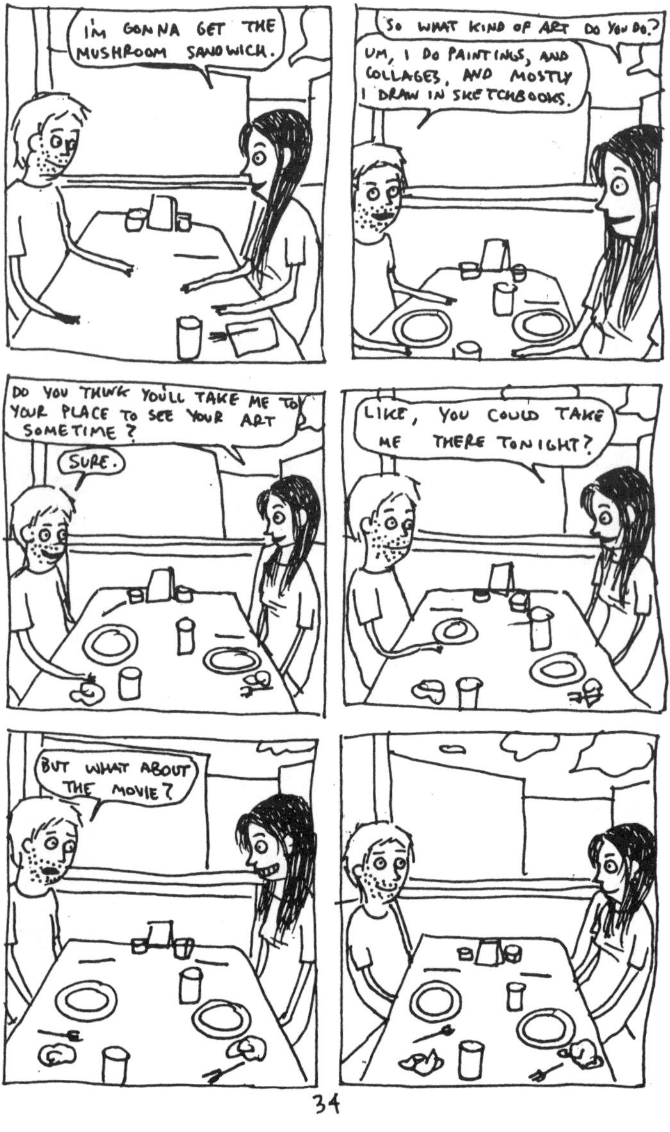
I'M GONNA GET THE MUSHROOM SANDWICH.
SO WHAT KIND OF ART DO YOU DO?
UM, I DO PAINTINGS, AND COLLAGES, AND MOSTLY I DRAW IN SKETCHBOOKS.
DO YOU THINK YOU'LL TAKE ME TO YOUR PLACE TO SEE YOUR ART SOMETIME?
SURE.
LIKE, YOU COULD TAKE ME THERE TONIGHT?
BUT WHAT ABOUT THE MOVIE?

LOOKING AT ART

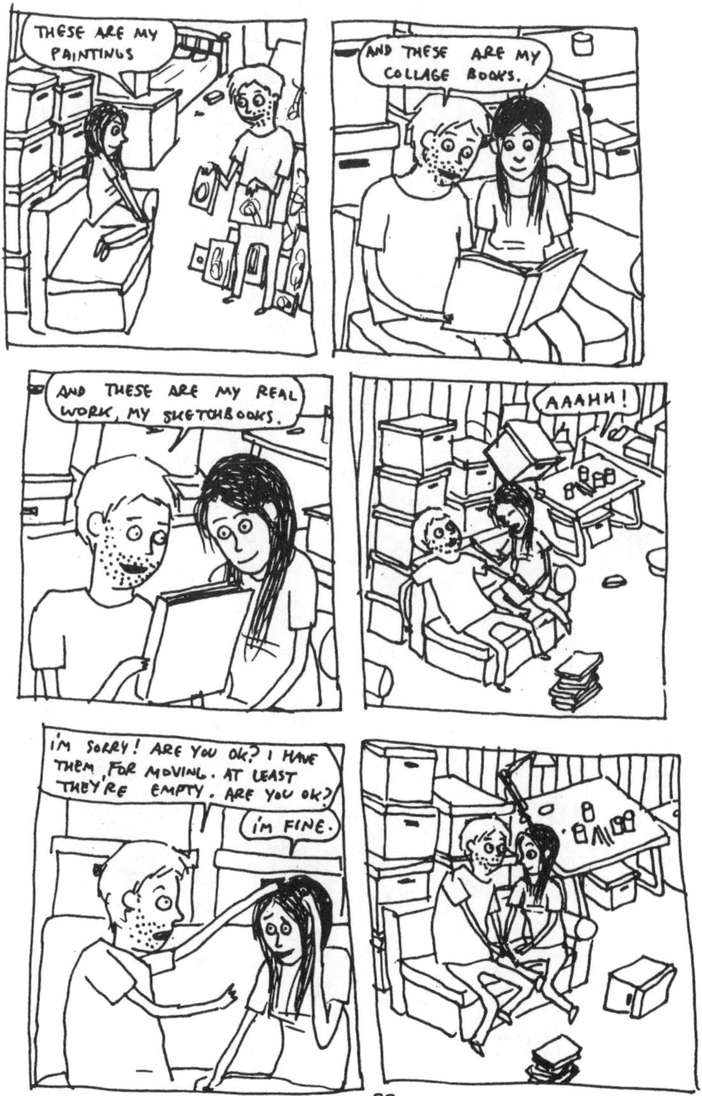

THESE ARE MY PAINTINGS
AND THESE ARE MY COLLAGE BOOKS.
AND THESE ARE MY REAL WORK, MY SKETCHBOOKS.
AAAHH!
I'M SORRY! ARE YOU OK? I HAVE THEM FOR MOVING. AT LEAST THEY'RE EMPTY. ARE YOU OK?
I'M FINE.

AMERICAN BEAUTY

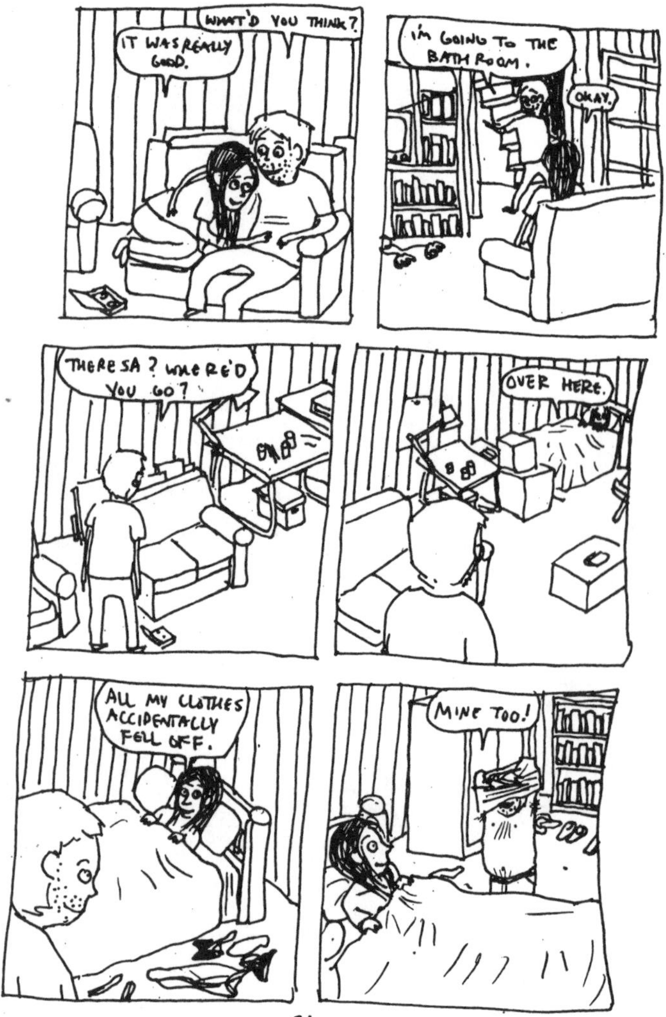
WHAT'D YOU THINK?
IT WAS REALLY GOOD.
I'M GOING TO THE BATHROOM.
OKAY.
THERESA? WHERE'D YOU GO?
OVER HERE.
ALL MY CLOTHES ACCIDENTALLY FELL OFF.
MINE TOO!

PACING

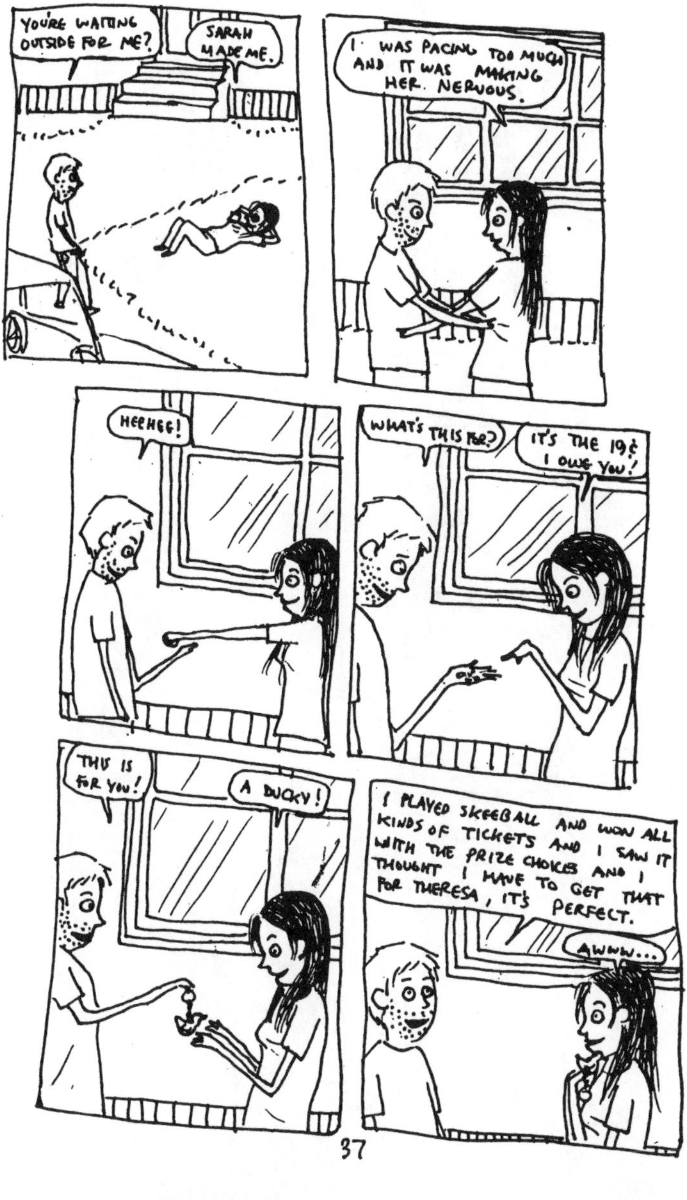

YOU'RE WAITING OUTSIDE FOR ME?
SARAH MADE ME.
I WAS PACING TOO MUCH AND IT WAS MAKING HER NERVOUS.
HEEHEE!
WHAT'S THIS FOR?
IT'S THE 19¢ I OWE YOU!
THIS IS FOR YOU!
A DUCKY!
I PLAYED SKEEBALL AND WON ALL KINDS OF TICKETS AND I SAW IT WITH THE PRIZE CHOICES AND I THOUGHT I HAVE TO GET THAT FOR THERESA, IT'S PERFECT.
AWWW...

FINGERS

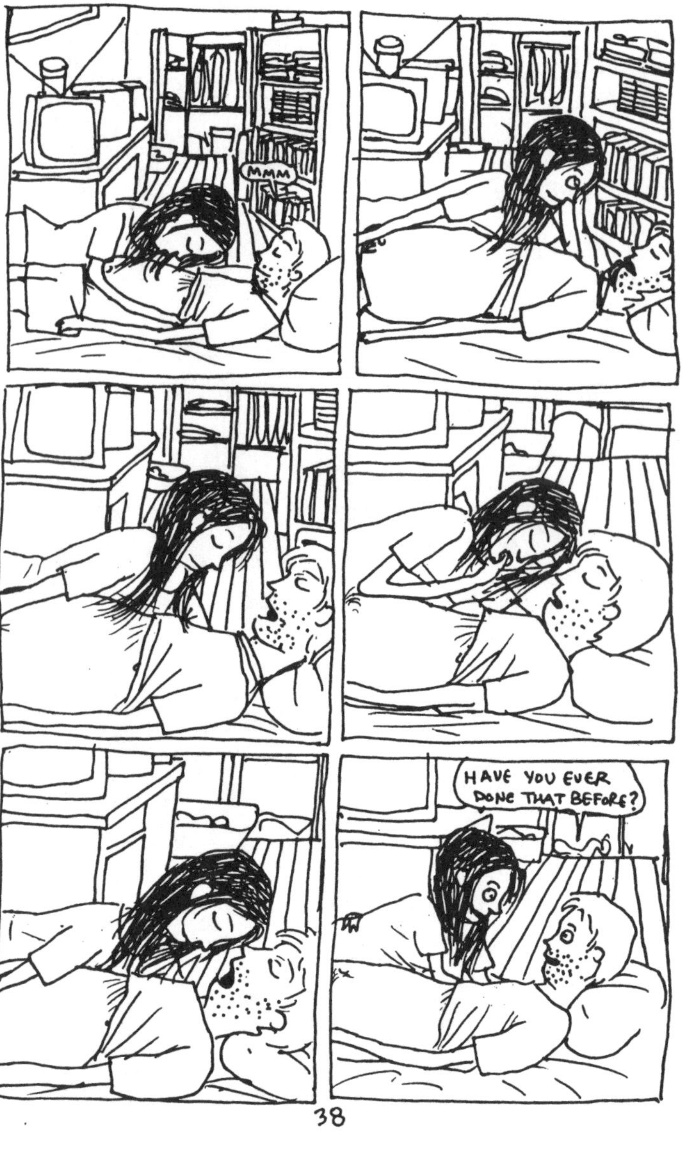
MMM
HAVE YOU EVER DONE THAT BEFORE?

THE CAMPER

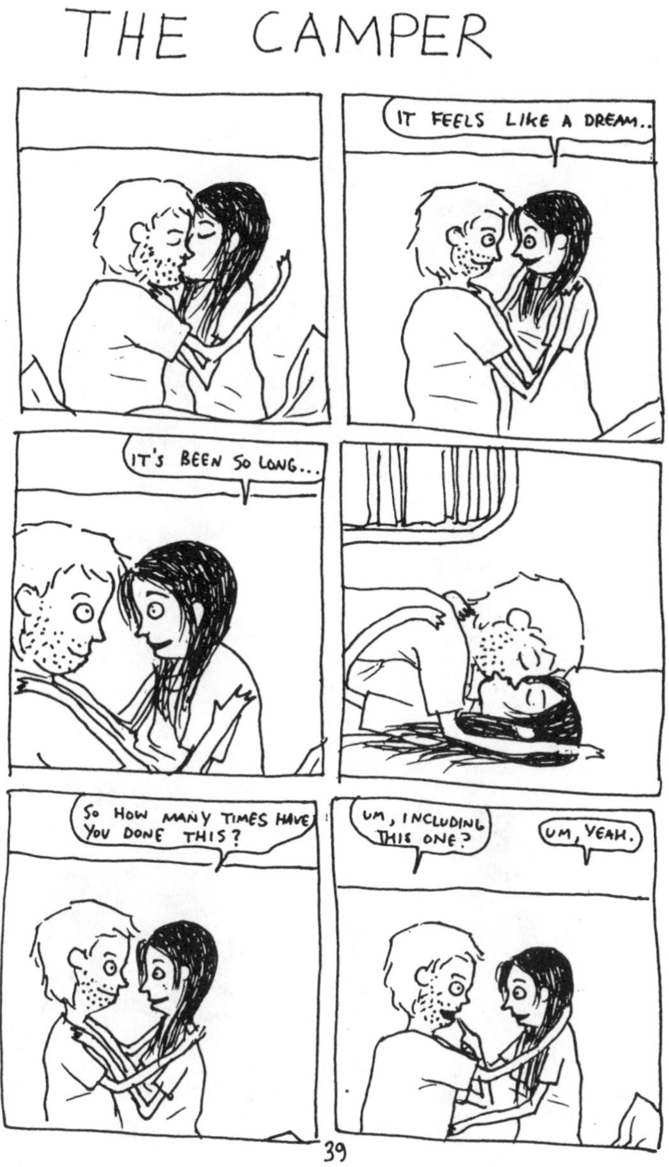

IT FEELS LIKE A DREAM..
IT'S BEEN SO LONG...
SO HOW MANY TIMES HAVE YOU DONE THIS?
UM, INCLUDING THIS ONE?
UM, YEAH.

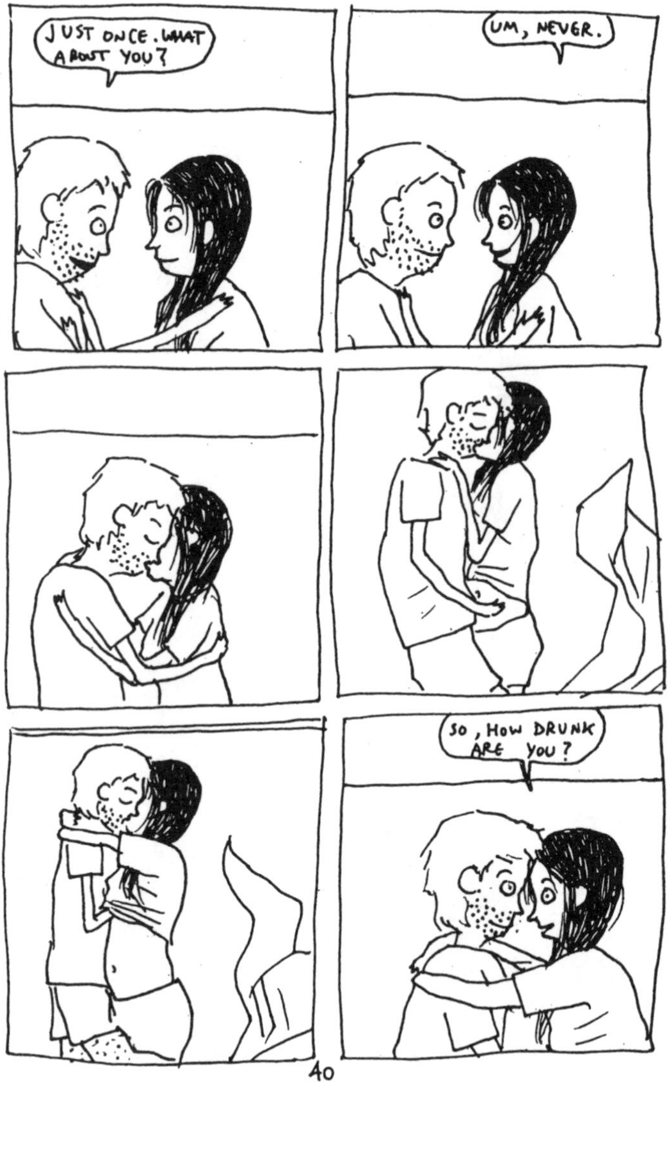
JUST ONCE. WHAT ABOUT YOU?
UM, NEVER.
SO, HOW DRUNK ARE YOU?

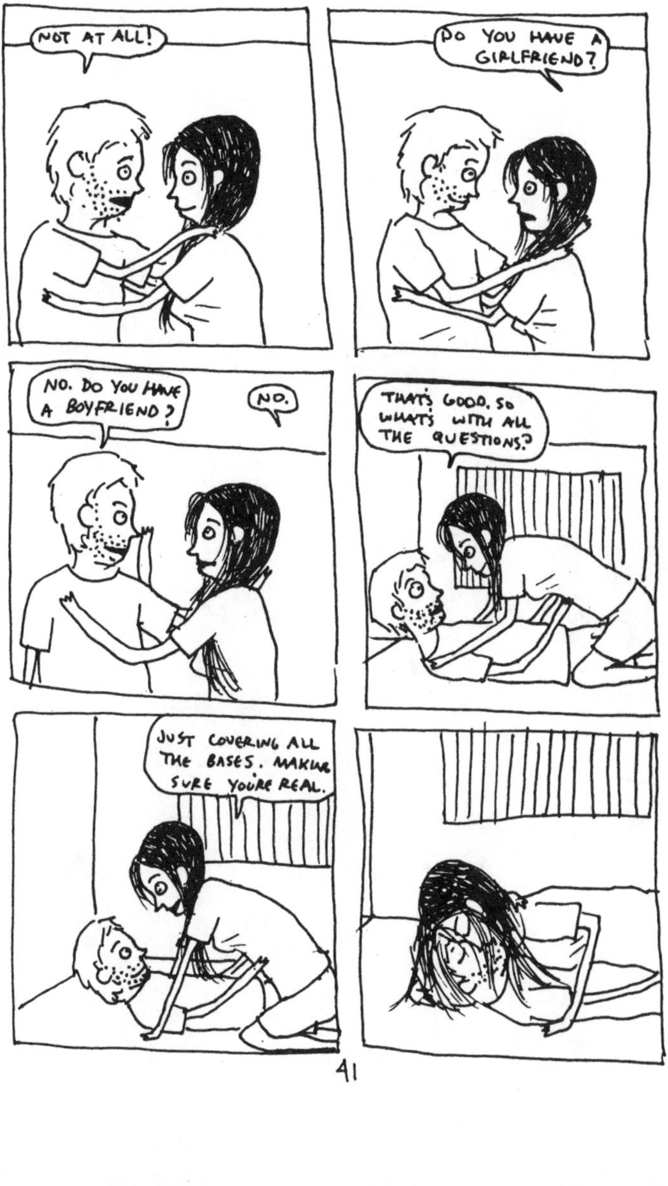
NOT AT ALL!
DO YOU HAVE A GIRLFRIEND?
NO. DO YOU HAVE A BOYFRIEND?
NO.
THAT'S GOOD. SO WHAT'S WITH ALL THE QUESTIONS?
JUST COVERING ALL THE BASES. MAKING SURE YOU'RE REAL.

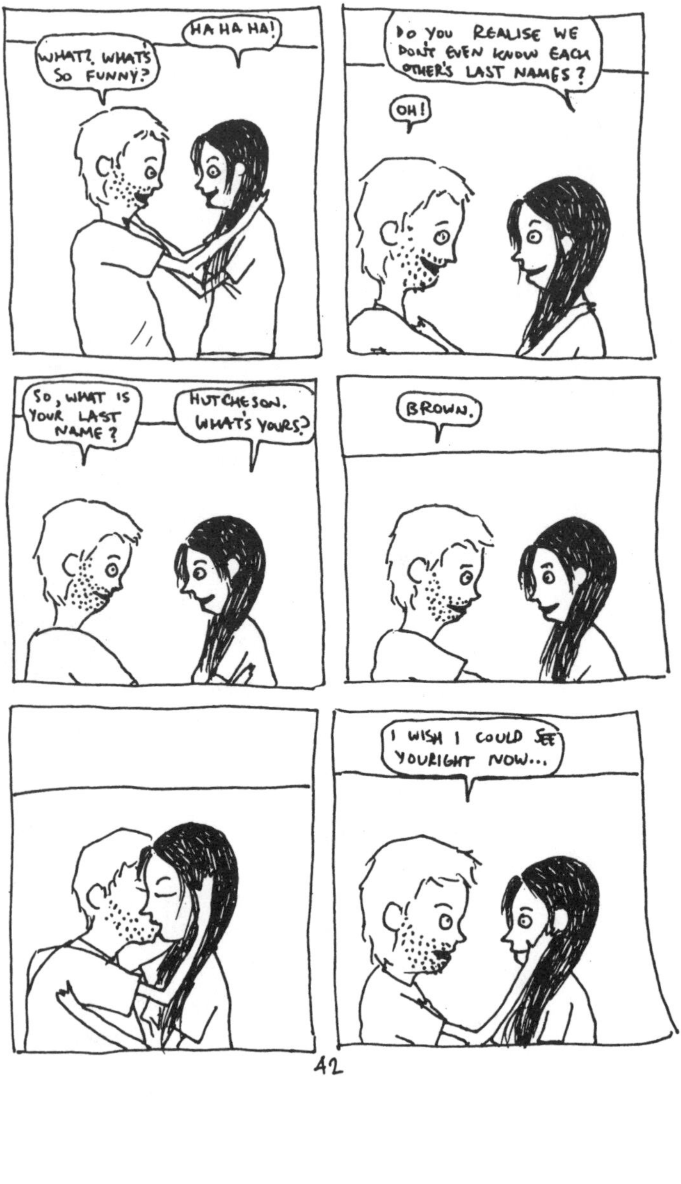
WHAT? WHAT'S SO FUNNY?
HA HA HA!
DO YOU REALISE WE DON'T EVEN KNOW EACH OTHER'S LAST NAMES?
OH!
SO, WHAT IS YOUR LAST NAME?
HUTCHESON. WHAT'S YOURS?
BROWN.
I WISH I COULD SEE YOU RIGHT NOW...

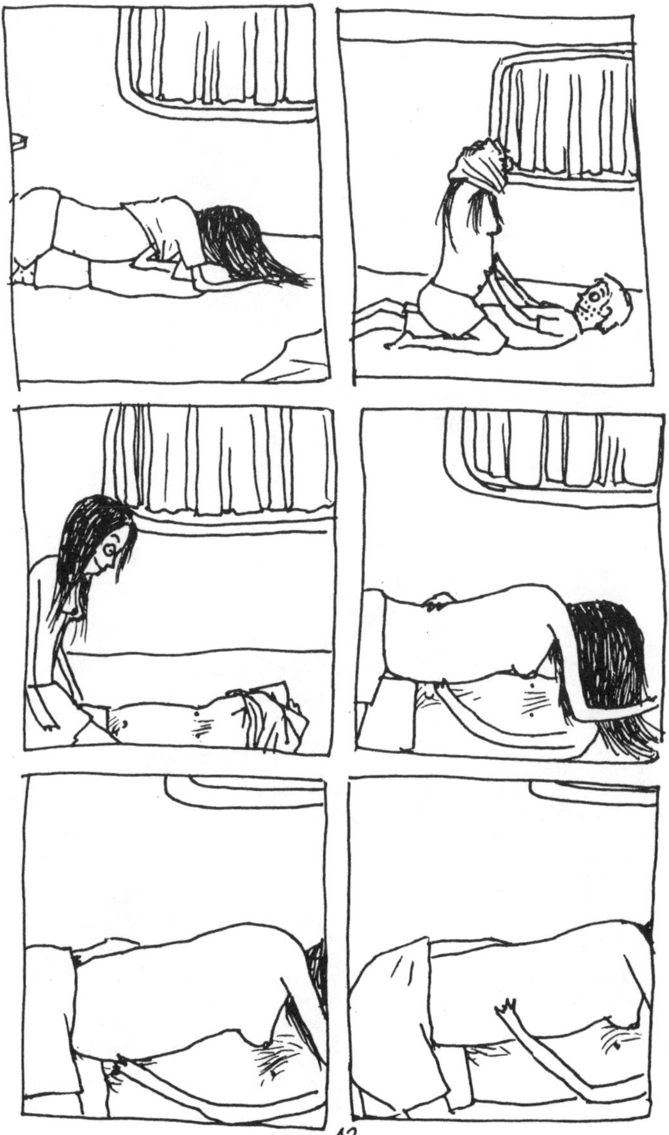

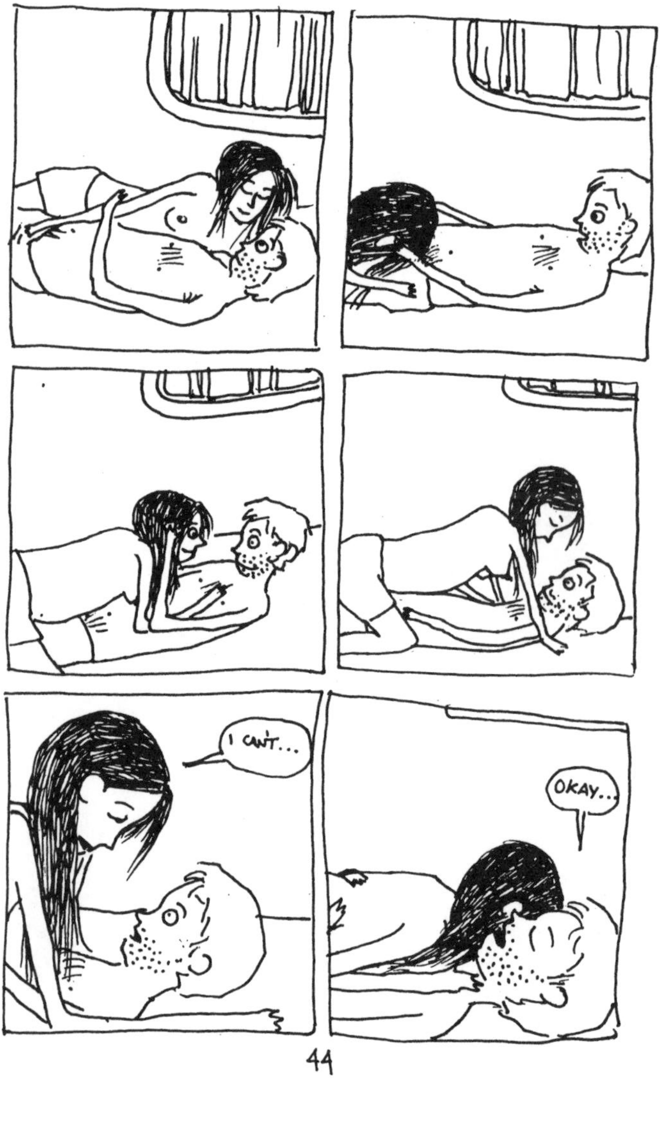
I CAN'T...
OKAY...

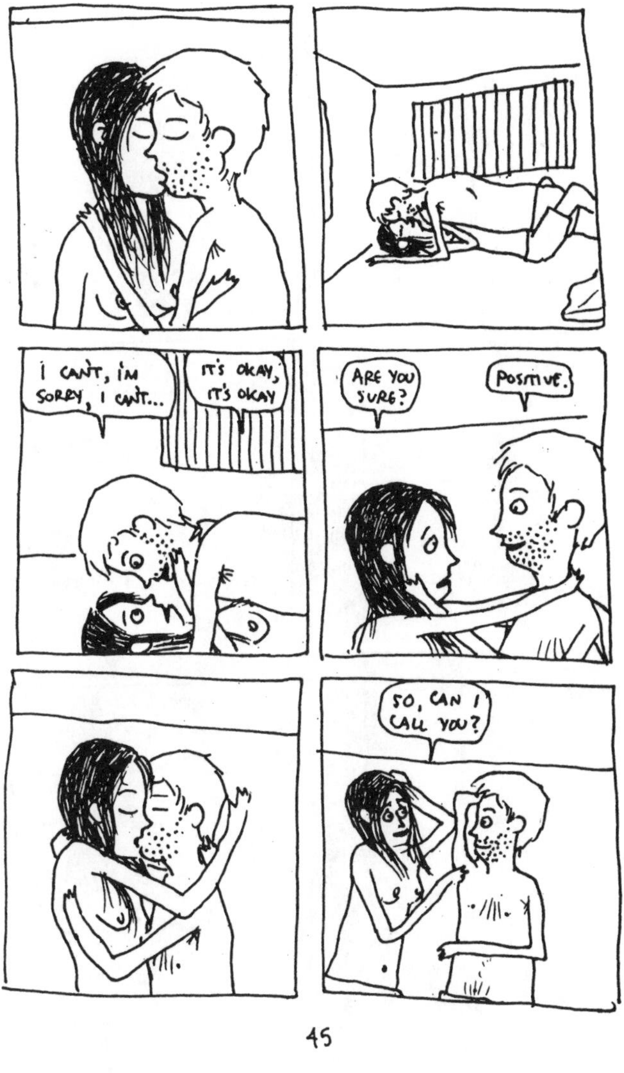
I CAN'T, I'M SORRY, I CAN'T...
IT'S OKAY, IT'S OKAY
ARE YOU SURE?
POSITIVE.
SO, CAN I CALL YOU?

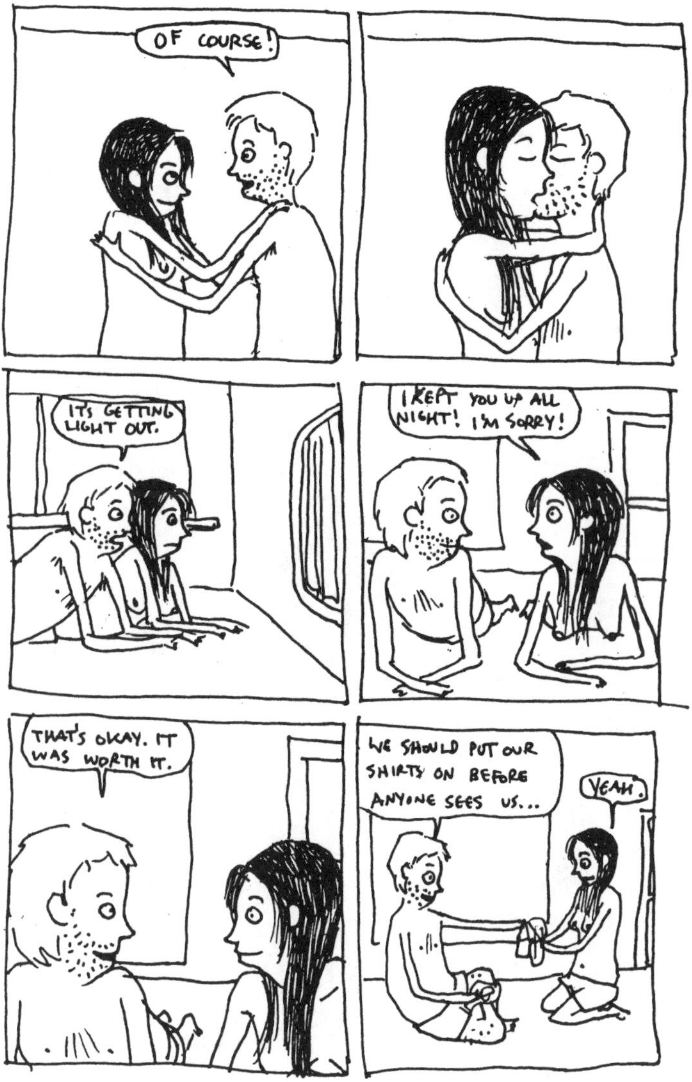
OF COURSE!
IT'S GETTING LIGHT OUT.
I KEPT YOU UP ALL NIGHT! I'M SORRY!
THAT'S OKAY. IT WAS WORTH IT.
WE SHOULD PUT OUR SHIRTS ON BEFORE ANYONE SEES US...
YEAH.

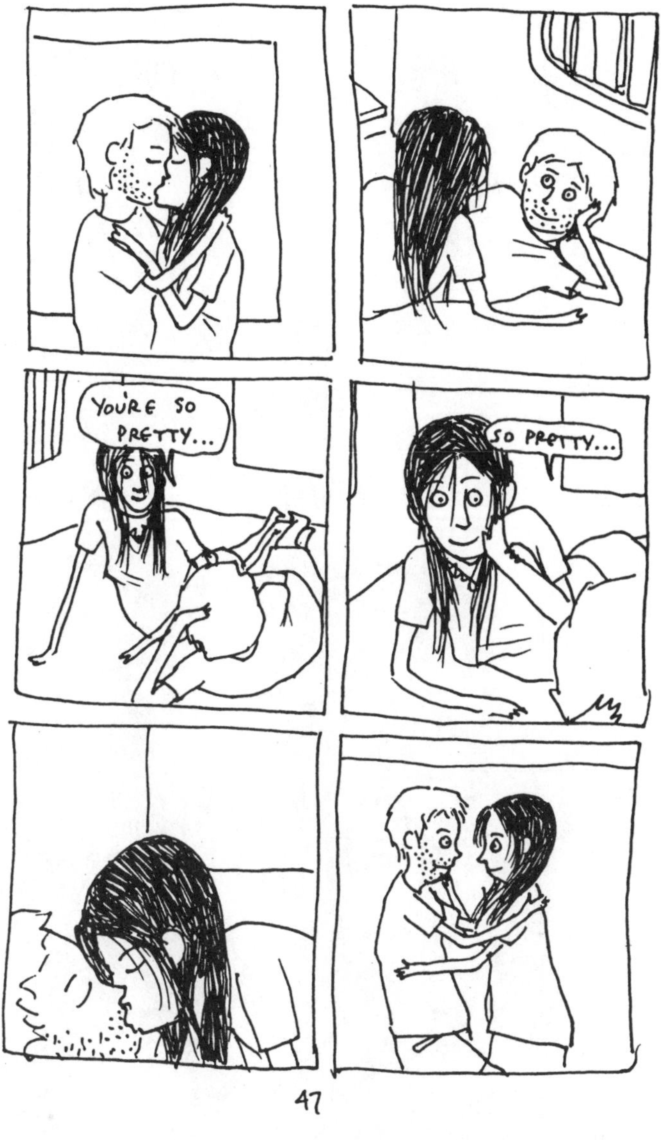
YOU'RE SO PRETTY...
SO PRETTY...

I FARTED

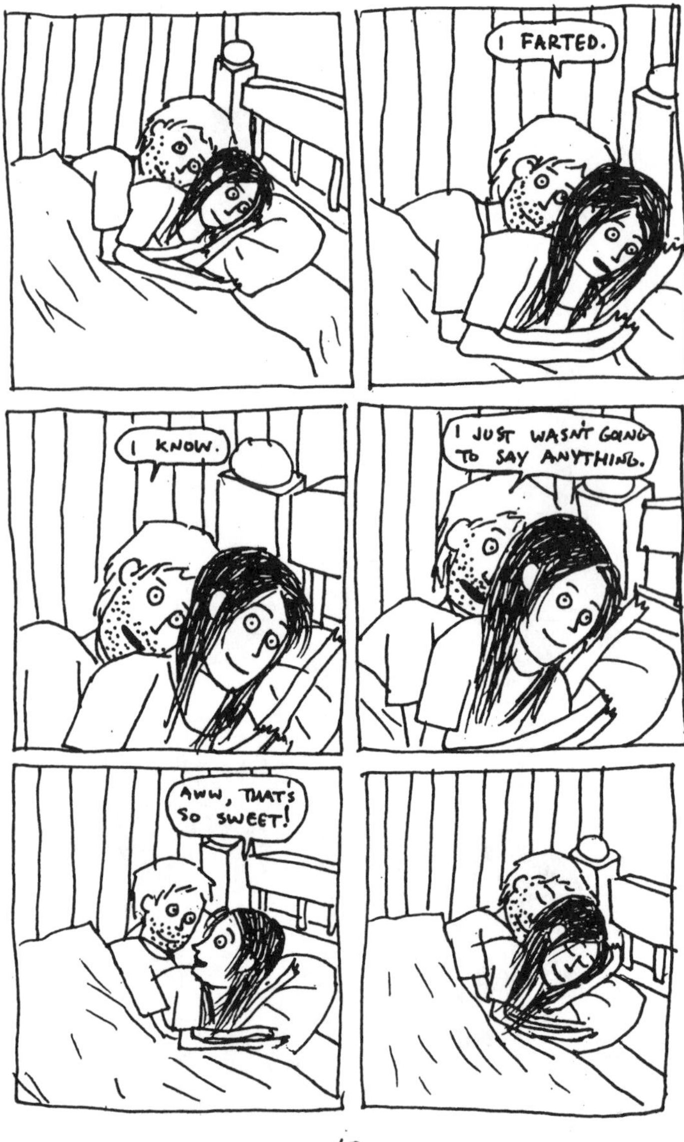
I FARTED.
I KNOW.
I JUST WASN'T GOING TO SAY ANYTHING.
AWW, THAT'S SO SWEET!

FAT

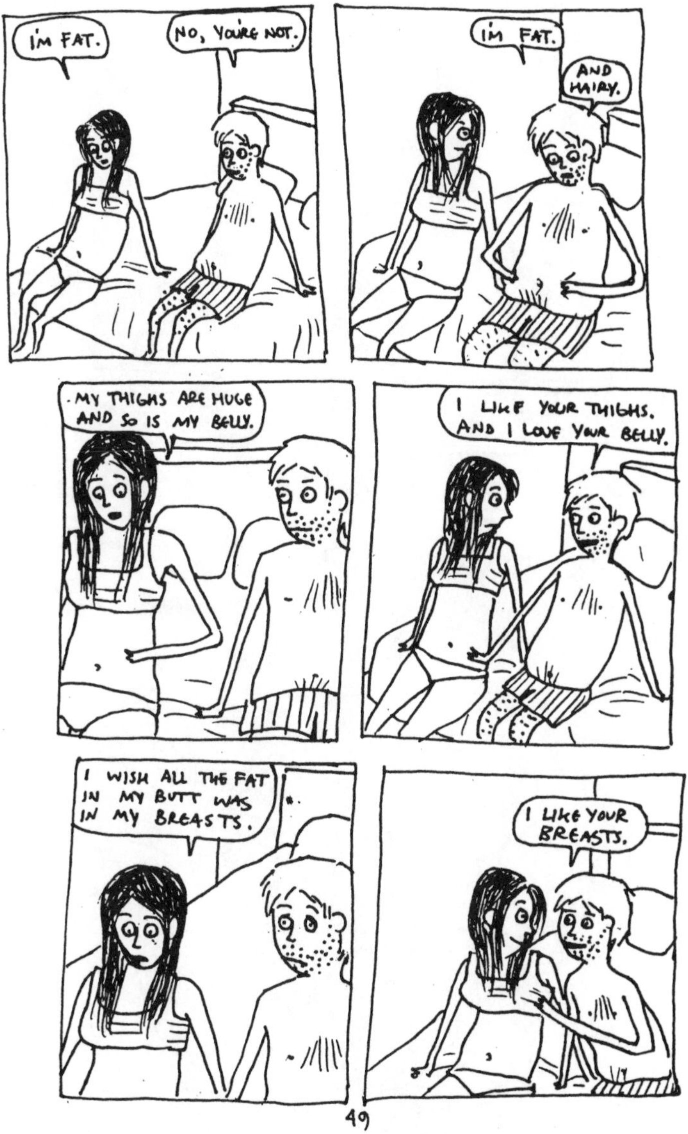
I'M FAT.
NO, YOU'RE NOT.
I'M FAT.
AND HAIRY.
MY THIGHS ARE HUGE AND SO IS MY BELLY.
I LIKE YOUR THIGHS. AND I LOVE YOUR BELLY.
I WISH ALL THE FAT IN MY BUTT WAS IN MY BREASTS.
I LIKE YOUR BREASTS.

JET GIRL

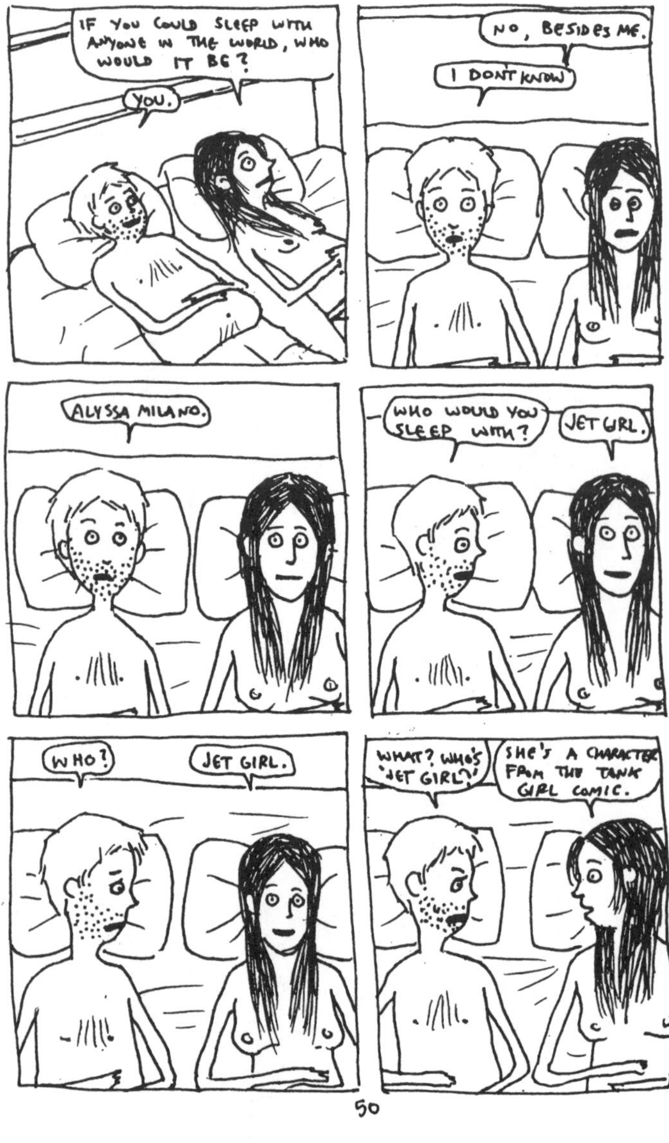
IF YOU COULD SLEEP WITH ANYONE IN THE WORLD, WHO WOULD IT BE?
YOU.
NO, BESIDES ME.
I DON'T KNOW
ALYSSA MILANO.
WHO WOULD YOU SLEEP WITH?
JET GIRL.
WHO?
JET GIRL.
WHAT? WHO'S 'JET GIRL'?
SHE'S A CHARACTER FROM THE TANK GIRL COMIC.

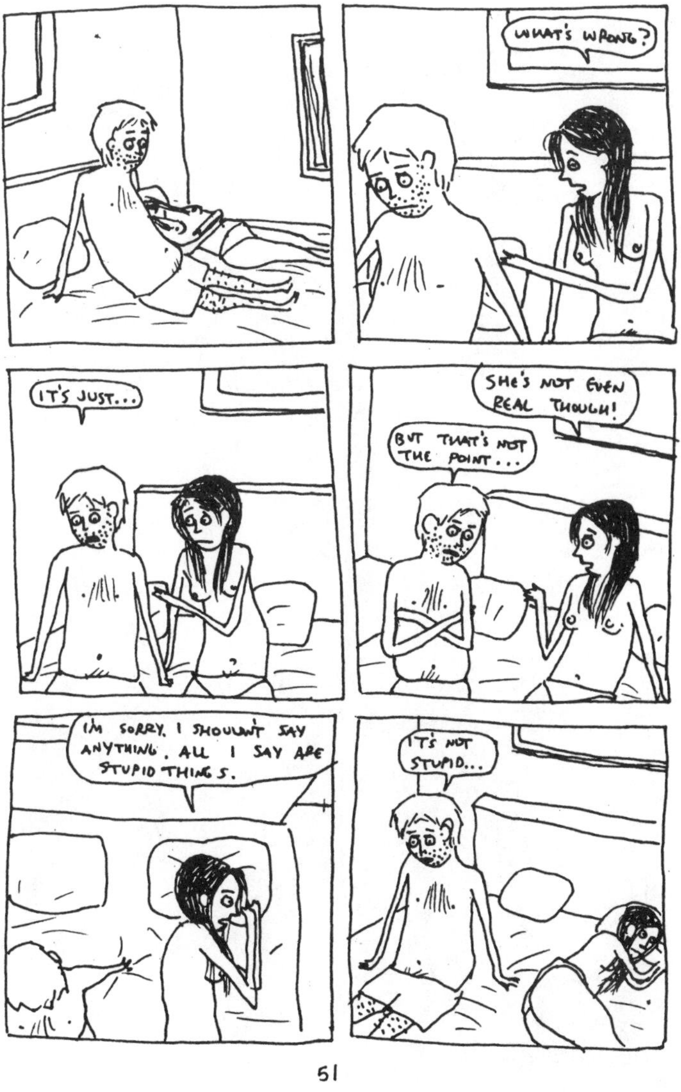
WHAT'S WRONG?
IT'S JUST...
SHE'S NOT EVEN REAL THOUGH!
BUT THAT'S NOT THE POINT...
I'M SORRY. I SHOULDN'T SAY ANYTHING. ALL I SAY ARE STUPID THINGS.
IT'S NOT STUPID...

I'M SORRY

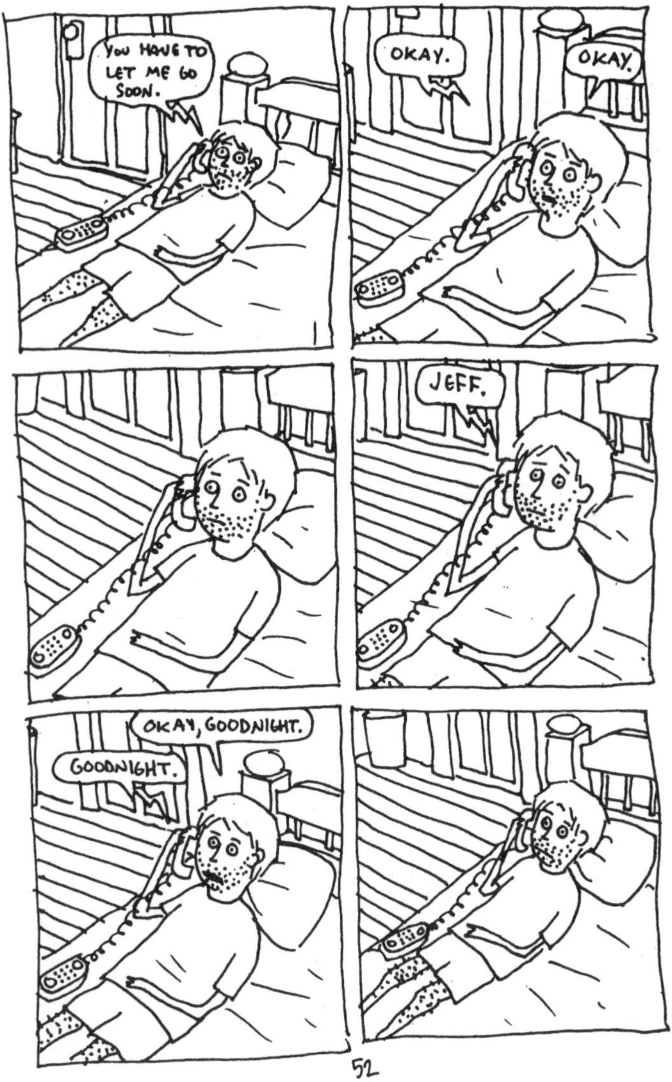
YOU HAVE TO LET ME GO SOON.
OKAY.
OKAY.
JEFF.
GOODNIGHT.
OKAY, GOODNIGHT.

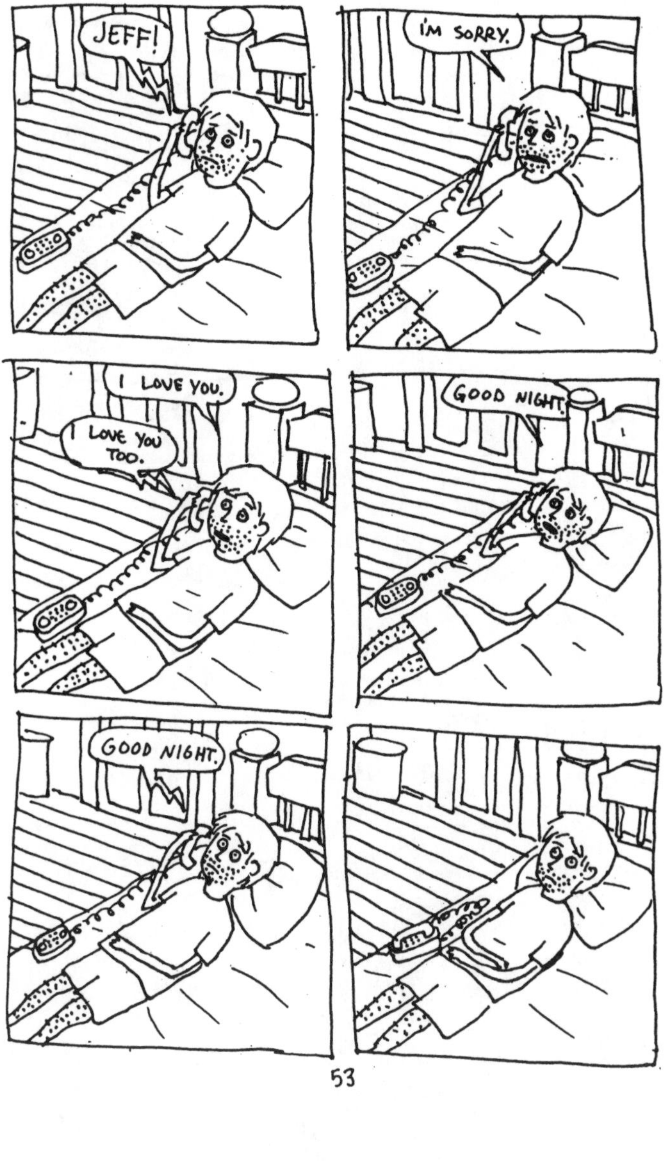
JEFF!
I'M SORRY.
I LOVE YOU.
I LOVE YOU TOO.
GOOD NIGHT.
GOOD NIGHT.

FOOZBALL

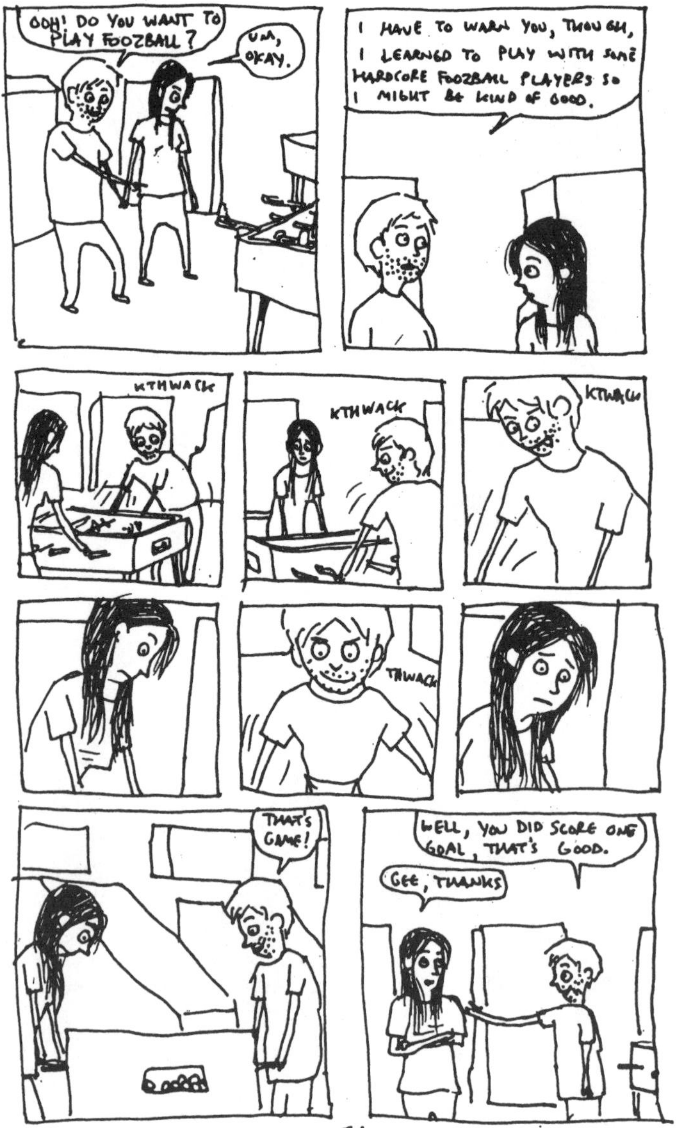
OOH! DO YOU WANT TO PLAY FOOZBALL?
UM, OKAY.
I HAVE TO WARN YOU, THOUGH, I LEARNED TO PLAY WITH SOME HARDCORE FOOZBALL PLAYERS SO I MIGHT BE KIND OF GOOD.
KTHWACK
KTHWACK
KTHWACK
THWACK
THAT'S GAME!
WELL, YOU DID SCORE ONE GOAL, THAT'S GOOD.
GEE, THANKS

X-MEN

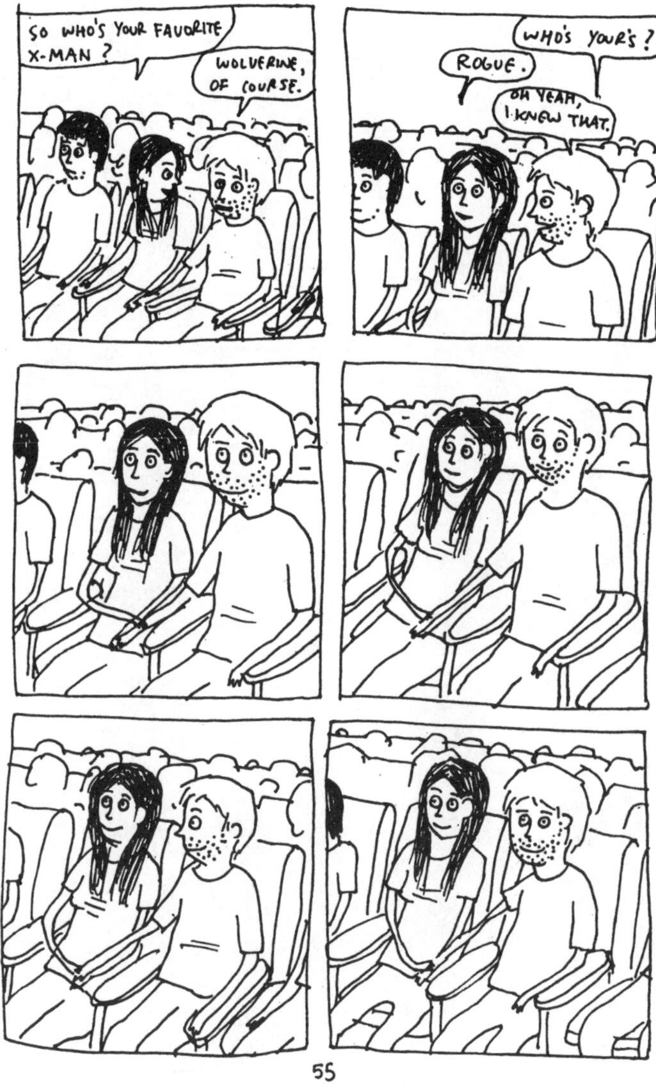
SO WHO'S YOUR FAVORITE X-MAN ?
WOLVERINE, OF COURSE.
WHO'S YOUR'S ?
ROGUE.
OH YEAH, I KNEW THAT.

DEXTER'S LABORATORY

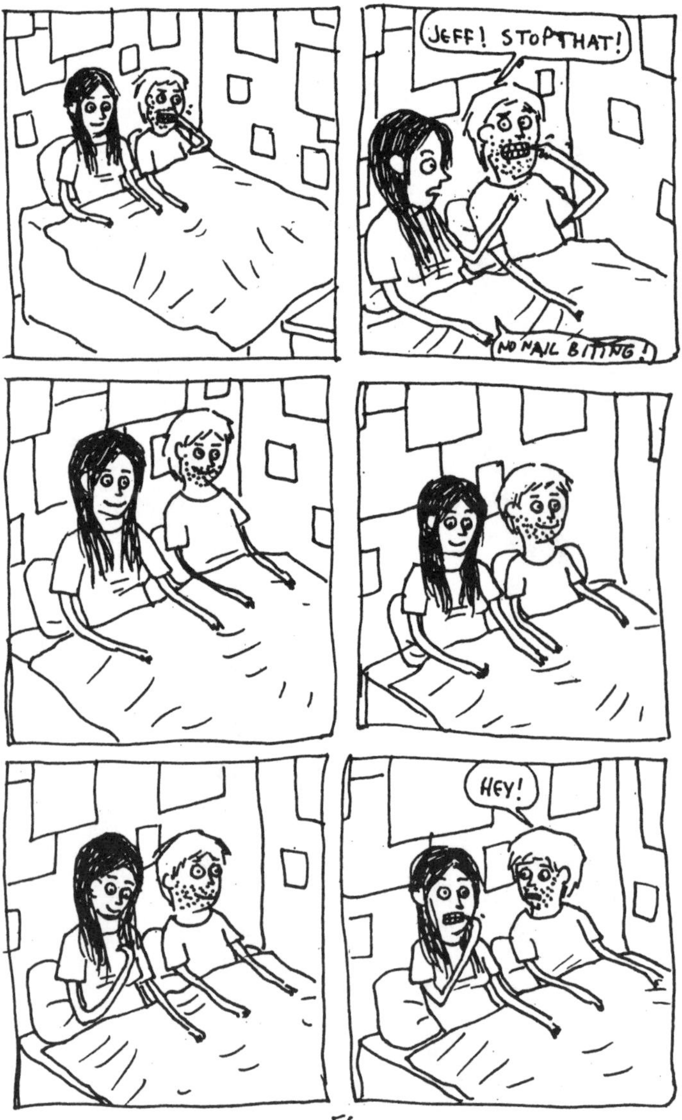
JEFF! STOP THAT!
NO NAIL BITING!
HEY!

BUT I WANT TO MAKE LOVE

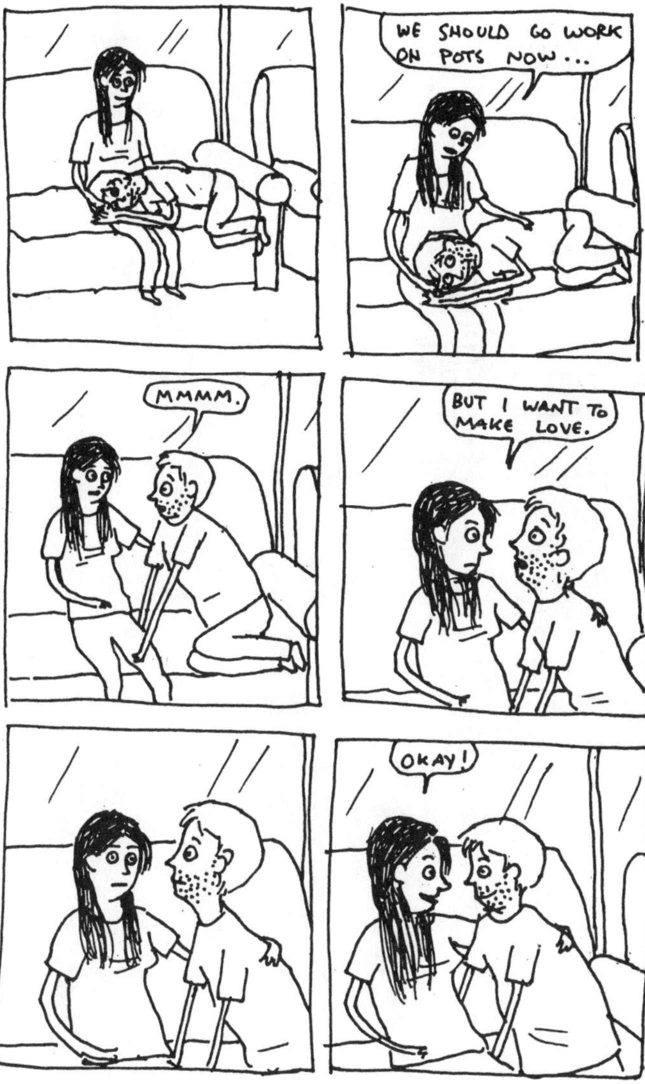
WE SHOULD GO WORK ON POTS NOW...
MMMM.
BUT I WANT TO MAKE LOVE.
OKAY!

GWEN

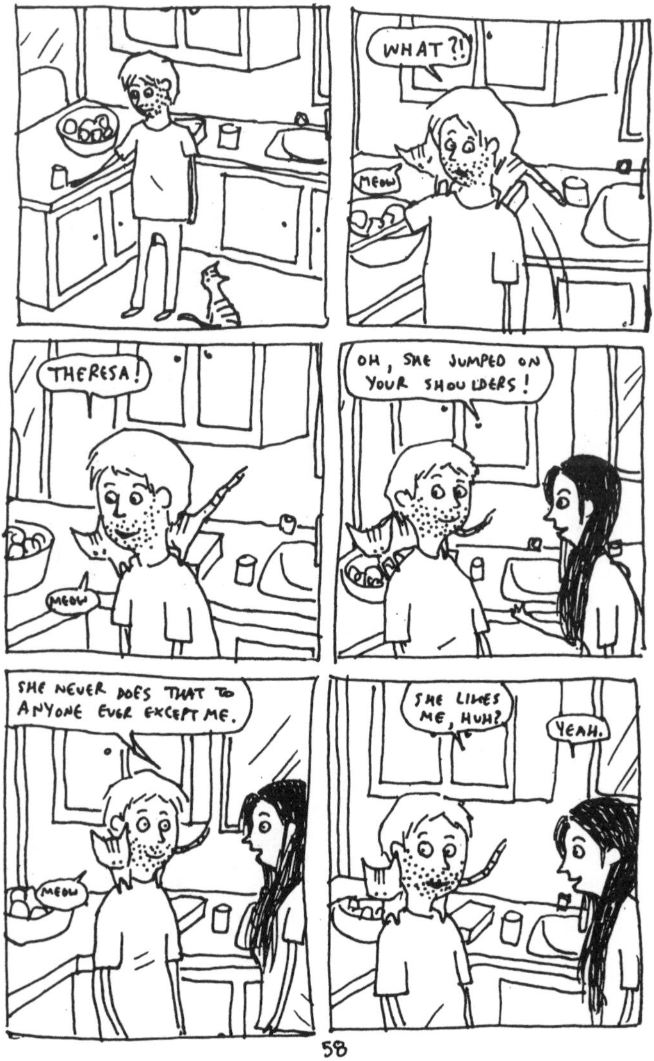
WHAT?!
MEOW
THERESA!
MEOW
OH, SHE JUMPED ON YOUR SHOULDERS!
SHE NEVER DOES THAT TO ANYONE EVER EXCEPT ME.
MEOW
SHE LIKES ME, HUH?
YEAH.

SEXY OUTFIT

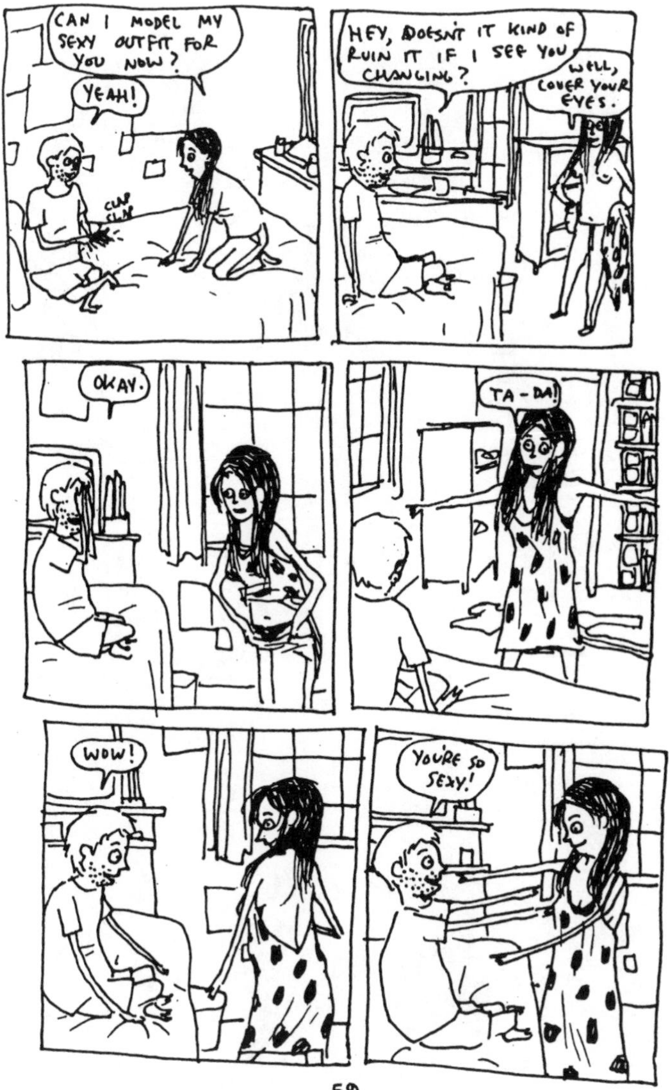
CAN I MODEL MY SEXY OUTFIT FOR YOU NOW?
YEAH!
HEY, DOESN'T IT KIND OF RUIN IT IF I SEE YOU CHANGING?
WELL, COVER YOUR EYES.
OKAY.
TA-DA!
WOW!
YOU'RE SO SEXY!

AIR HOCKEY

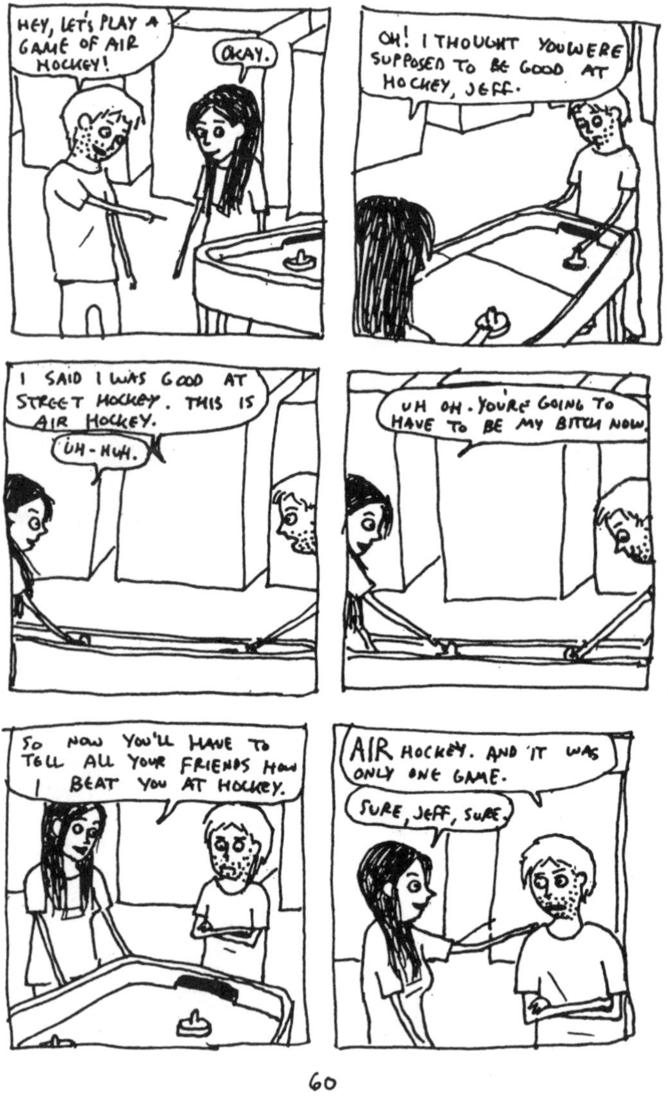
HEY, LET'S PLAY A GAME OF AIR HOCKEY!
OKAY.
OH! I THOUGHT YOU WERE SUPPOSED TO BE GOOD AT HOCKEY, JEFF.
I SAID I WAS GOOD AT STREET HOCKEY. THIS IS AIR HOCKEY.
UH-HUH.
UH OH. YOU'RE GOING TO HAVE TO BE MY BITCH NOW.
SO NOW YOU'LL HAVE TO TELL ALL YOUR FRIENDS HOW I BEAT YOU AT HOCKEY.
AIR HOCKEY. AND IT WAS ONLY ONE GAME.
SURE, JEFF, SURE.

THERESA DOES ART, TOO

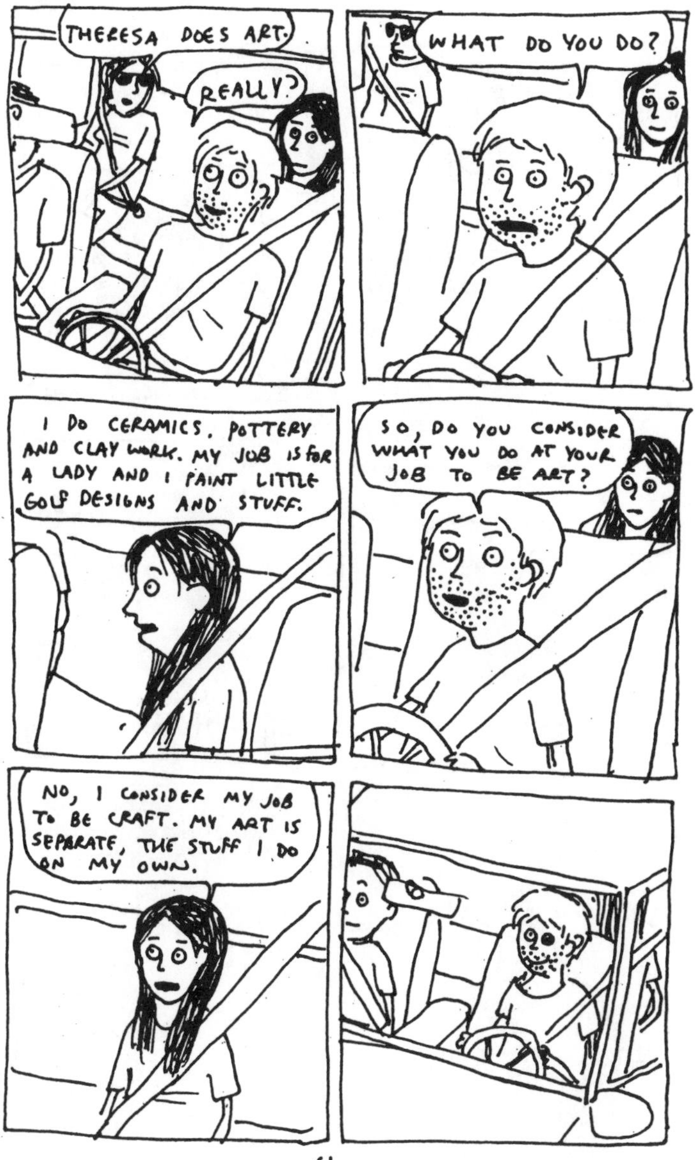
THERESA DOES ART.
REALLY?
WHAT DO YOU DO?
I DO CERAMICS, POTTERY AND CLAY WORK. MY JOB IS FOR A LADY AND I PAINT LITTLE GOLF DESIGNS AND STUFF.
SO, DO YOU CONSIDER WHAT YOU DO AT YOUR JOB TO BE ART?
NO, I CONSIDER MY JOB TO BE CRAFT. MY ART IS SEPARATE, THE STUFF I DO ON MY OWN.

NOW BOARDING

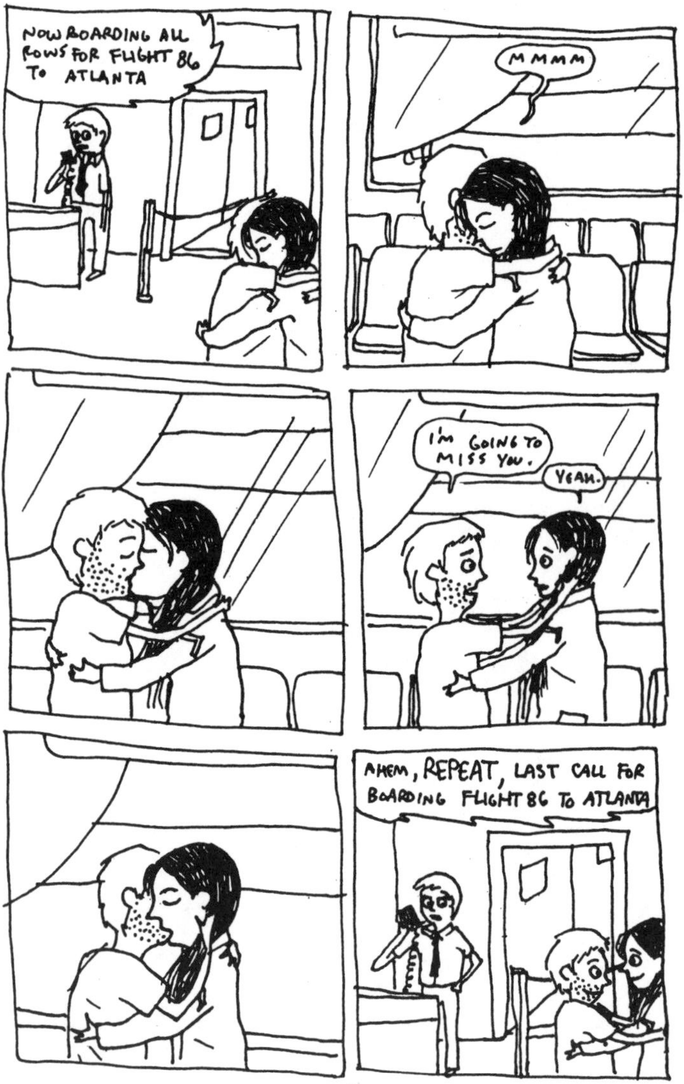
NOW BOARDING ALL ROWS FOR FLIGHT 86 TO ATLANTA
MMMM
I'M GOING TO MISS YOU.
YEAH.
AHEM, REPEAT, LAST CALL FOR BOARDING FLIGHT 86 TO ATLANTA

HURT ME

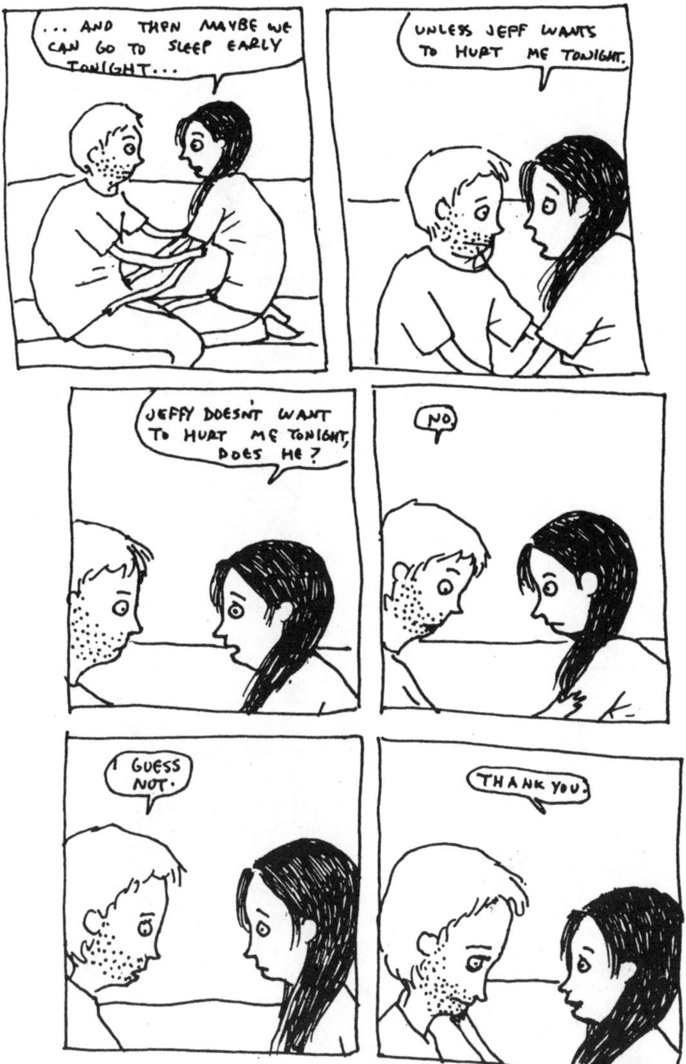
... AND THEN MAYBE WE CAN GO TO SLEEP EARLY TONIGHT...
UNLESS JEFF WANTS TO HURT ME TONIGHT.
JEFFY DOESN'T WANT TO HURT ME TONIGHT, DOES HE?
NO.
I GUESS NOT.
THANK YOU.

ALEVE

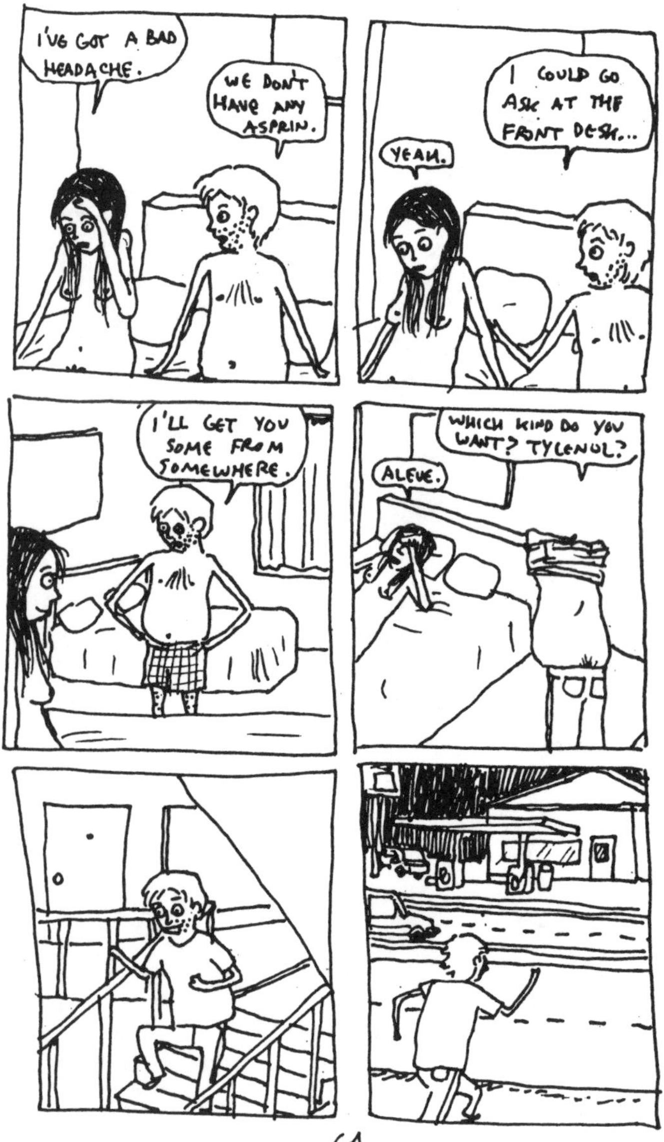
I'VE GOT A BAD HEADACHE.
WE DON'T HAVE ANY ASPRIN.
I COULD GO ASK AT THE FRONT DESK...
YEAH.
I'LL GET YOU SOME FROM SOMEWHERE.
WHICH KIND DO YOU WANT? TYLENOL?
ALEVE.

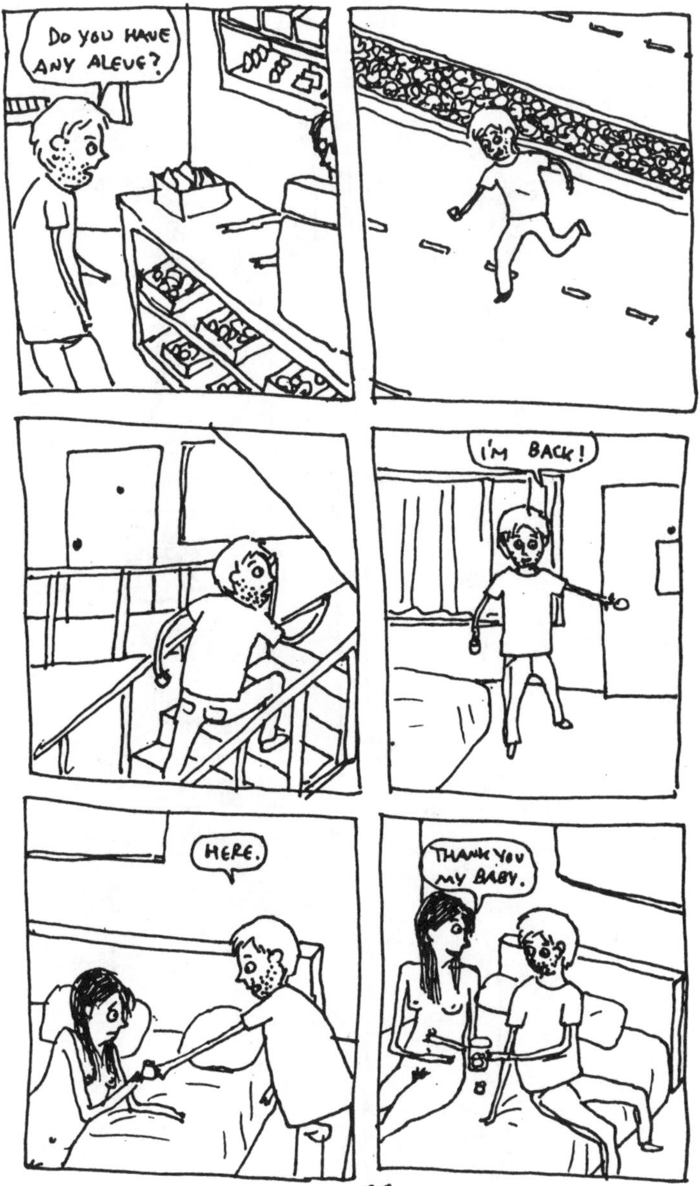
DO YOU HAVE ANY ALEVE?
I'M BACK!
HERE.
THANK YOU MY BABY.

APX. SIX A.M.

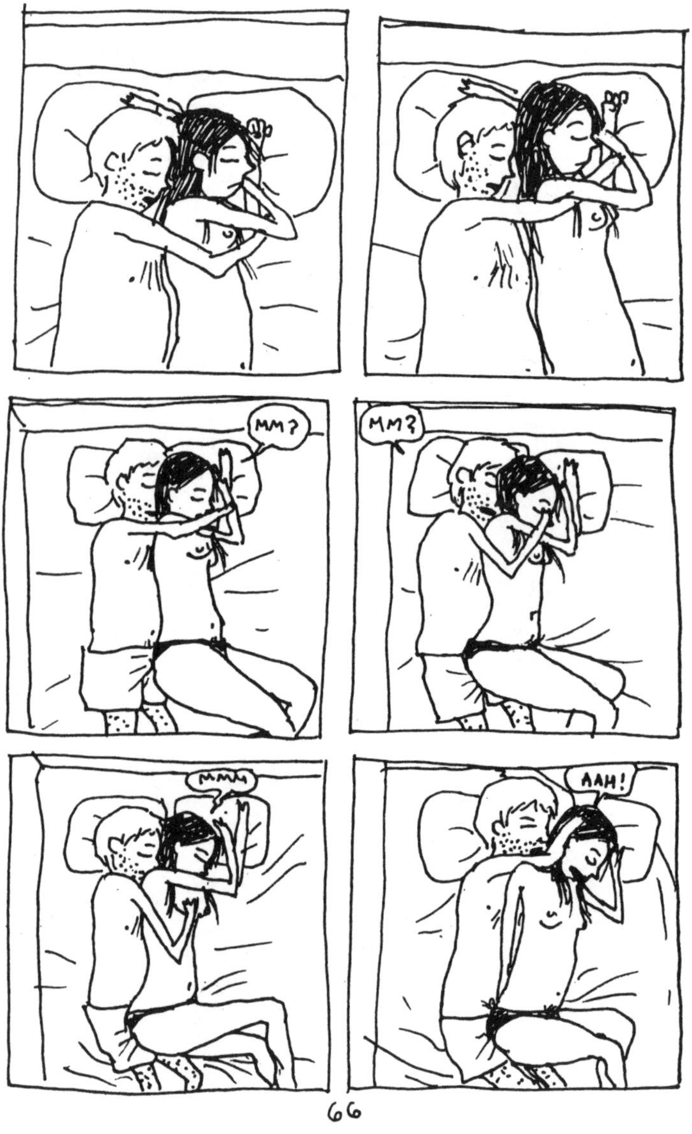
MM?
MM?
MMM
AAH!

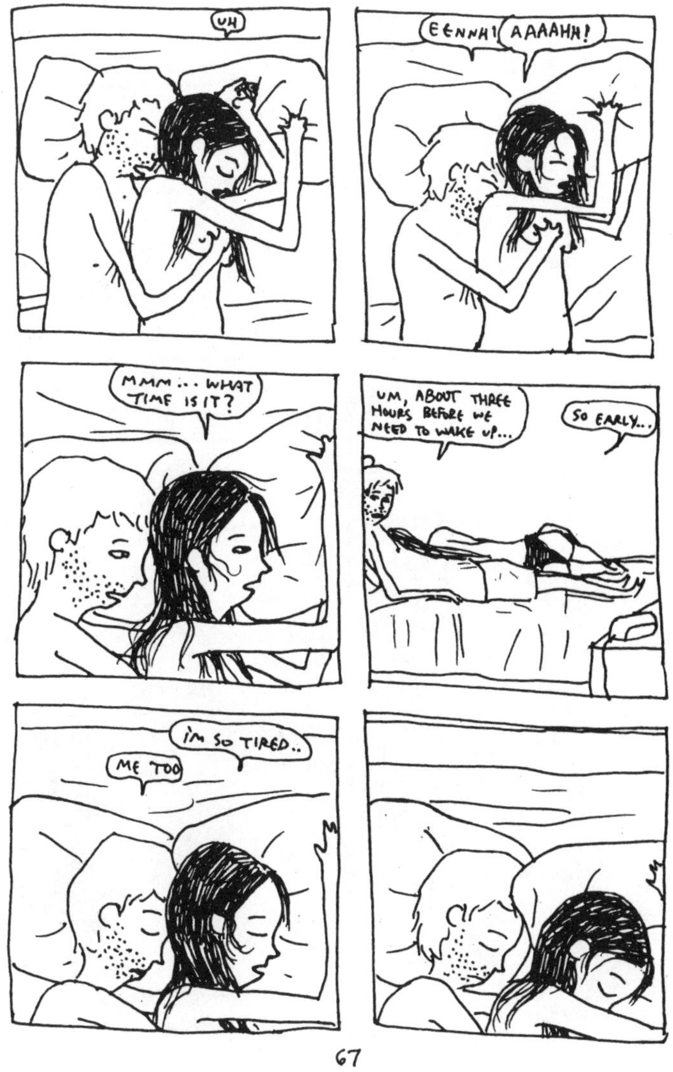
UH
EENNH!
AAAAHH!
MMM... WHAT TIME IS IT?
UM, ABOUT THREE HOURS BEFORE WE NEED TO WAKE UP...
SO EARLY...
I'M SO TIRED..
ME TOO

CONDOMS

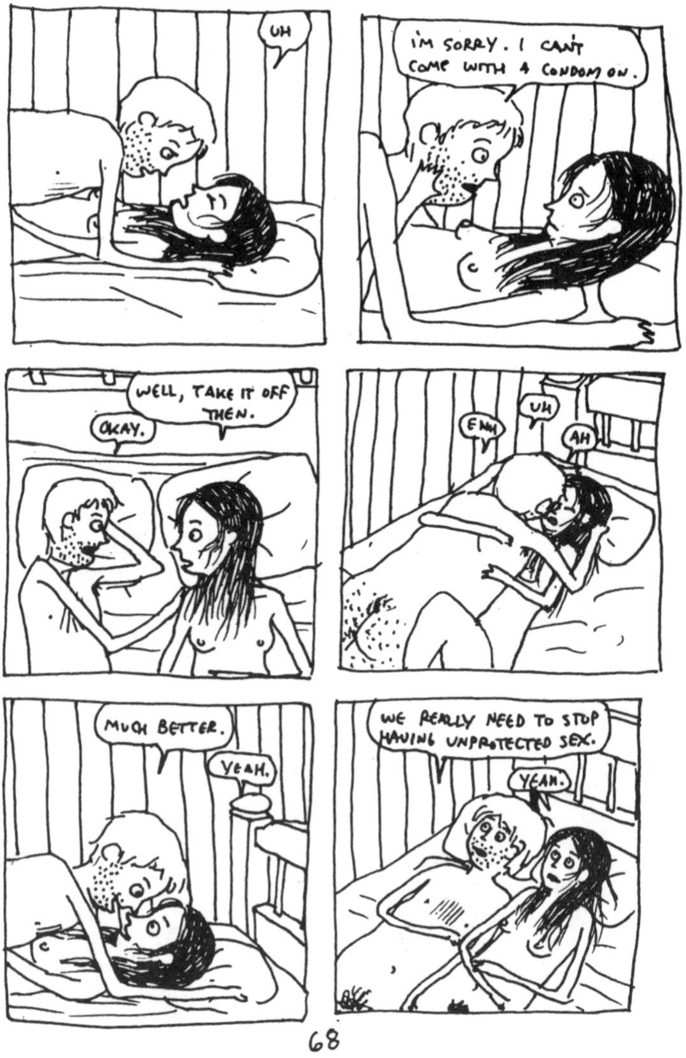
UH
I'M SORRY. I CAN'T COME WITH A CONDOM ON.
WELL, TAKE IT OFF THEN.
OKAY.
ENH
UH
AH
MUCH BETTER.
YEAH.
WE REALLY NEED TO STOP HAVING UNPROTECTED SEX.
YEAH.

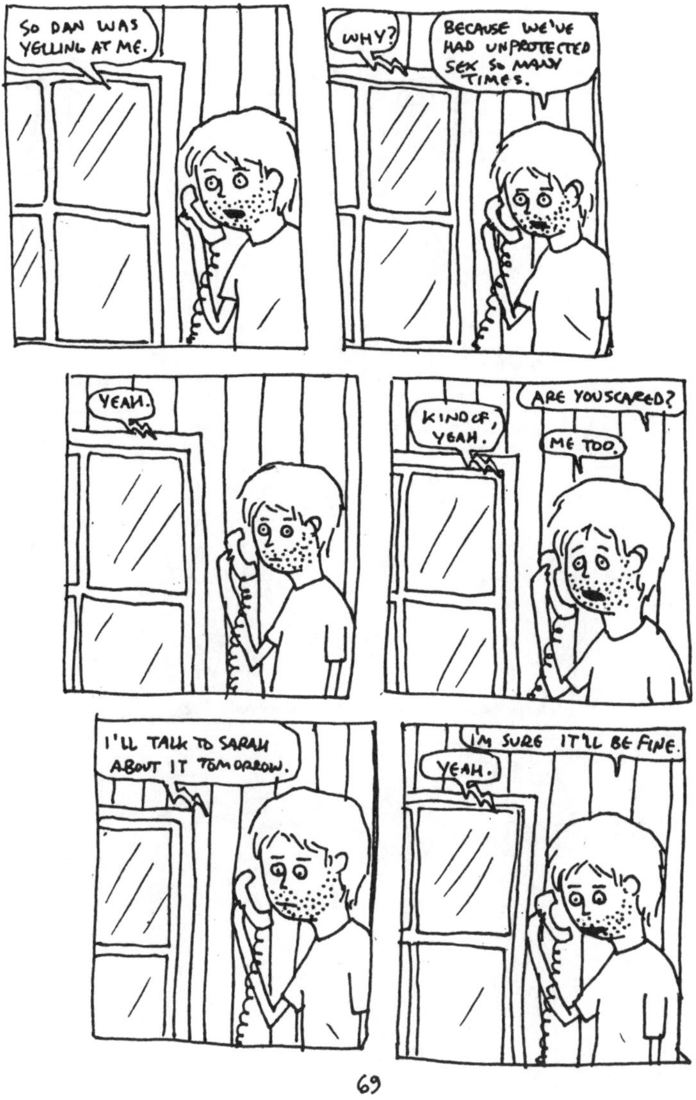
SO DAN WAS YELLING AT ME.
WHY?
BECAUSE WE'VE HAD UNPROTECTED SEX SO MANY TIMES.
YEAH.
ARE YOU SCARED?
KIND OF, YEAH.
ME TOO.
I'LL TALK TO SARAH ABOUT IT TOMORROW.
I'M SURE IT'LL BE FINE.
YEAH.

PERIODS

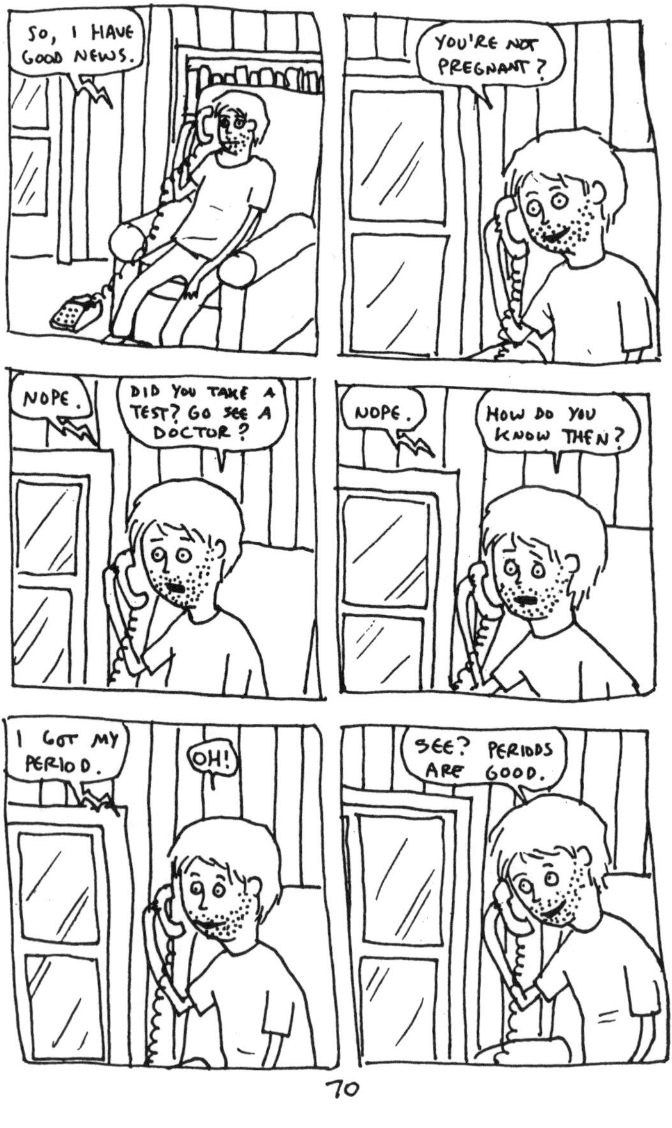
SO, I HAVE GOOD NEWS.
YOU'RE NOT PREGNANT?
NOPE.
DID YOU TAKE A TEST? GO SEE A DOCTOR?
NOPE.
HOW DO YOU KNOW THEN?
I GOT MY PERIOD.
OH!
SEE? PERIODS ARE GOOD.

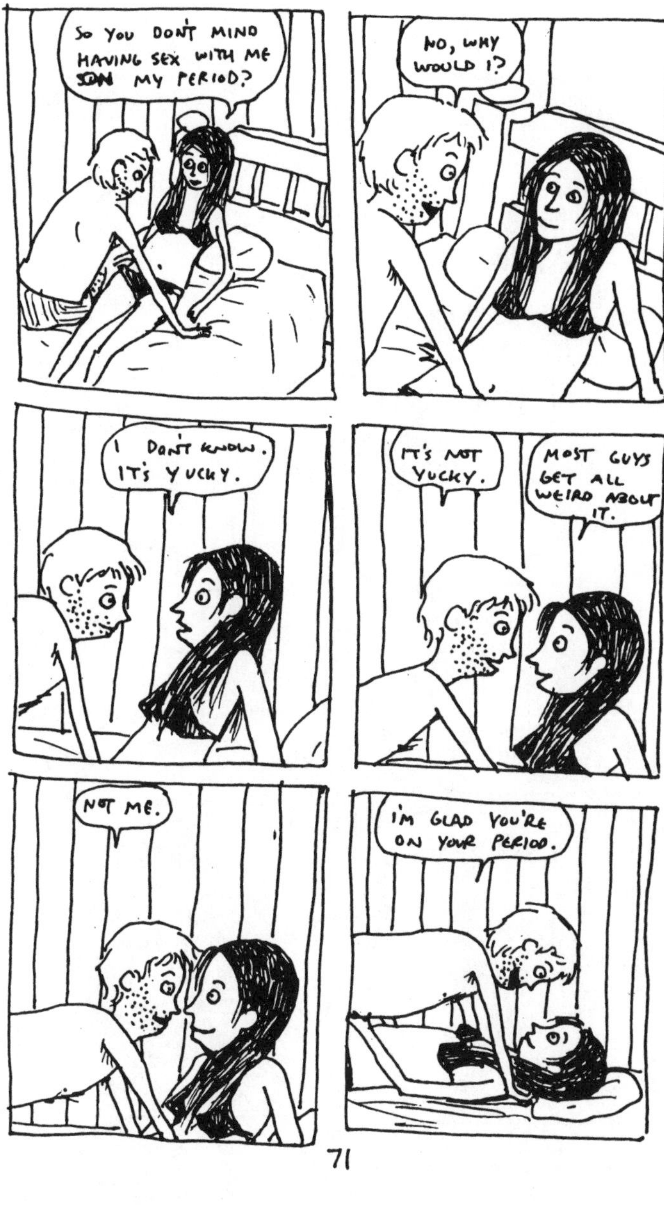

SO YOU DON'T MIND HAVING SEX WITH ME ON MY PERIOD?
NO, WHY WOULD I?
I DON'T KNOW. IT'S YUCKY.
IT'S NOT YUCKY.
MOST GUYS GET ALL WEIRD ABOUT IT.
NOT ME.
I'M GLAD YOU'RE ON YOUR PERIOD.

FOAM

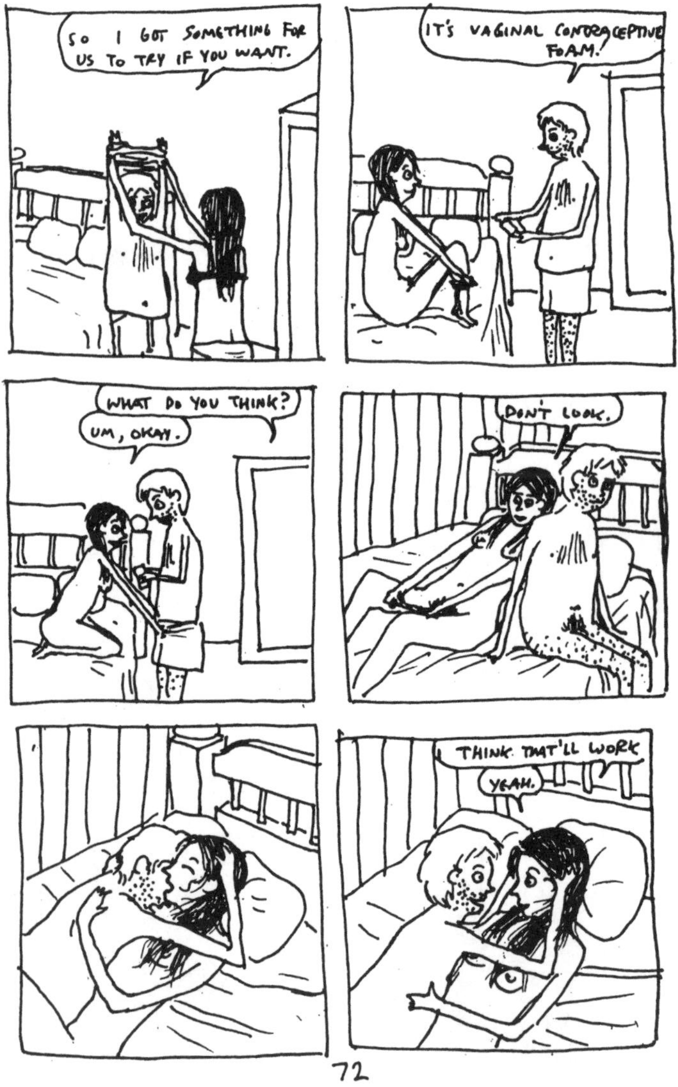
SO I GOT SOMETHING FOR US TO TRY IF YOU WANT.
IT'S VAGINAL CONTRACEPTIVE FOAM.
WHAT DO YOU THINK?
UM, OKAY.
DON'T LOOK.
THINK THAT'LL WORK
YEAH.

DON'T TOUCH ME

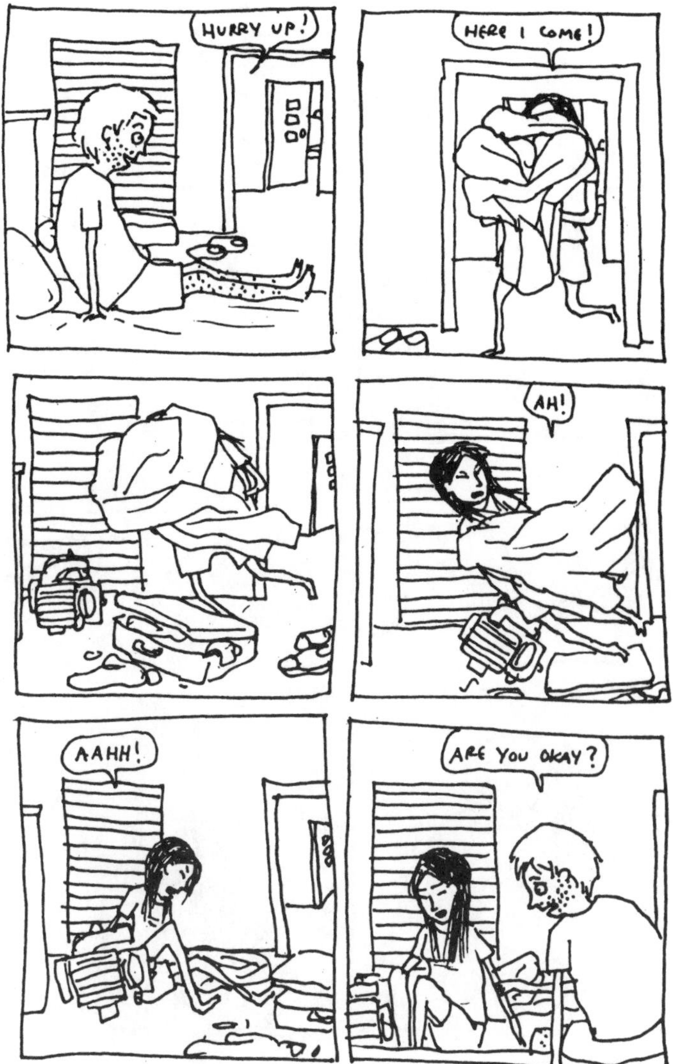
HURRY UP!
HERE I COME!
AH!
AAHH!
ARE YOU OKAY?

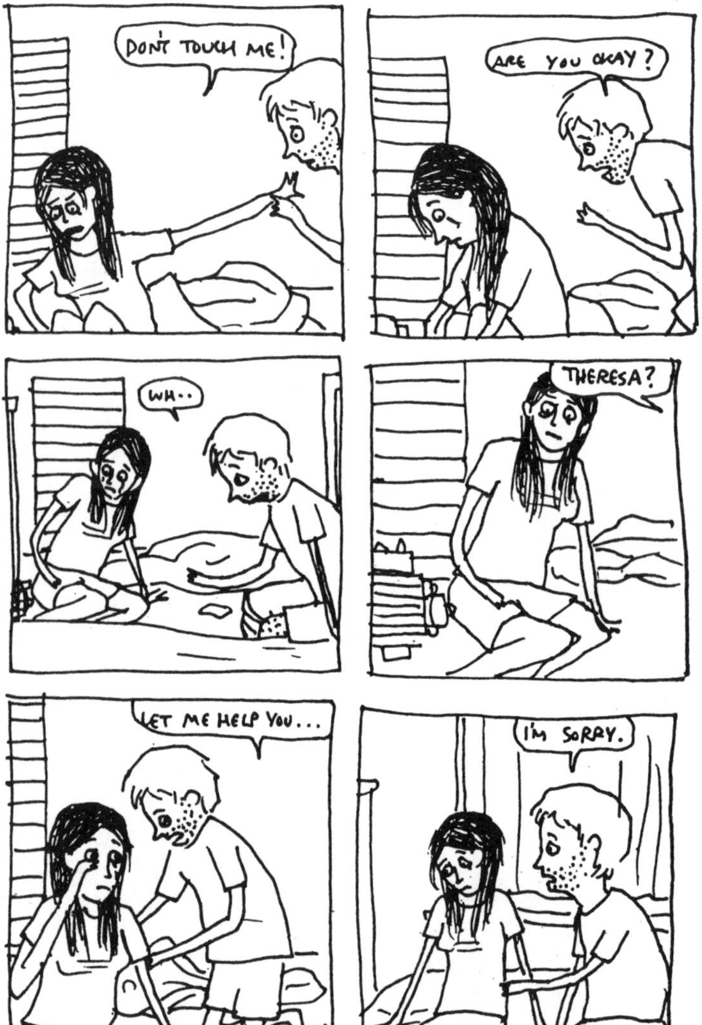
DON'T TOUCH ME!
ARE YOU OKAY?
WH..
THERESA?
LET ME HELP YOU...
I'M SORRY.

I'M SORRY. ARE YOU OKAY?
LET ME SEE.
HERE, LET ME RUB IT.
IT'S NOT YOUR FAULT.
I'M SORRY.
I'M SORRY.
I'M SORRY.

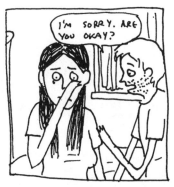

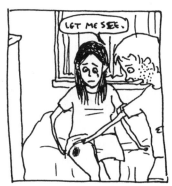

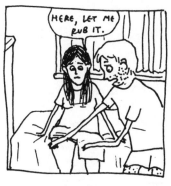

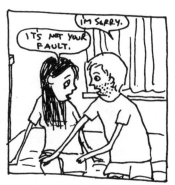

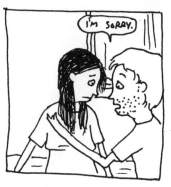

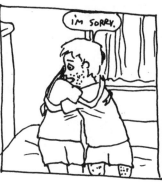

WHAT DID YOU THINK OF ME?

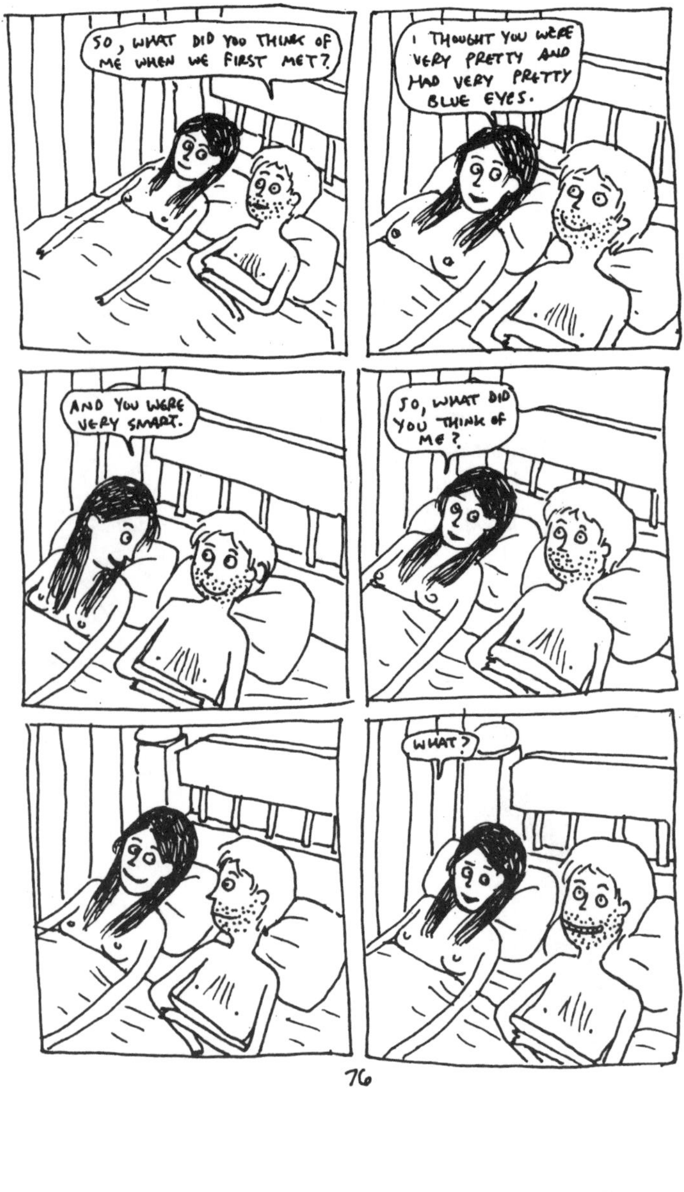
SO, WHAT DID YOU THINK OF ME WHEN WE FIRST MET?
I THOUGHT YOU WERE VERY PRETTY AND HAD VERY PRETTY BLUE EYES.
AND YOU WERE VERY SMART.
SO, WHAT DID YOU THINK OF ME?
WHAT?

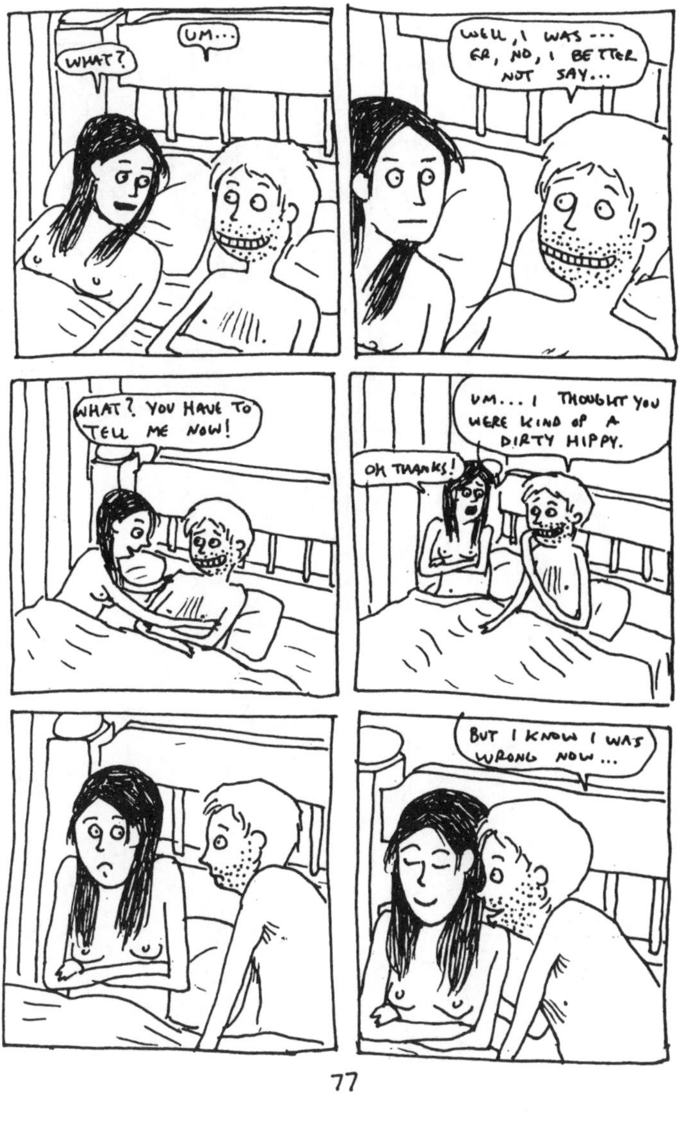
WHAT?
UM...
WELL, I WAS... ER, NO, I BETTER NOT SAY...
WHAT? YOU HAVE TO TELL ME NOW!
UM... I THOUGHT YOU WERE KIND OF A DIRTY HIPPY.
OH THANKS!
BUT I KNOW I WAS WRONG NOW...

HICCUPS

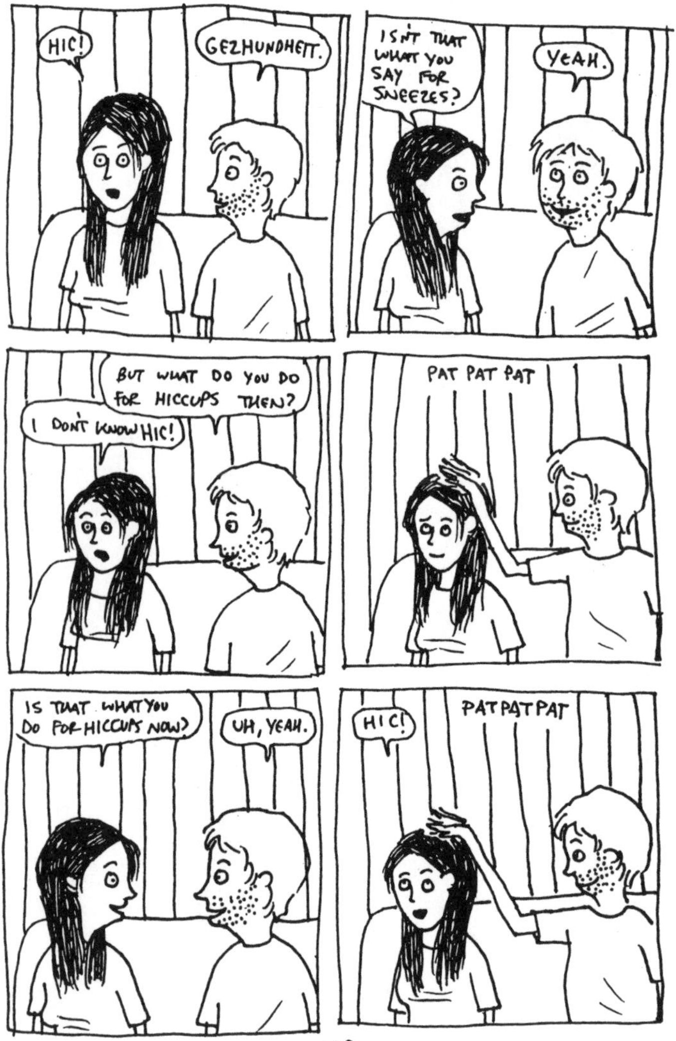
HIC!
GEZHUNDHEIT.
ISN'T THAT WHAT YOU SAY FOR SNEEZES?
YEAH.
BUT WHAT DO YOU DO FOR HICCUPS THEN?
I DON'T KNOW HIC!
PAT PAT PAT
IS THAT WHAT YOU DO FOR HICCUPS NOW?
UH, YEAH.
HIC!
PATPATPAT

DAY LILLIES

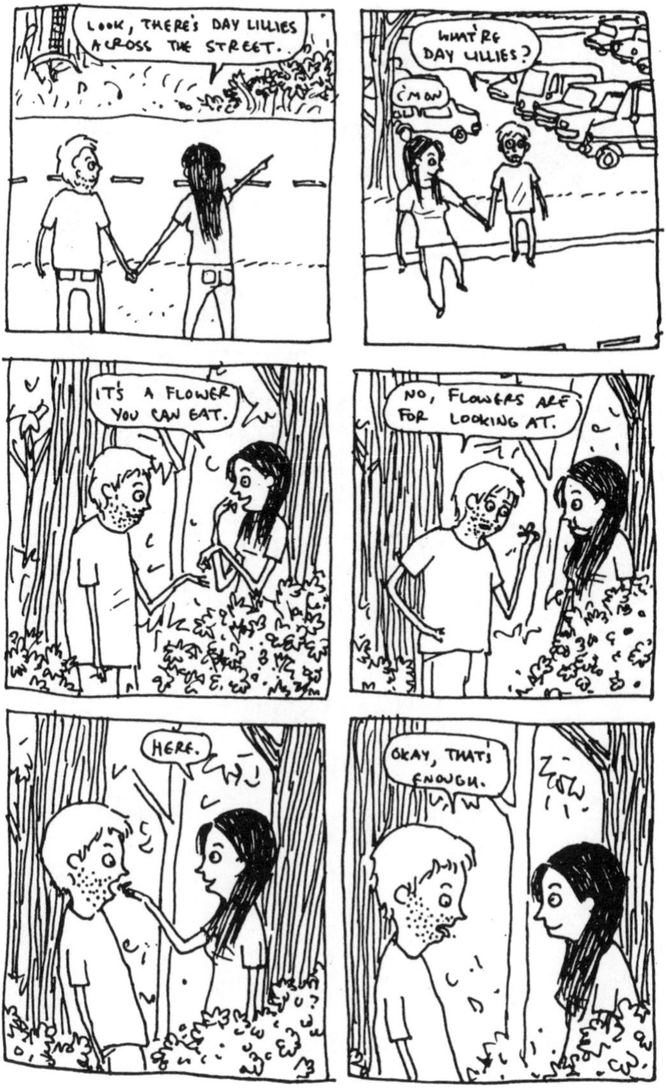
LOOK, THERE'S DAY LILLIES ACROSS THE STREET.
WHAT'RE DAY LILLIES?
C'MON
IT'S A FLOWER YOU CAN EAT.
NO, FLOWERS ARE FOR LOOKING AT.
HERE.
OKAY, THAT'S ENOUGH.

ROACHES

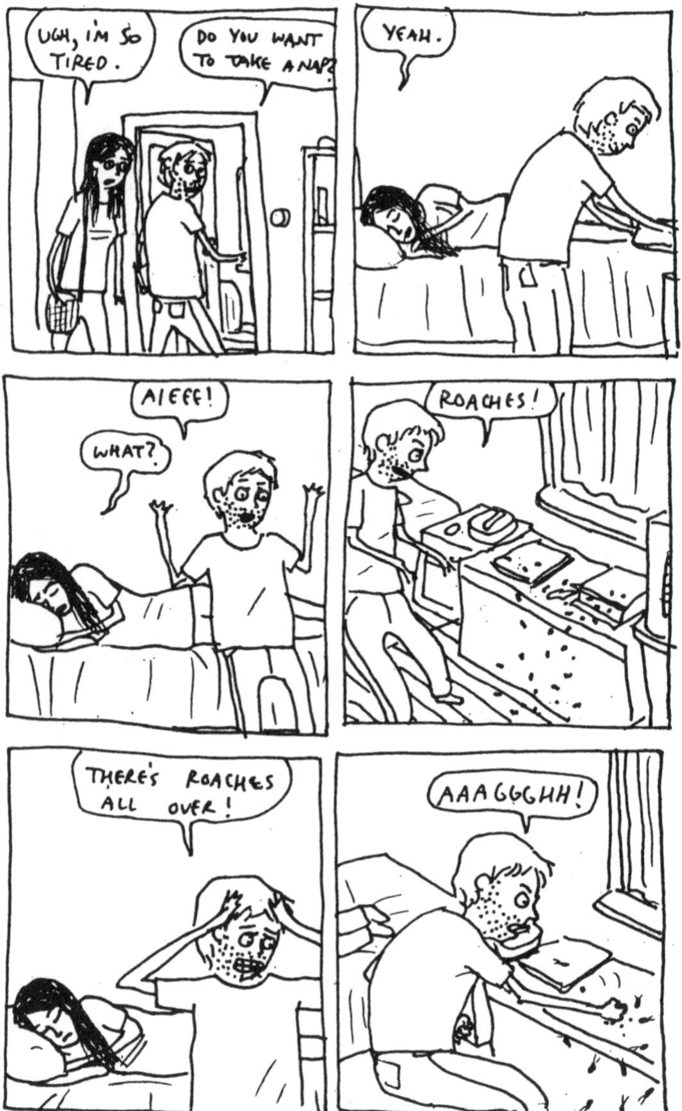
UGH, I'M SO TIRED.
DO YOU WANT TO TAKE A NAP?
YEAH.
AIEEE!
WHAT?
ROACHES!
THERE'S ROACHES ALL OVER!
AAAGGGHH!

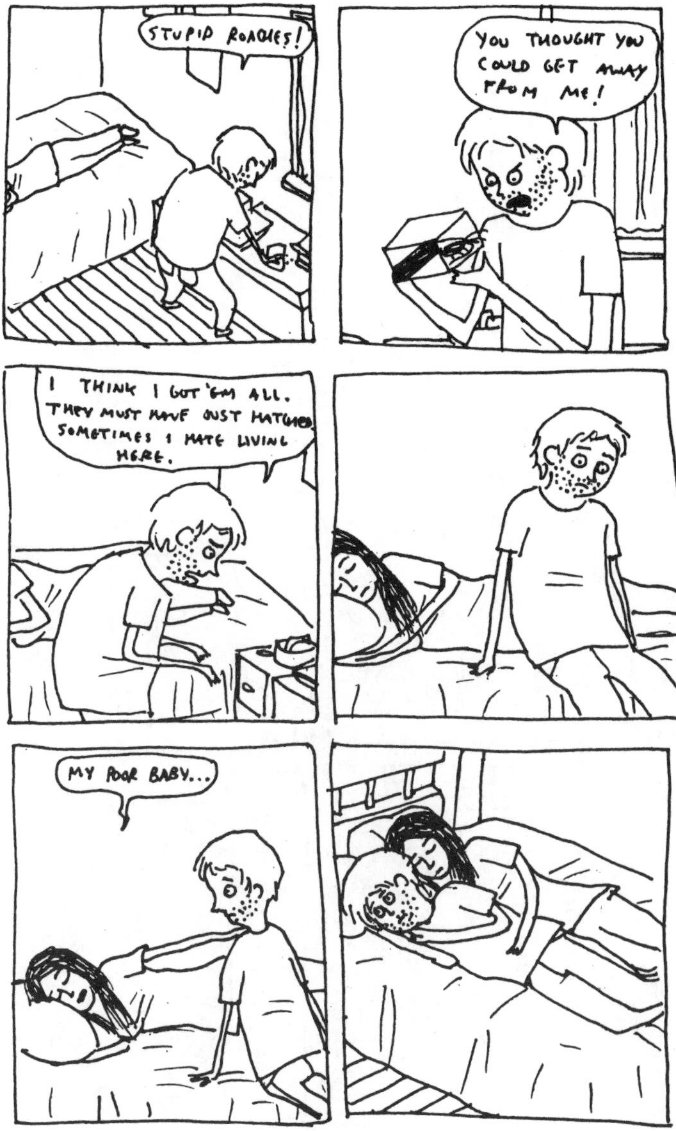
STUPID ROACHES!
YOU THOUGHT YOU COULD GET AWAY FROM ME!
I THINK I GOT 'EM ALL. THEY MUST HAVE JUST HATCHED. SOMETIMES I HATE LIVING HERE.
MY POOR BABY...

CAMPING

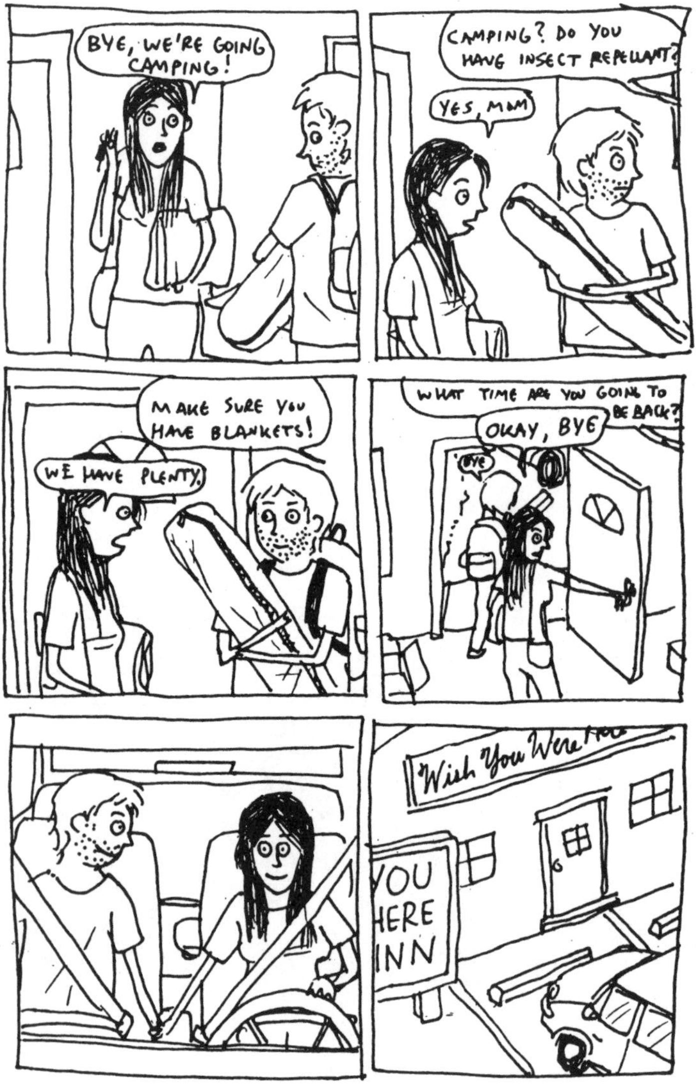
BYE, WE'RE GOING CAMPING!
CAMPING? DO YOU HAVE INSECT REPELLANT?
YES, MOM
MAKE SURE YOU HAVE BLANKETS!
WE HAVE PLENTY.
WHAT TIME ARE YOU GOING TO BE BACK?
OKAY, BYE
BYE
Wish You Were Here
YOU HERE INN

MY LITTLE BOOK

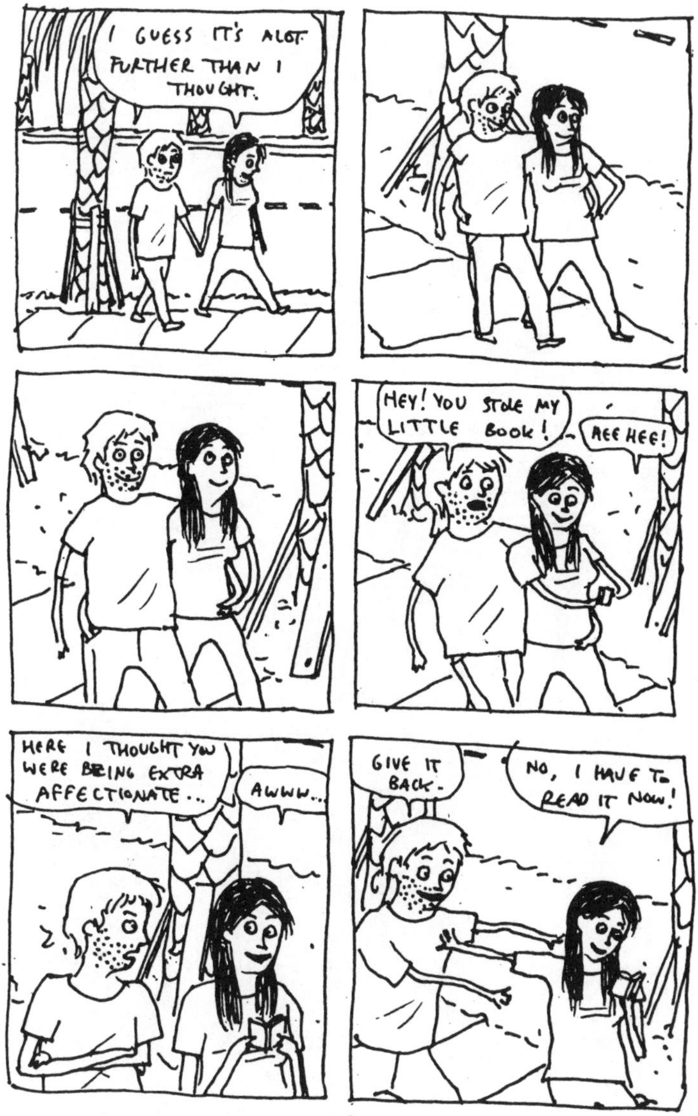

I GUESS IT'S ALOT FURTHER THAN I THOUGHT.
HEY! YOU STOLE MY LITTLE BOOK!
HEE HEE!
HERE I THOUGHT YOU WERE BEING EXTRA AFFECTIONATE...
AWWW...
GIVE IT BACK.
NO, I HAVE TO READ IT NOW!

THE PLACEMAT

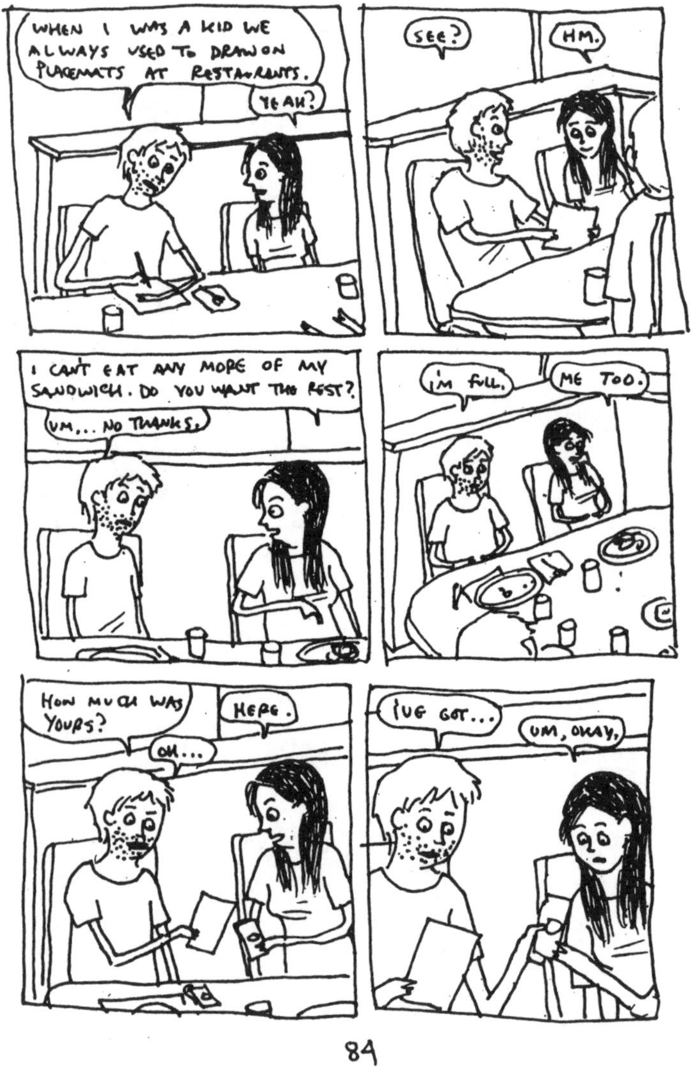
WHEN I WAS A KID WE ALWAYS USED TO DRAW ON PLACEMATS AT RESTAURANTS.
YEAH?
SEE?
HM.
I CAN'T EAT ANY MORE OF MY SANDWICH. DO YOU WANT THE REST?
UM... NO THANKS.
I'M FULL.
ME TOO.
HOW MUCH WAS YOURS?
HERE.
OH...
I'VE GOT...
UM, OKAY.

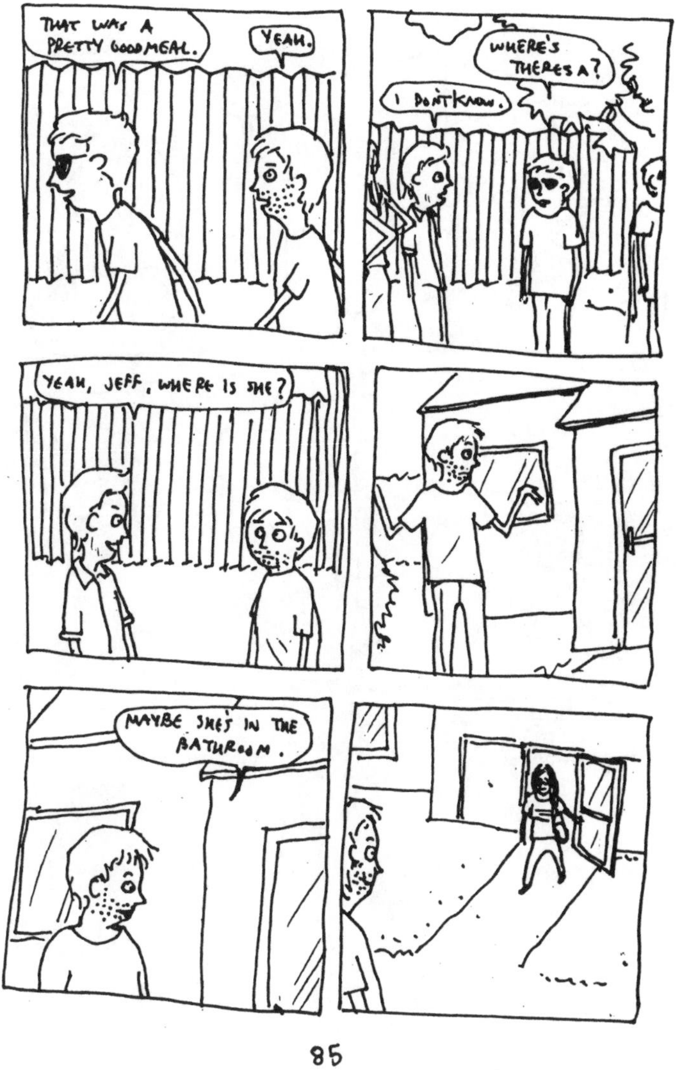
THAT WAS A PRETTY GOOD MEAL.
YEAH.
WHERE'S THERESA?
I DON'T KNOW.
YEAH, JEFF, WHERE IS SHE?
MAYBE SHE'S IN THE BATHROOM.

FLORIDA

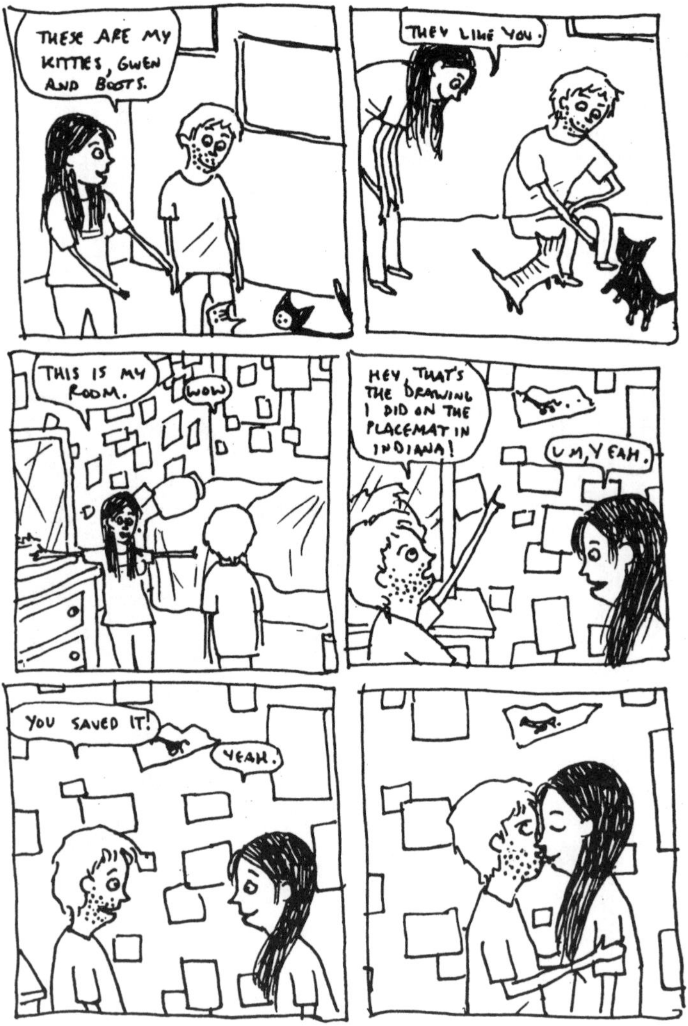
THESE ARE MY KITTIES, GWEN AND BOOTS.
THEY LIKE YOU.
THIS IS MY ROOM.
WOW
HEY, THAT'S THE DRAWING I DID ON THE PLACEMAT IN INDIANA!
UM, YEAH.
YOU SAVED IT!
YEAH.

A SHORT GOODBYE

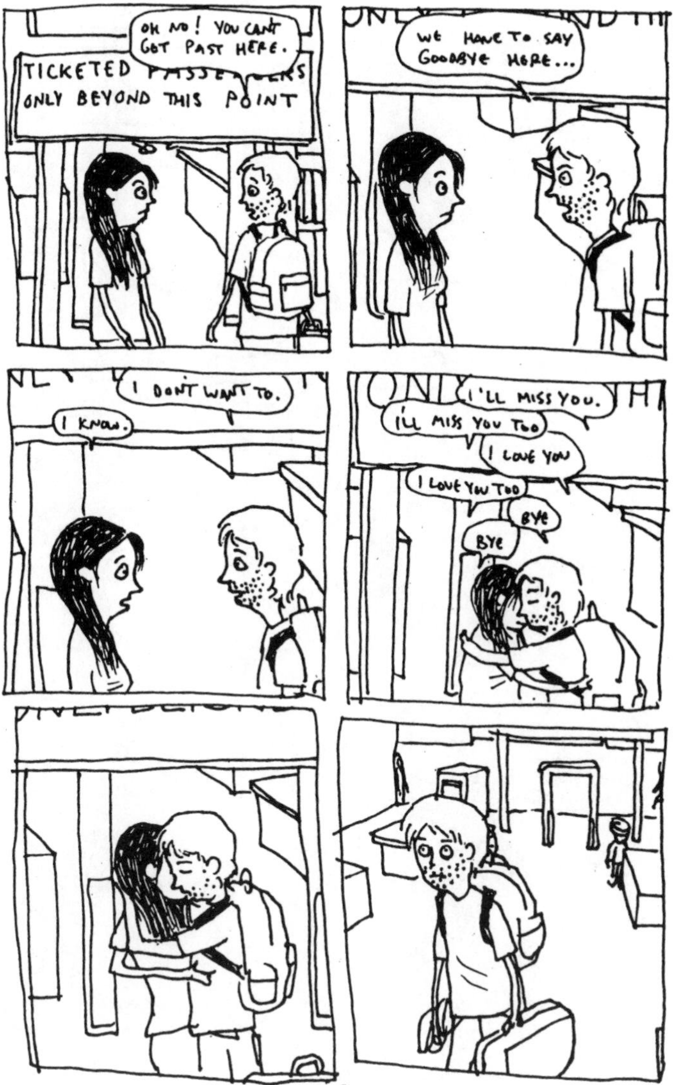
OH NO! YOU CAN'T GET PAST HERE.
TICKETED
ONLY BEYOND THIS POINT
WE HAVE TO SAY GOODBYE HERE...
I DON'T WANT TO.
I KNOW.
I'LL MISS YOU.
I'LL MISS YOU TOO
I LOVE YOU
I LOVE YOU TOO
BYE
BYE

ART HISTORY

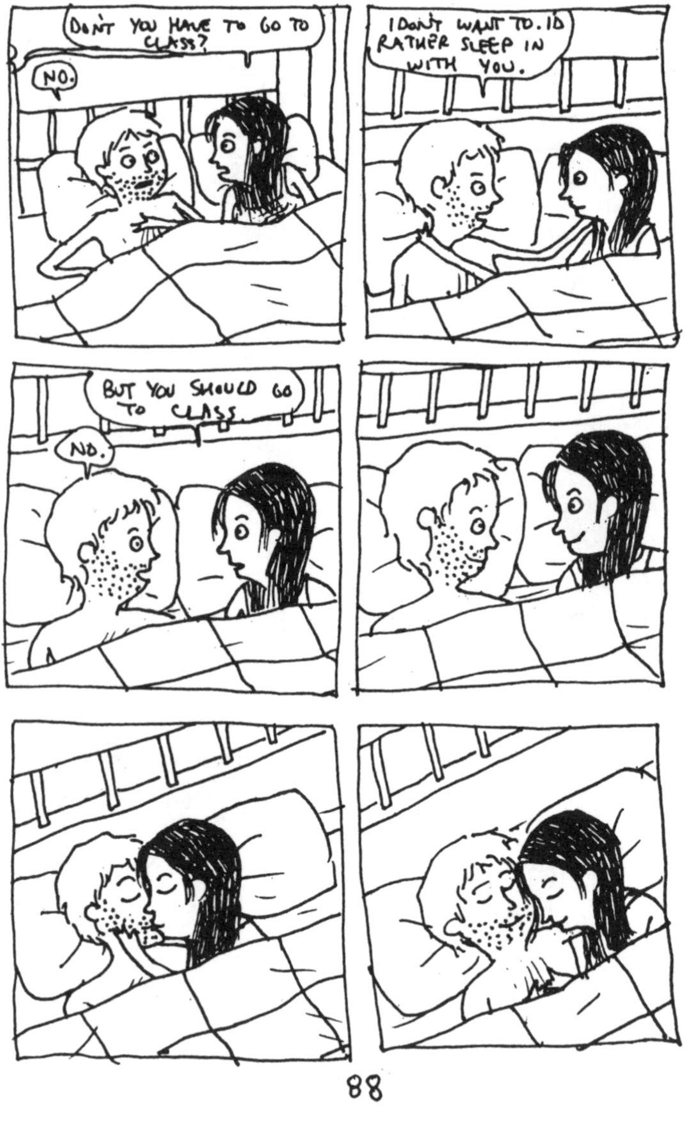
DON'T YOU HAVE TO GO TO CLASS?
NO.
I DON'T WANT TO. I'D RATHER SLEEP IN WITH YOU.
BUT YOU SHOULD GO TO CLASS.
NO.

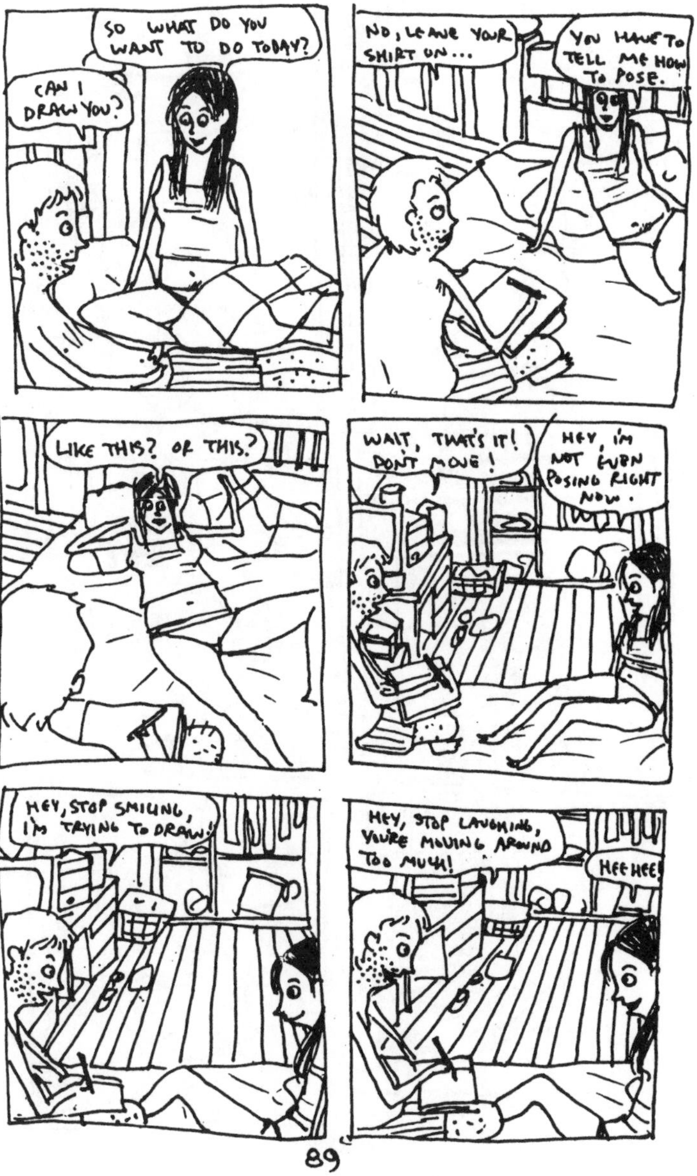
SO WHAT DO YOU WANT TO DO TODAY?
CAN I DRAW YOU?
NO, LEAVE YOUR SHIRT ON...
YOU HAVE TO TELL ME HOW TO POSE.
LIKE THIS? OR THIS?
WAIT, THAT'S IT! DONT MOVE!
HEY, I'M NOT EVEN POSING RIGHT NOW.
HEY, STOP SMILING, I'M TRYING TO DRAW!
HEY, STOP LAUGHING, YOU'RE MOVING AROUND TOO MUCH!
HEE HEE!

FRIDAY

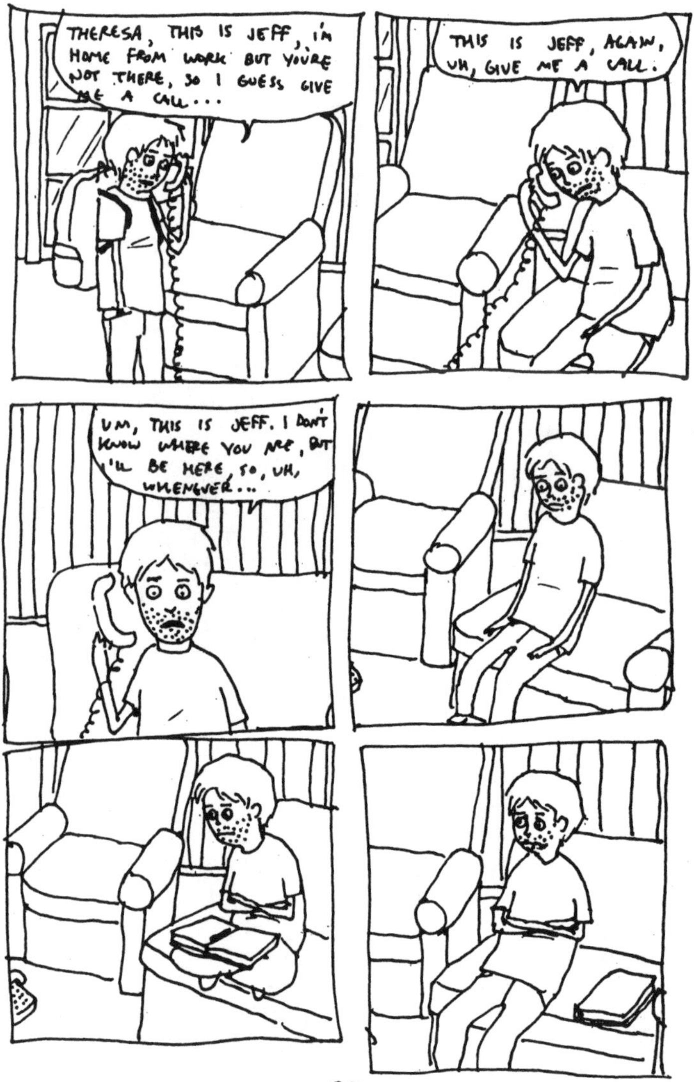
THERESA, THIS IS JEFF, I'M HOME FROM WORK BUT YOU'RE NOT THERE, SO I GUESS GIVE ME A CALL...
THIS IS JEFF, AGAIN, UH, GIVE ME A CALL.
UM, THIS IS JEFF. I DON'T KNOW WHERE YOU ARE, BUT I'LL BE HERE, SO, UH, WHENEVER...

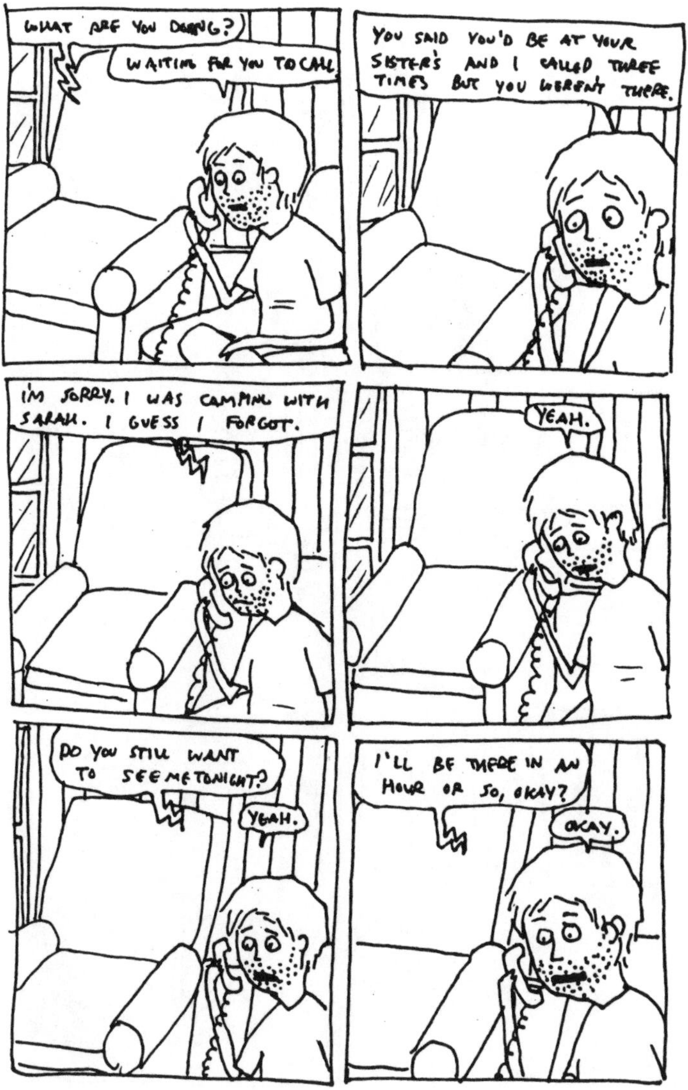
WHAT ARE YOU DOING?
WAITING FOR YOU TO CALL
YOU SAID YOU'D BE AT YOUR SISTER'S AND I CALLED THREE TIMES BUT YOU WEREN'T THERE.
I'M SORRY. I WAS CAMPING WITH SARAH. I GUESS I FORGOT.
YEAH.
DO YOU STILL WANT TO SEE ME TONIGHT?
YEAH.
I'LL BE THERE IN AN HOUR OR SO, OKAY?
OKAY.

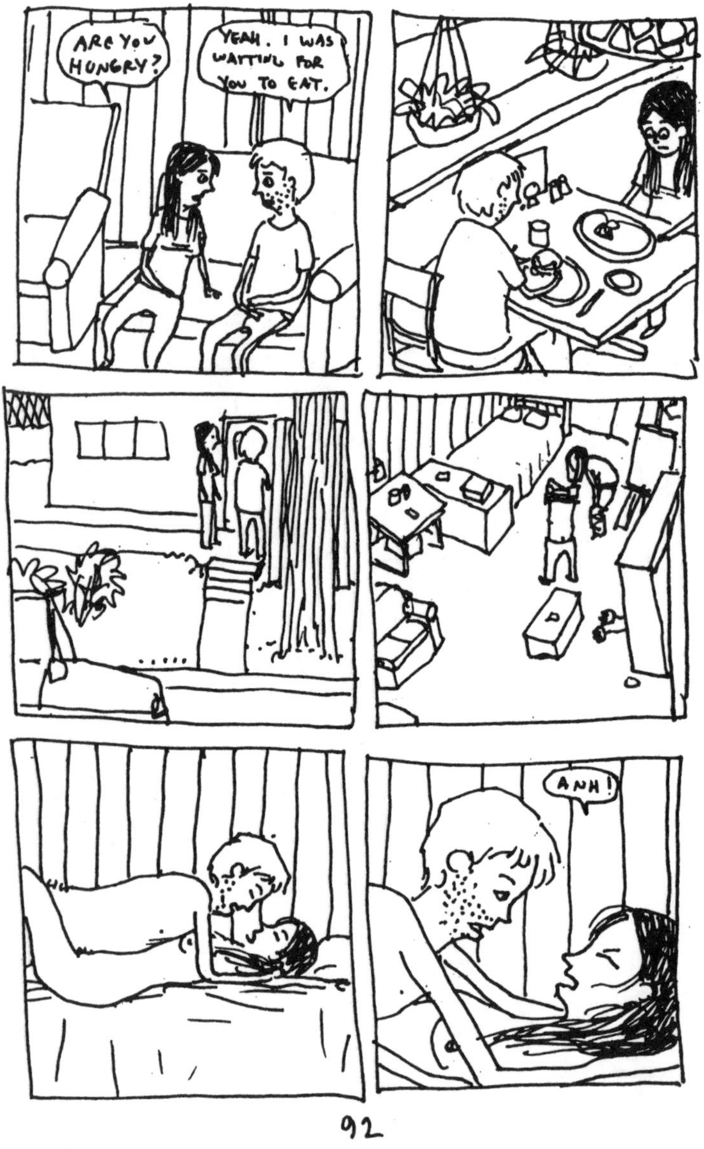
ARE YOU HUNGRY?
YEAH. I WAS WAITING FOR YOU TO EAT.
ANH!

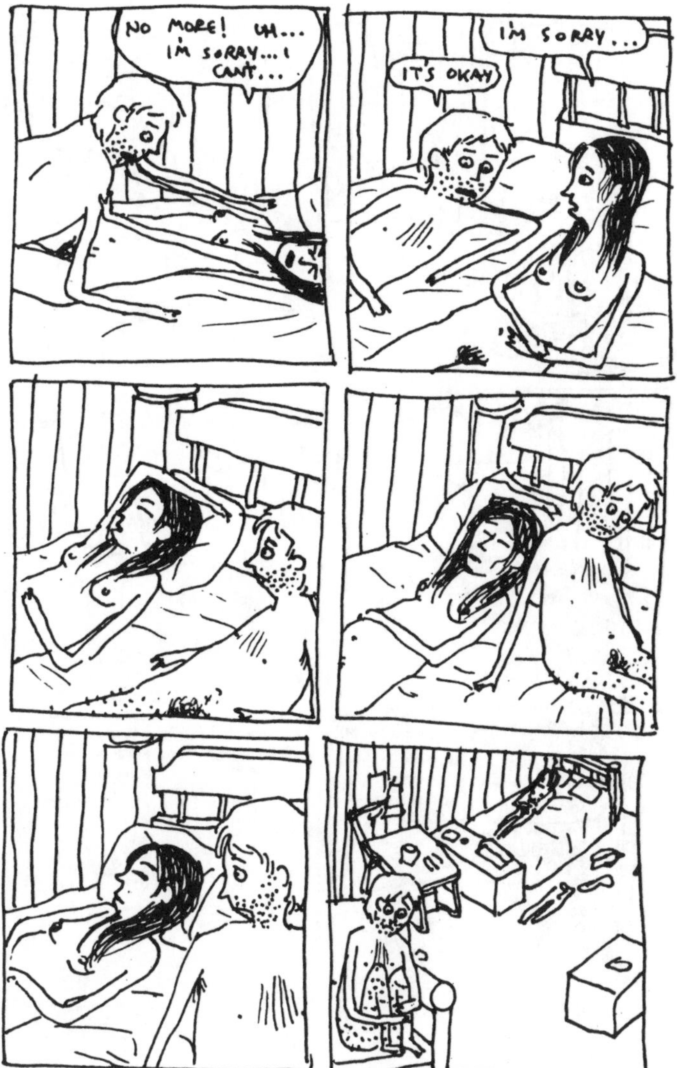
NO MORE! UH... I'M SORRY... I CAN'T...
I'M SORRY...
IT'S OKAY

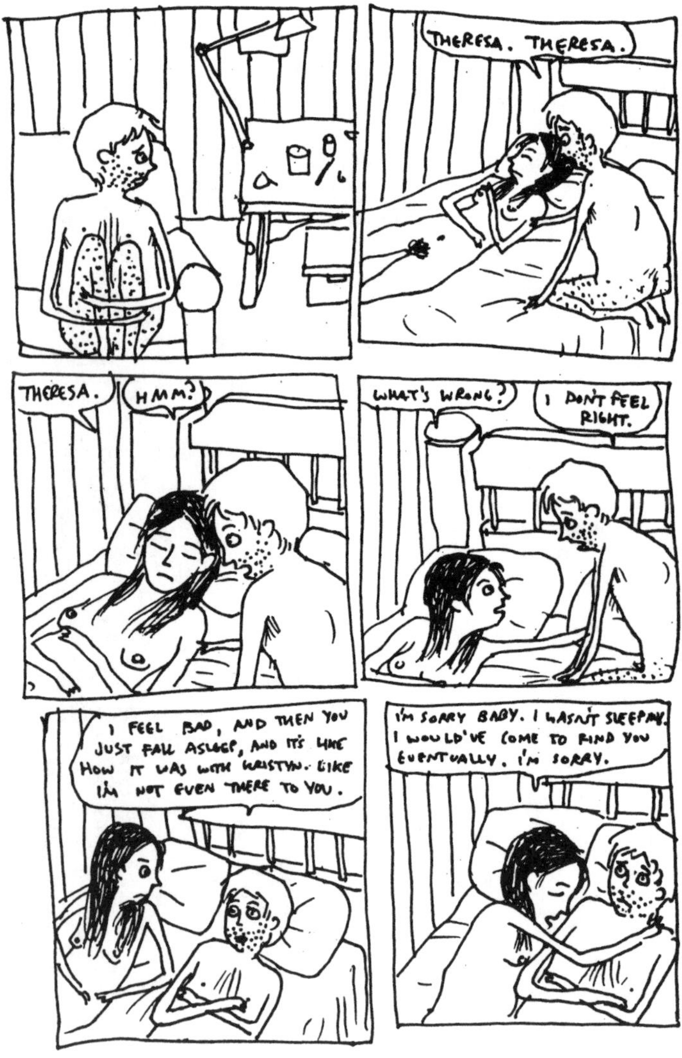
THERESA. THERESA.
THERESA.
HMM?
WHAT'S WRONG?
I DON'T FEEL RIGHT.
I FEEL BAD, AND THEN YOU JUST FALL ASLEEP, AND IT'S LIKE HOW IT WAS WITH KRISTYN. LIKE I'M NOT EVEN THERE TO YOU.
I'M SORRY BABY. I WASN'T SLEEPING. I WOULD'VE COME TO FIND YOU EVENTUALLY. I'M SORRY.

A CAR RIDE

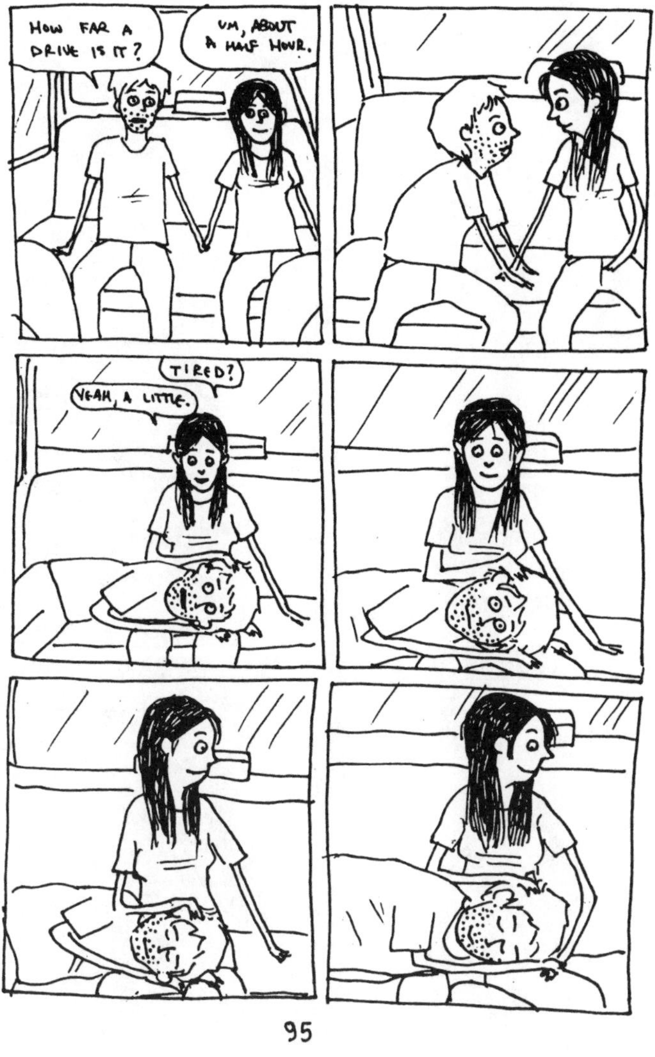
HOW FAR A DRIVE IS IT?
UM, ABOUT A HALF HOUR.
TIRED?
YEAH, A LITTLE.

SAUGATUCK

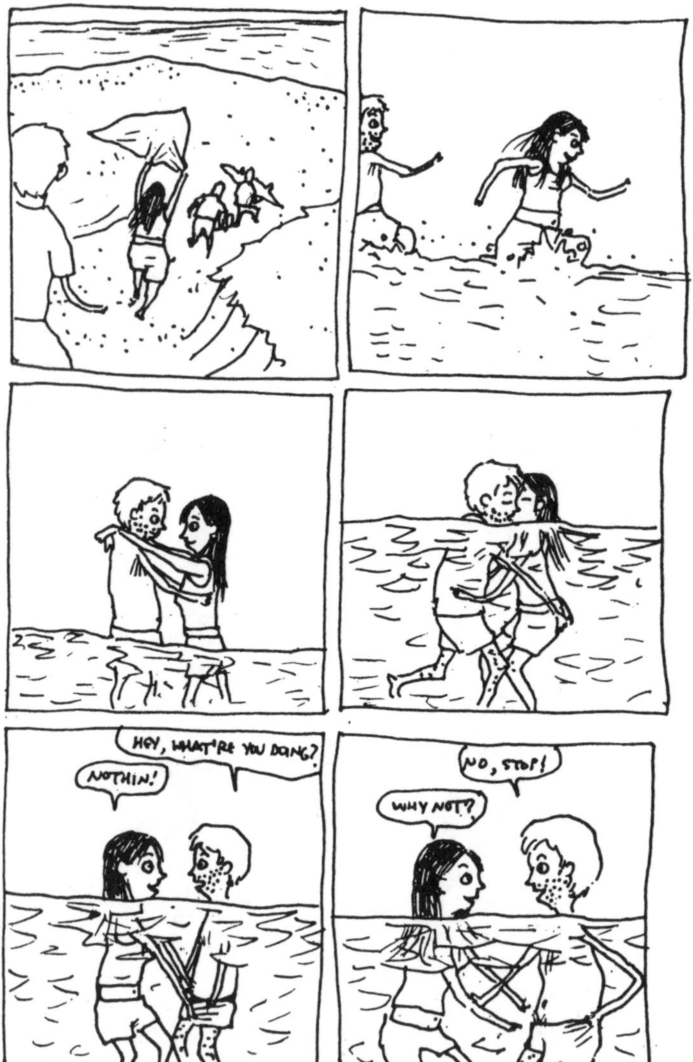
HEY, WHAT'RE YOU DOING?
NOTHIN'!
NO, STOP!
WHY NOT?

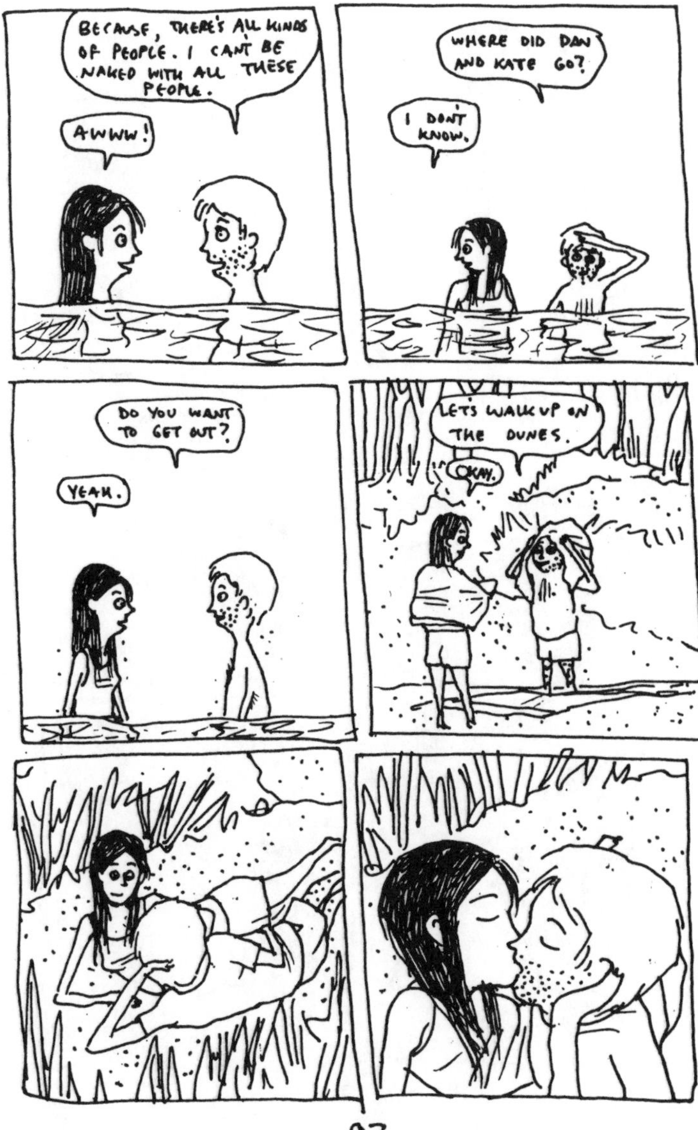
BECAUSE, THERE'S ALL KINDS OF PEOPLE. I CAN'T BE NAKED WITH ALL THESE PEOPLE.
AWWW!
WHERE DID DAN AND KATE GO?
I DON'T KNOW.
DO YOU WANT TO GET OUT?
YEAH.
LETS WALK UP ON THE DUNES.
OKAY.

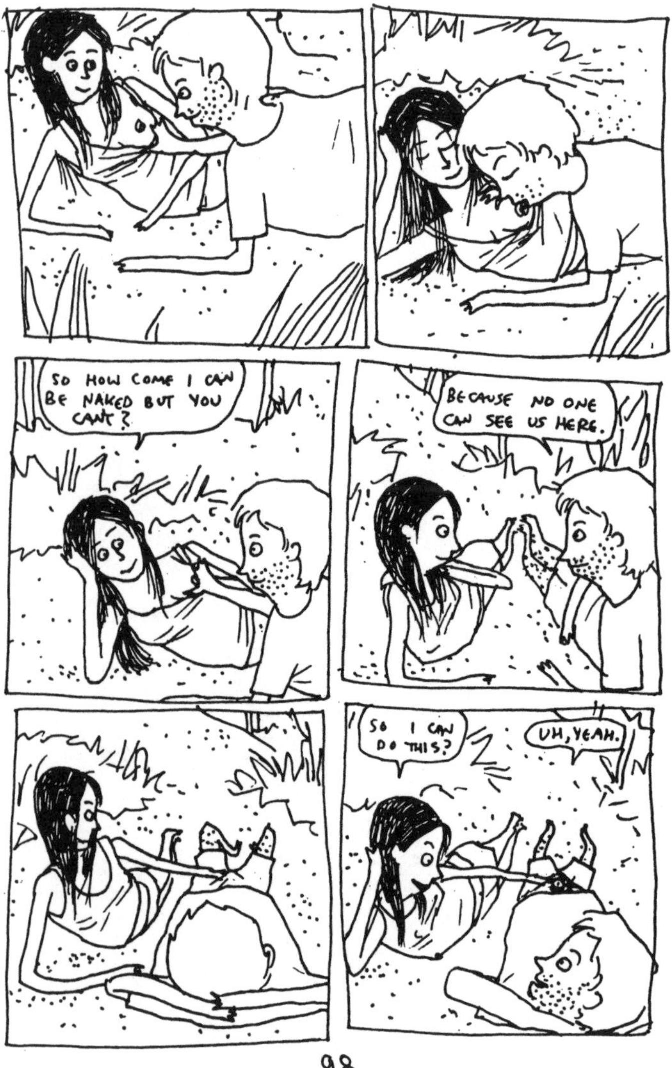
SO HOW COME I CAN BE NAKED BUT YOU CAN'T?
BECAUSE NO ONE CAN SEE US HERE.
SO I CAN DO THIS?
UH, YEAH.

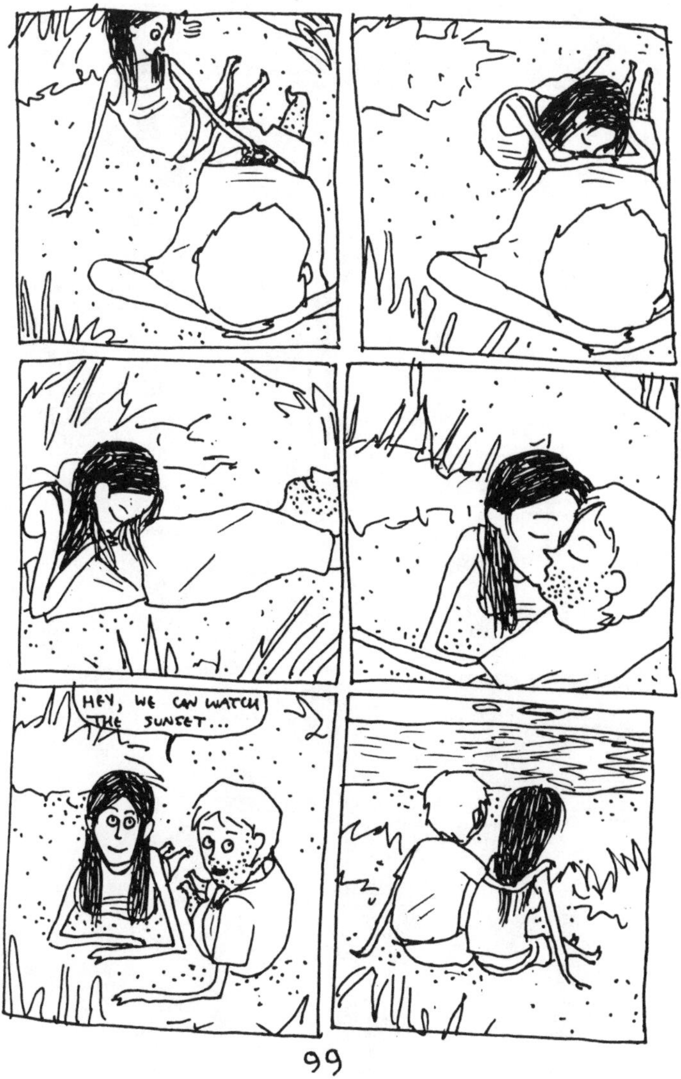
HEY, WE CAN WATCH THE SUNSET...

PHONE NUMBER

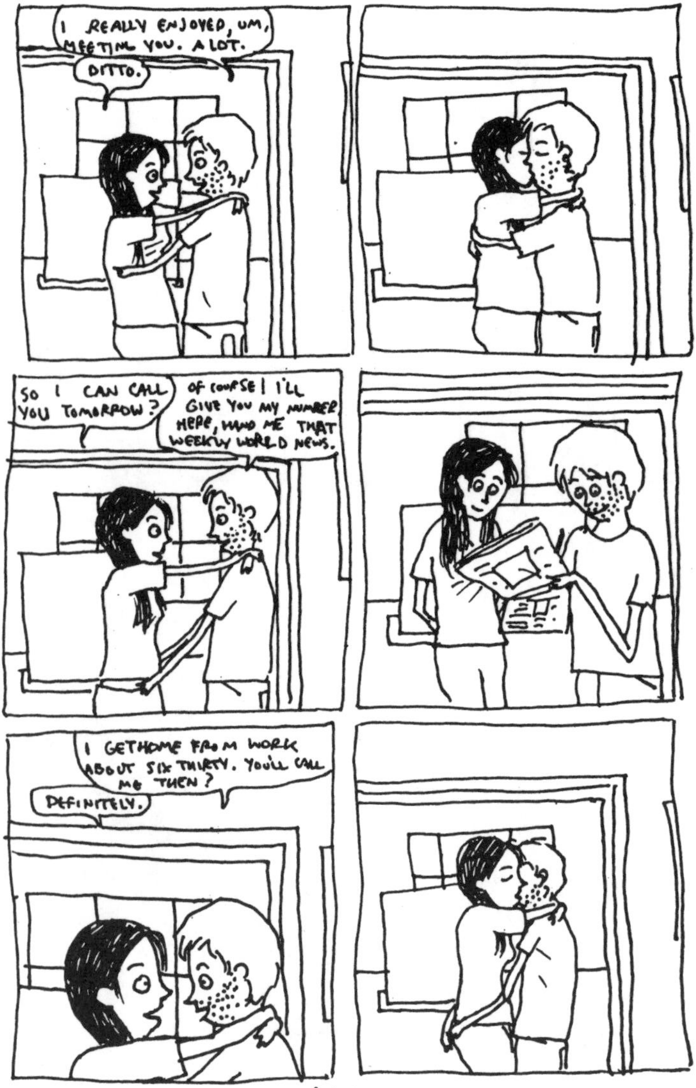
I REALLY ENJOYED, UM, MEETING YOU. A LOT.
DITTO.
SO I CAN CALL YOU TOMORROW?
OF COURSE! I'LL GIVE YOU MY NUMBER HERE, HAND ME THAT WEEKLY WORLD NEWS.
I GET HOME FROM WORK ABOUT SIX THIRTY. YOU'LL CALL ME THEN?
DEFINITELY.

SHARPIE TATTOOS

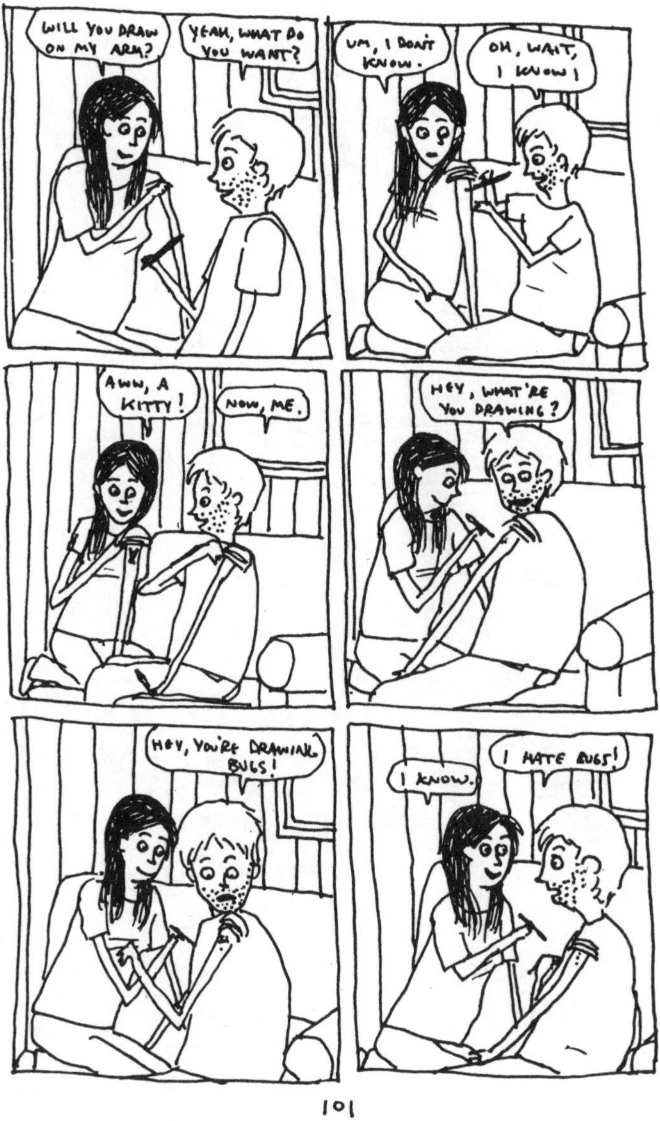
WILL YOU DRAW ON MY ARM?
YEAH, WHAT DO YOU WANT?
UM, I DON'T KNOW.
OH, WAIT, I KNOW!
AWW, A KITTY!
NOW, ME.
HEY, WHAT'RE YOU DRAWING?
HEY, YOU'RE DRAWING BUGS!
I KNOW.
I HATE BUGS!

LET'S GO SWIMMING

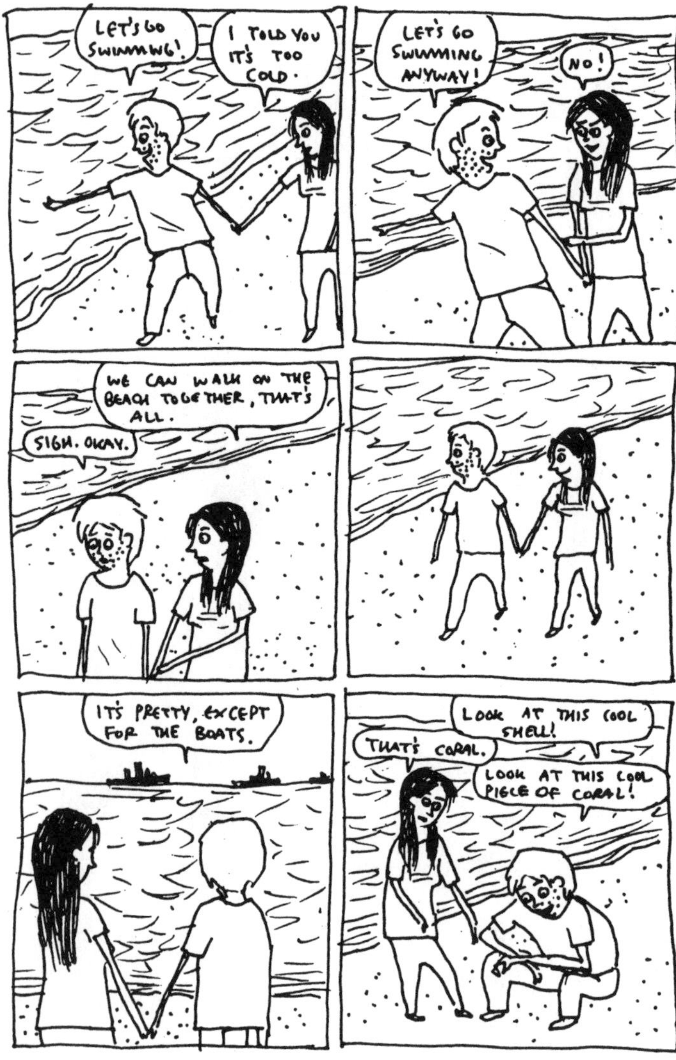

LET'S GO SWIMMING!
I TOLD YOU IT'S TOO COLD.
LET'S GO SWIMMING ANYWAY!
NO!
WE CAN WALK ON THE BEACH TOGETHER, THAT'S ALL.
SIGH. OKAY.
IT'S PRETTY, EXCEPT FOR THE BOATS.
LOOK AT THIS COOL SHELL!
THAT'S CORAL.
LOOK AT THIS COOL PIECE OF CORAL!

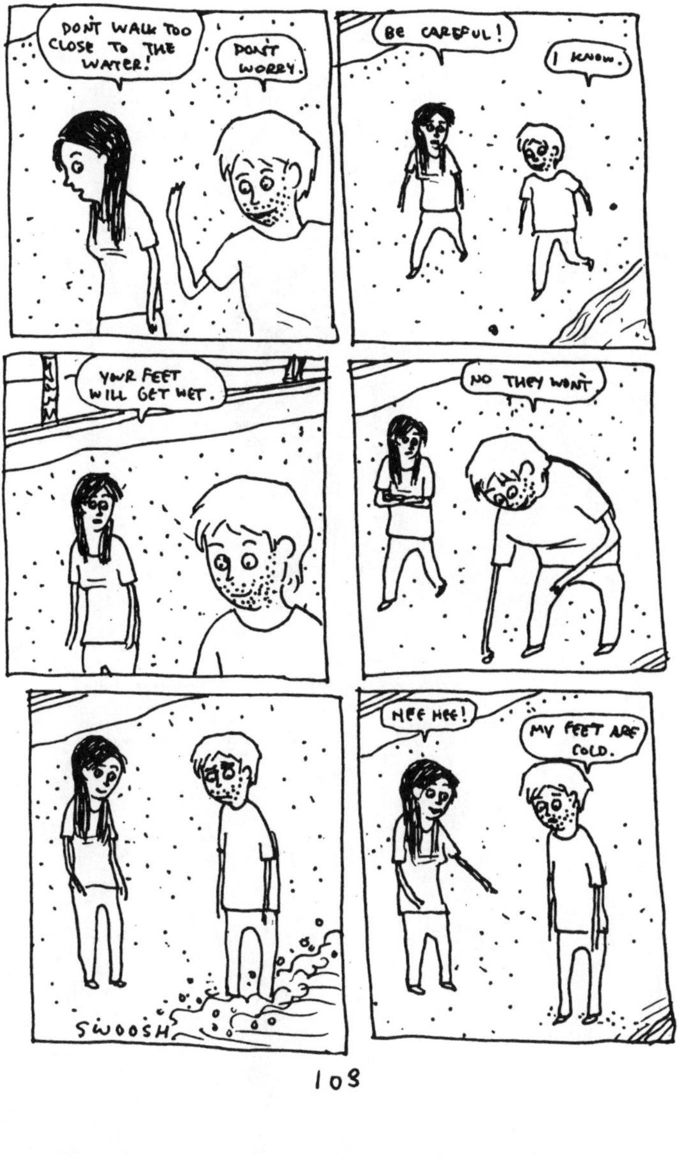
DON'T WALK TOO CLOSE TO THE WATER!
DON'T WORRY.
BE CAREFUL!
I KNOW.
YOUR FEET WILL GET WET.
NO THEY WON'T
SWOOSH
HEE HEE!
MY FEET ARE COLD.

[redacted]

SKETCHBOOKS

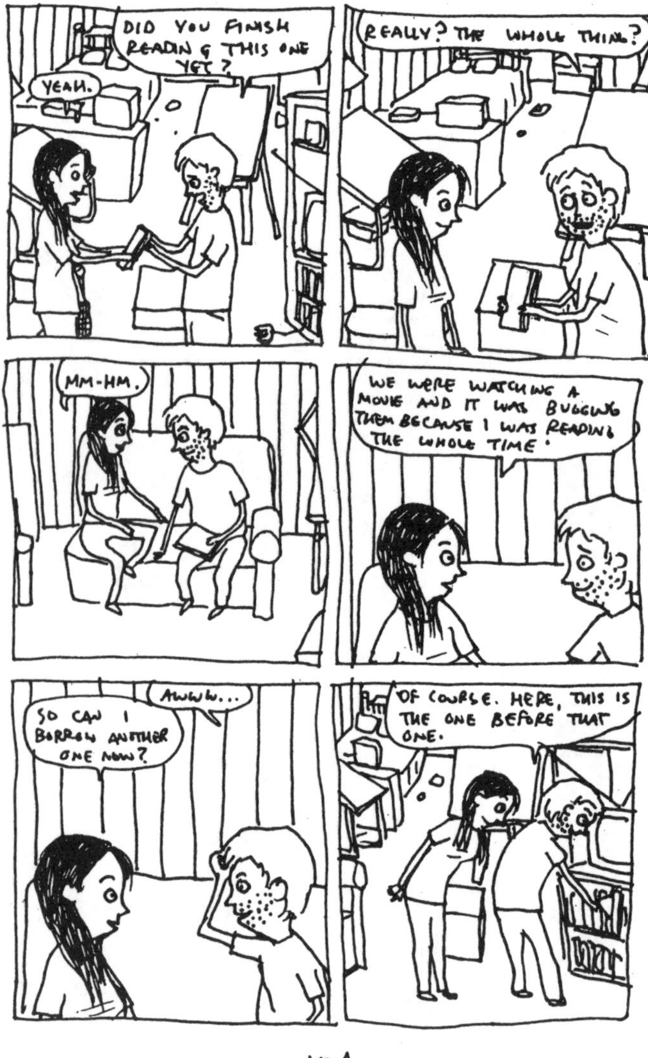
DID YOU FINISH READING THIS ONE YET?
YEAH.
REALLY? THE WHOLE THING?
MM-HM.
WE WERE WATCHING A MOVIE AND IT WAS BUGGING THEM BECAUSE I WAS READING THE WHOLE TIME.
AWWW...
SO CAN I BORROW ANOTHER ONE NOW?
OF COURSE. HERE, THIS IS THE ONE BEFORE THAT ONE.

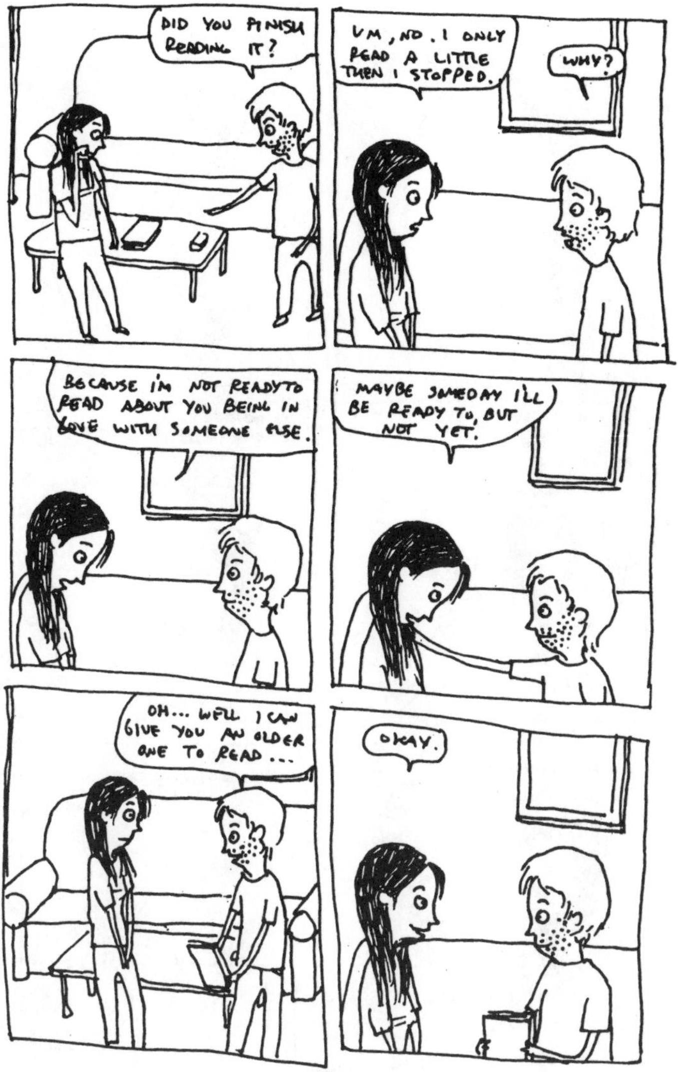
DID YOU FINISH READING IT?
UM, NO. I ONLY READ A LITTLE THEN I STOPPED.
WHY?
BECAUSE I'M NOT READY TO READ ABOUT YOU BEING IN LOVE WITH SOMEONE ELSE.
MAYBE SOMEDAY I'LL BE READY TO, BUT NOT YET.
OH... WELL I CAN GIVE YOU AN OLDER ONE TO READ...
OKAY.

[redacted]

A MORNING STORY

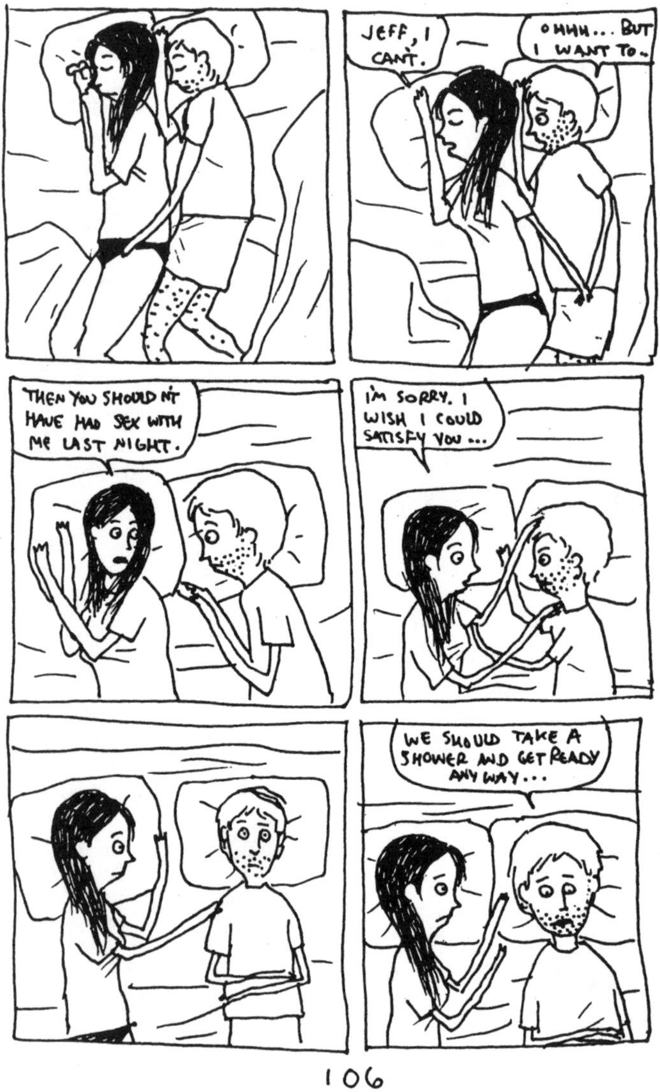
JEFF, I CAN'T.
OHHH... BUT I WANT TO..
THEN YOU SHOULDN'T HAVE HAD SEX WITH ME LAST NIGHT.
I'M SORRY. I WISH I COULD SATISFY YOU...
WE SHOULD TAKE A SHOWER AND GET READY ANYWAY...

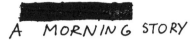

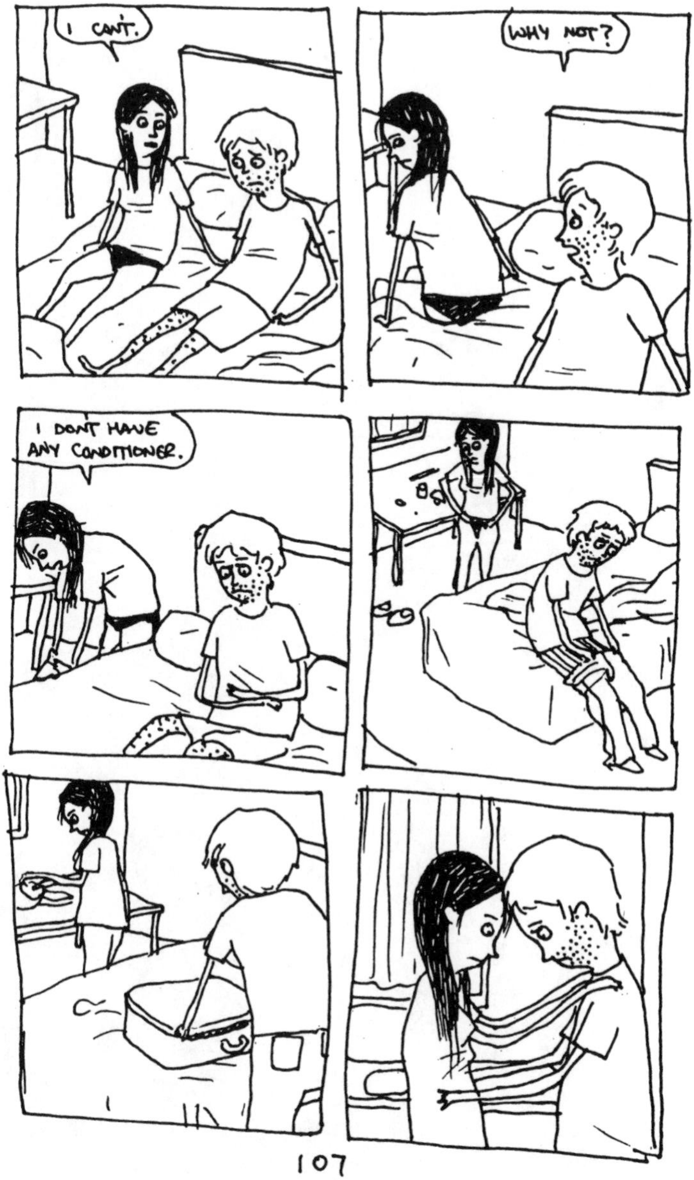
I CAN'T.
WHY NOT?
I DONT HAVE ANY CONDITIONER.

FARSCAPE

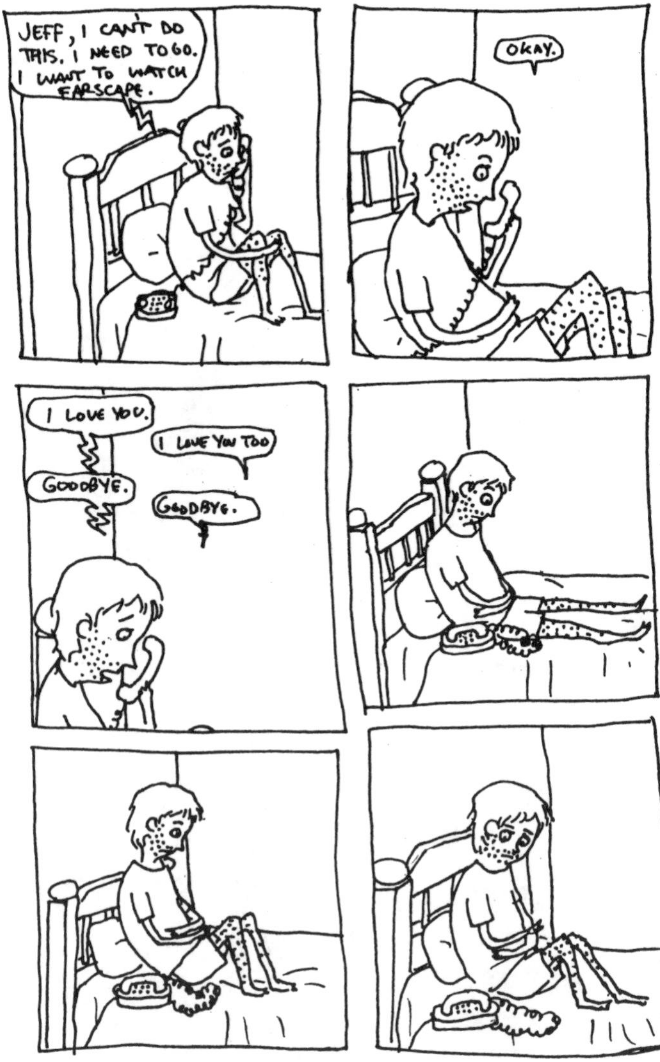
JEFF, I CAN'T DO THIS. I NEED TO GO. I WANT TO WATCH FARSCAPE.
OKAY.
I LOVE YOU.
I LOVE YOU TOO
GOODBYE.
GOODBYE.

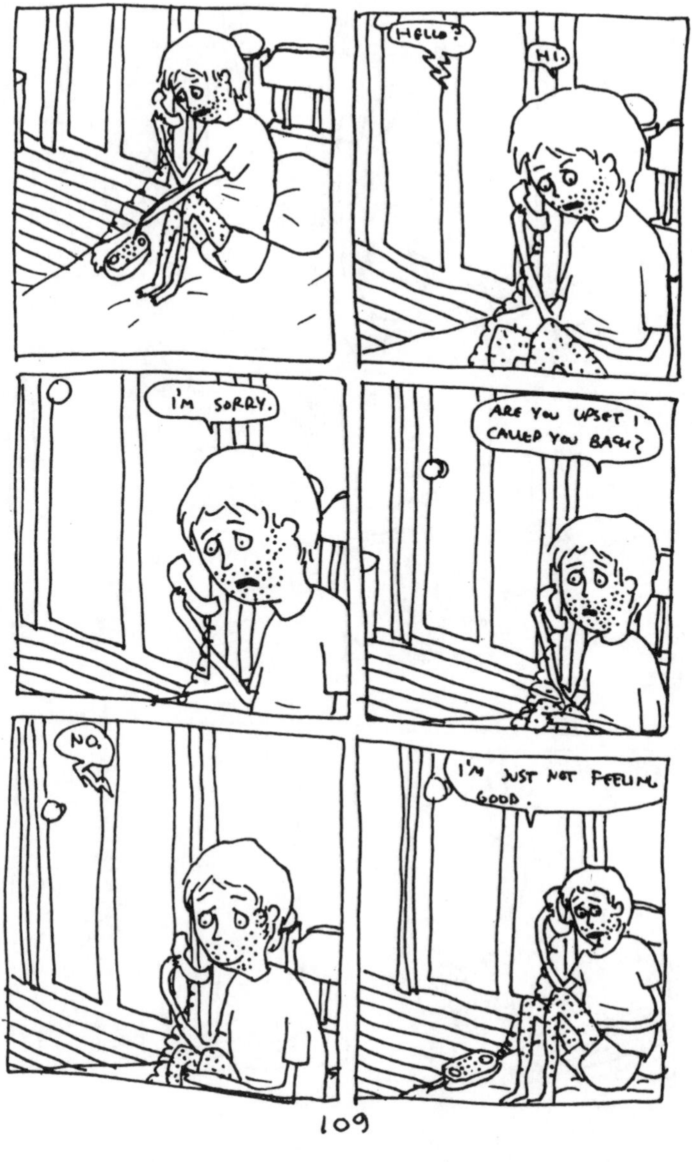
HELLO?
HI.
I'M SORRY.
ARE YOU UPSET I CALLED YOU BACK?
NO.
I'M JUST NOT FEELING GOOD.

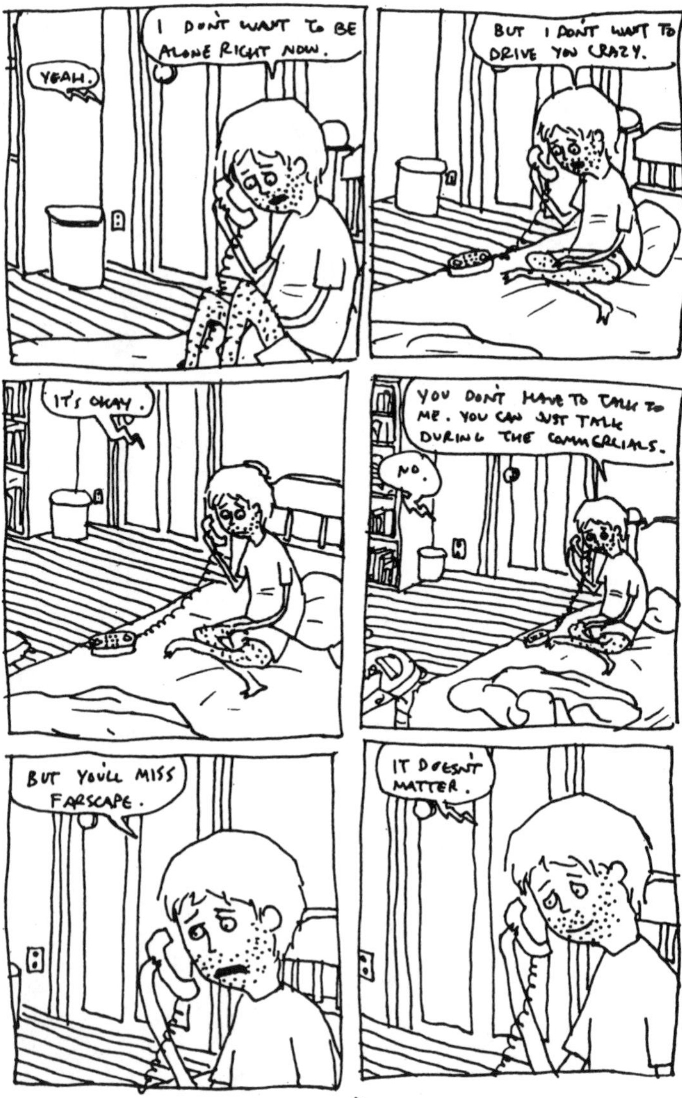
I DON'T WANT TO BE ALONE RIGHT NOW.
YEAH.
BUT I DON'T WANT TO DRIVE YOU CRAZY.
IT'S OKAY.
YOU DON'T HAVE TO TALK TO ME. YOU CAN JUST TALK DURING THE COMMERCIALS.
NO.
BUT YOU'LL MISS FARSCAPE.
IT DOESN'T MATTER.

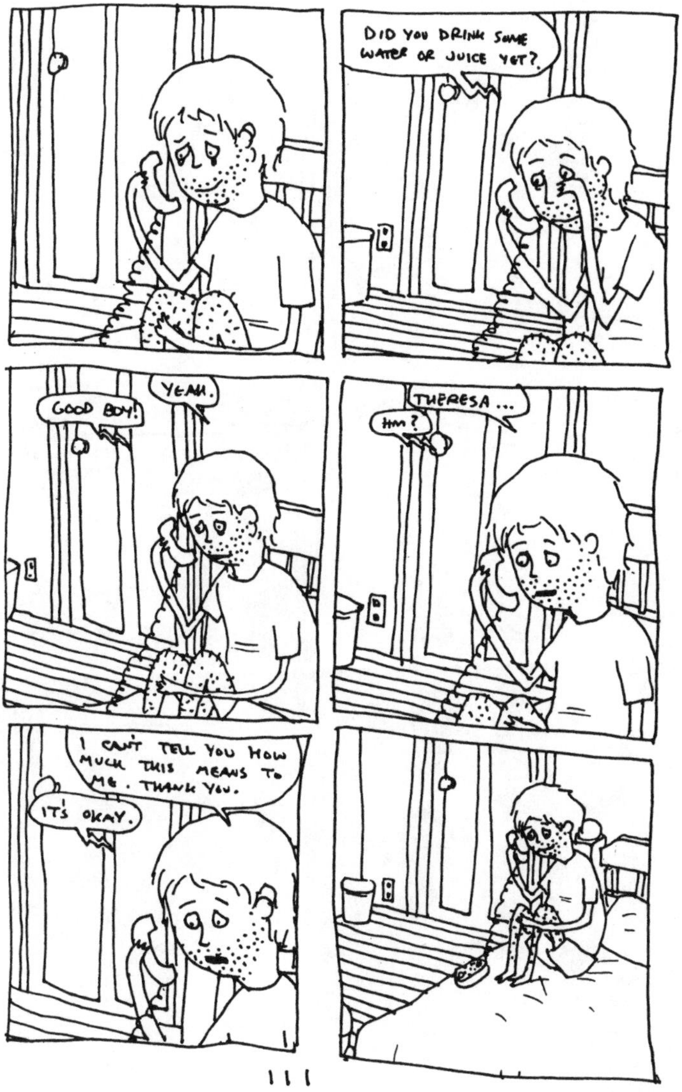

DID YOU DRINK SOME WATER OR JUICE YET?
YEAH.
GOOD BOY!
THERESA...
HM?
I CAN'T TELL YOU HOW MUCH THIS MEANS TO ME. THANK YOU.
IT'S OKAY.

THE NICE ROOM

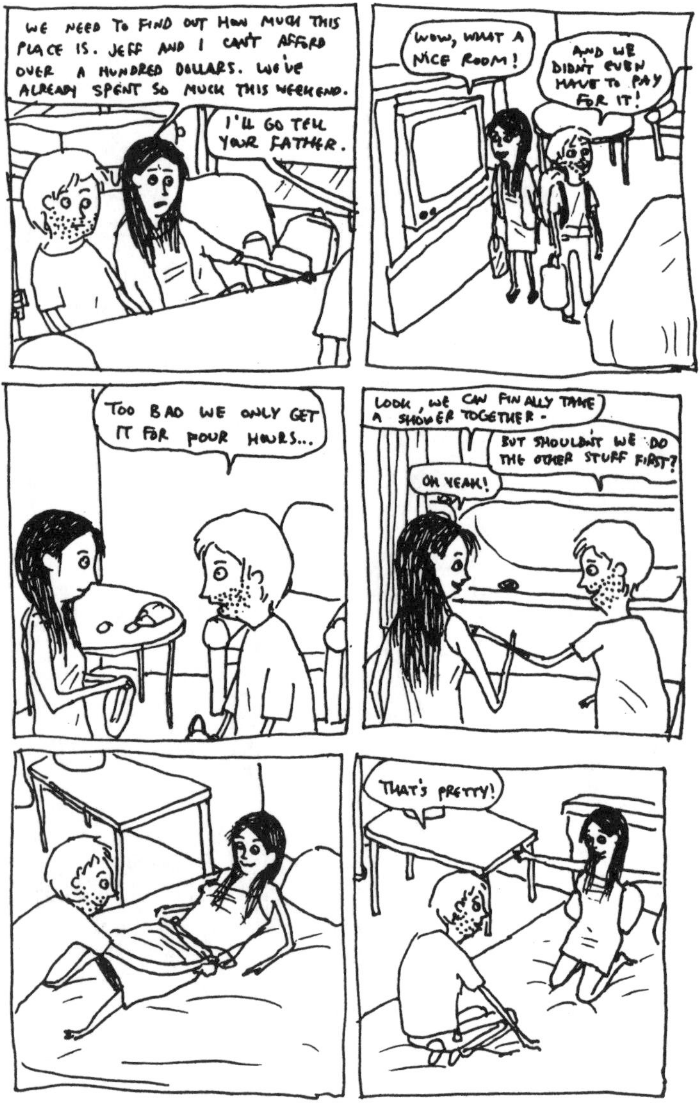

WE NEED TO FIND OUT HOW MUCH THIS PLACE IS. JEFF AND I CAN'T AFFORD OVER A HUNDRED DOLLARS. WE'VE ALREADY SPENT SO MUCH THIS WEEKEND.
I'LL GO TELL YOUR FATHER.
WOW, WHAT A NICE ROOM!
AND WE DIDN'T EVEN HAVE TO PAY FOR IT!
TOO BAD WE ONLY GET IT FOR FOUR HOURS...
LOOK, WE CAN FINALLY TAKE A SHOWER TOGETHER -
BUT SHOULDN'T WE DO THE OTHER STUFF FIRST?
OH YEAH!
THAT'S PRETTY!

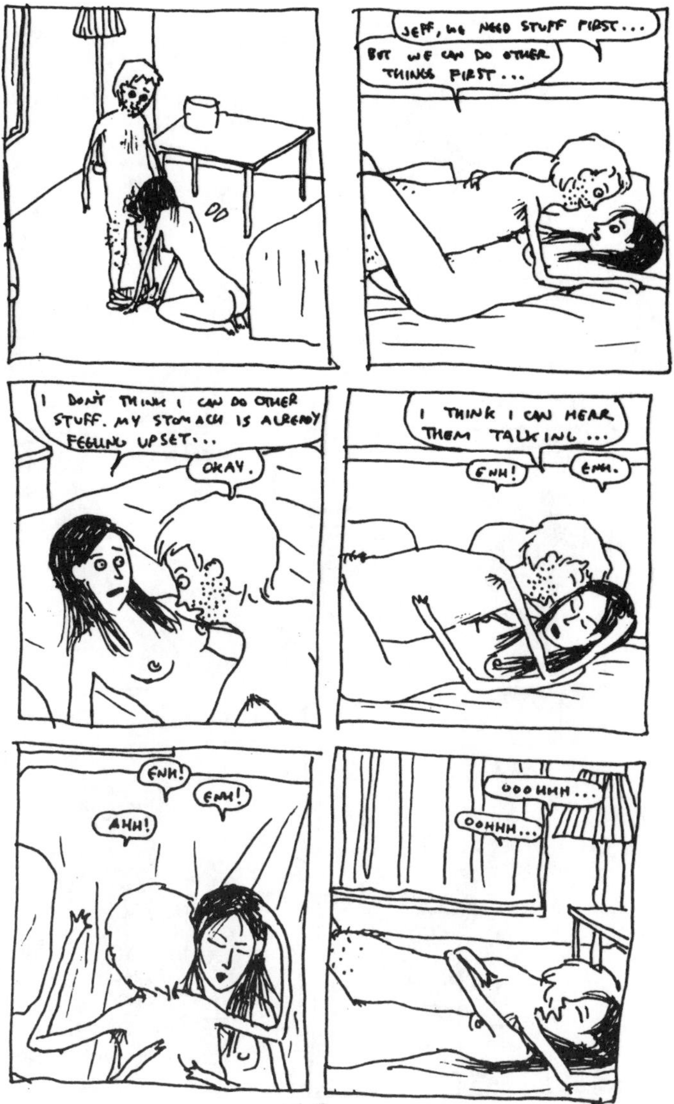
JEFF, WE NEED STUFF FIRST...
BUT WE CAN DO OTHER THINGS FIRST...
I DON'T THINK I CAN DO OTHER STUFF. MY STOMACH IS ALREADY FEELING UPSET...
OKAY.
I THINK I CAN HEAR THEM TALKING...
ENH!
ENH.
ENH!
ENH!
AHH!
OOOHHH...
OOHHH...

THE BATH

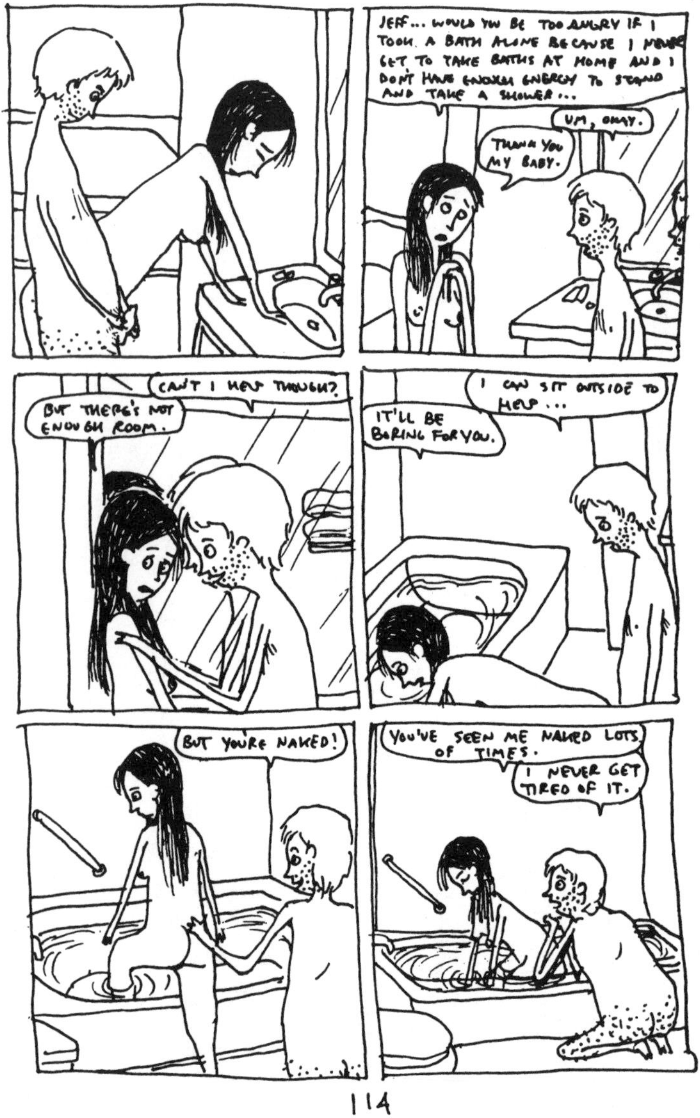
JEFF... WOULD YOU BE TOO ANGRY IF I TOOK A BATH ALONE BECAUSE I NEVER GET TO TAKE BATHS AT HOME AND I DON'T HAVE ENOUGH ENERGY TO STAND AND TAKE A SHOWER...
UM, OKAY.
THANK YOU MY BABY.
CAN'T I HELP THOUGH?
BUT THERE'S NOT ENOUGH ROOM.
I CAN SIT OUTSIDE TO HELP...
IT'LL BE BORING FOR YOU.
BUT YOU'RE NAKED!
YOU'VE SEEN ME NAKED LOTS OF TIMES.
I NEVER GET TIRED OF IT.

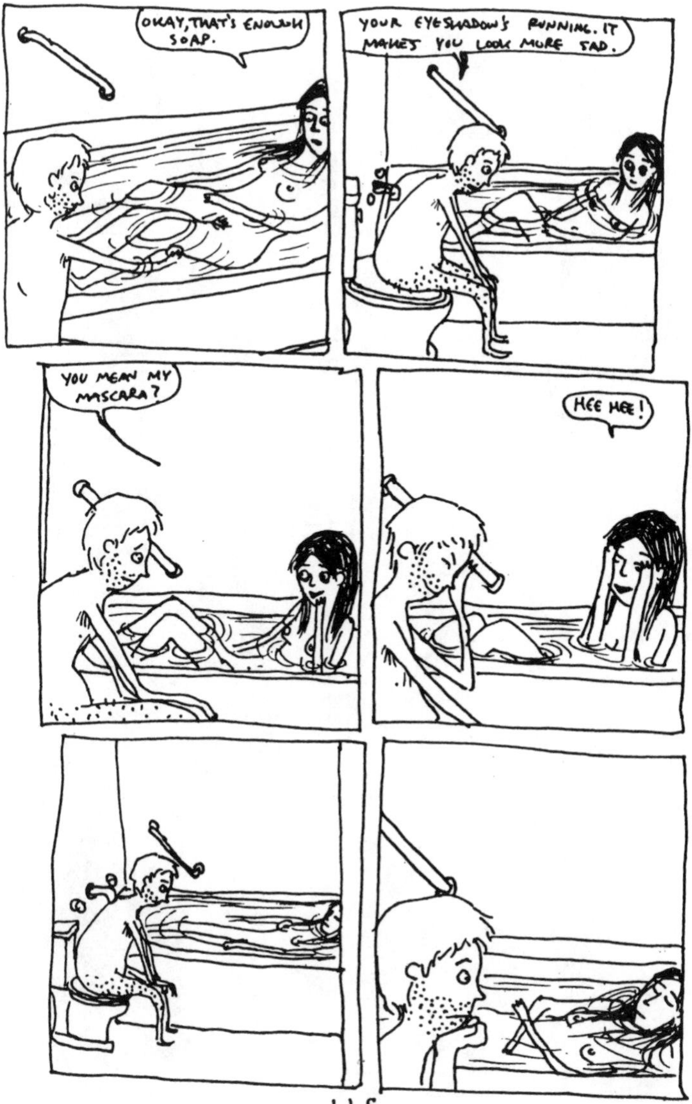
OKAY, THAT'S ENOUGH SOAP.
YOUR EYESHADOW'S RUNNING. IT MAKES YOU LOOK MORE SAD.
YOU MEAN MY MASCARA?
HEE HEE!

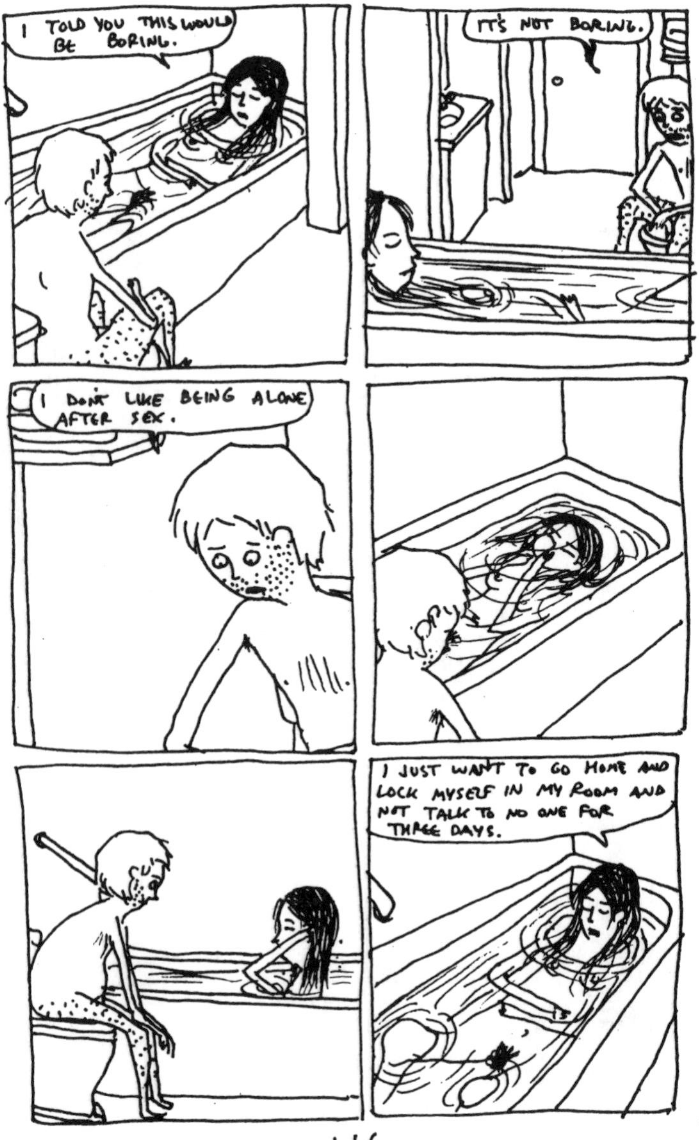
I TOLD YOU THIS WOULD BE BORING.
IT'S NOT BORING.
I DON'T LIKE BEING ALONE AFTER SEX.
I JUST WANT TO GO HOME AND LOCK MYSELF IN MY ROOM AND NOT TALK TO NO ONE FOR THREE DAYS.

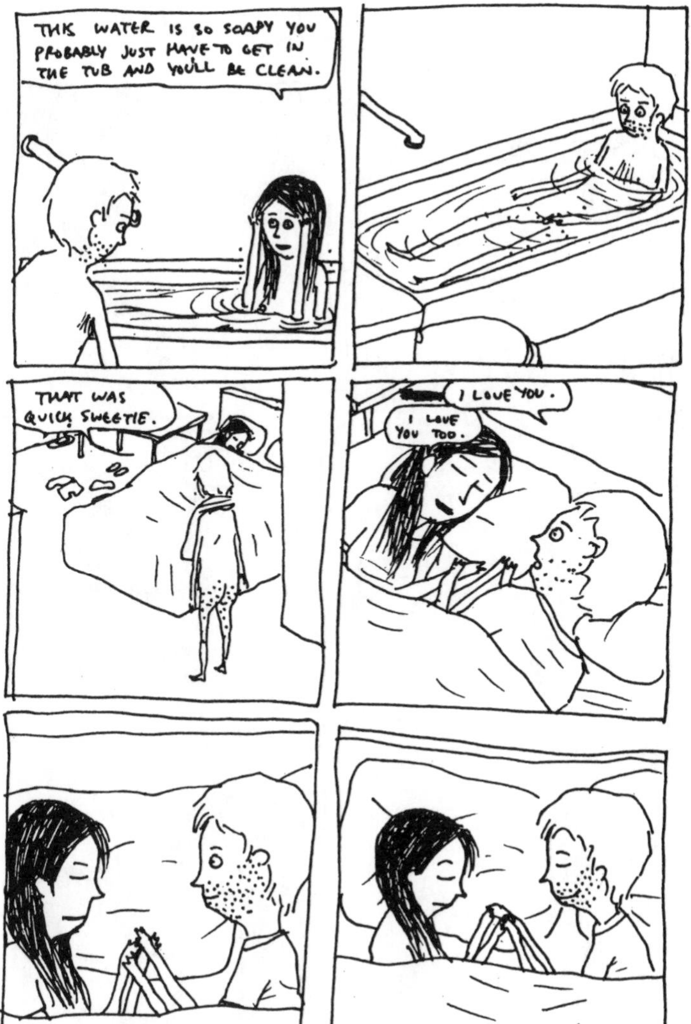
THIS WATER IS SO SOAPY YOU PROBABLY JUST HAVE TO GET IN THE TUB AND YOU'LL BE CLEAN.
THAT WAS QUICK SWEETIE.
I LOVE YOU.
I LOVE YOU TOO.

HAIRCUT

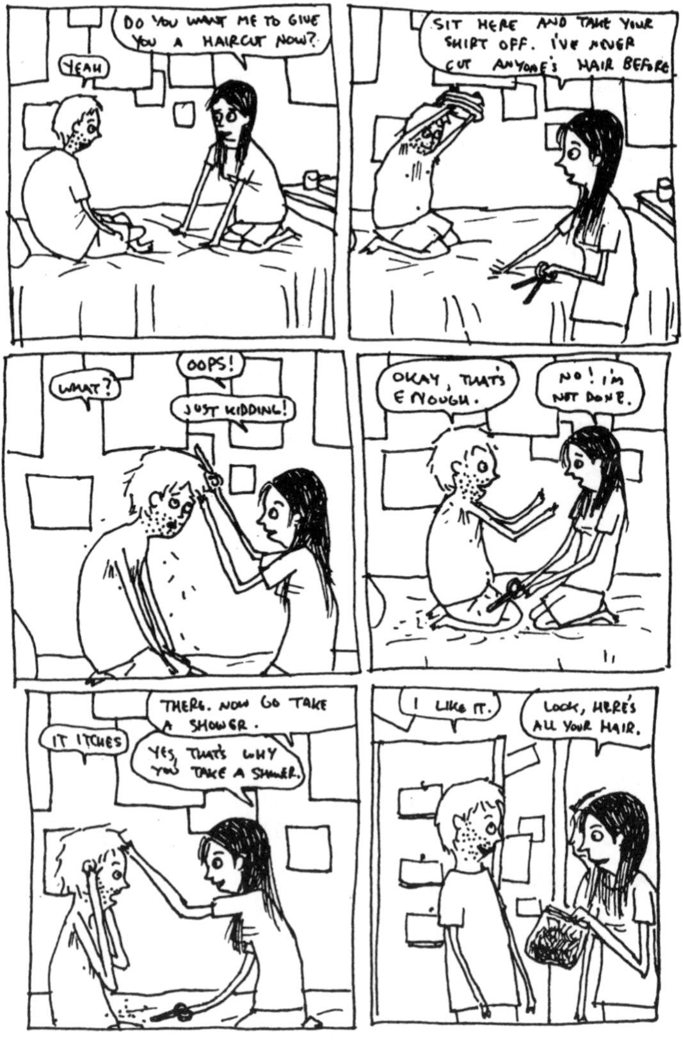
DO YOU WANT ME TO GIVE YOU A HAIRCUT NOW?
YEAH
SIT HERE AND TAKE YOUR SHIRT OFF. I'VE NEVER CUT ANYONE'S HAIR BEFORE
WHAT?
OOPS!
JUST KIDDING!
OKAY, THAT'S ENOUGH.
NO! I'M NOT DONE.
IT ITCHES
THERE. NOW GO TAKE A SHOWER.
YES, THAT'S WHY YOU TAKE A SHOWER.
I LIKE IT.
LOOK, HERE'S ALL YOUR HAIR.

GO-CARTS

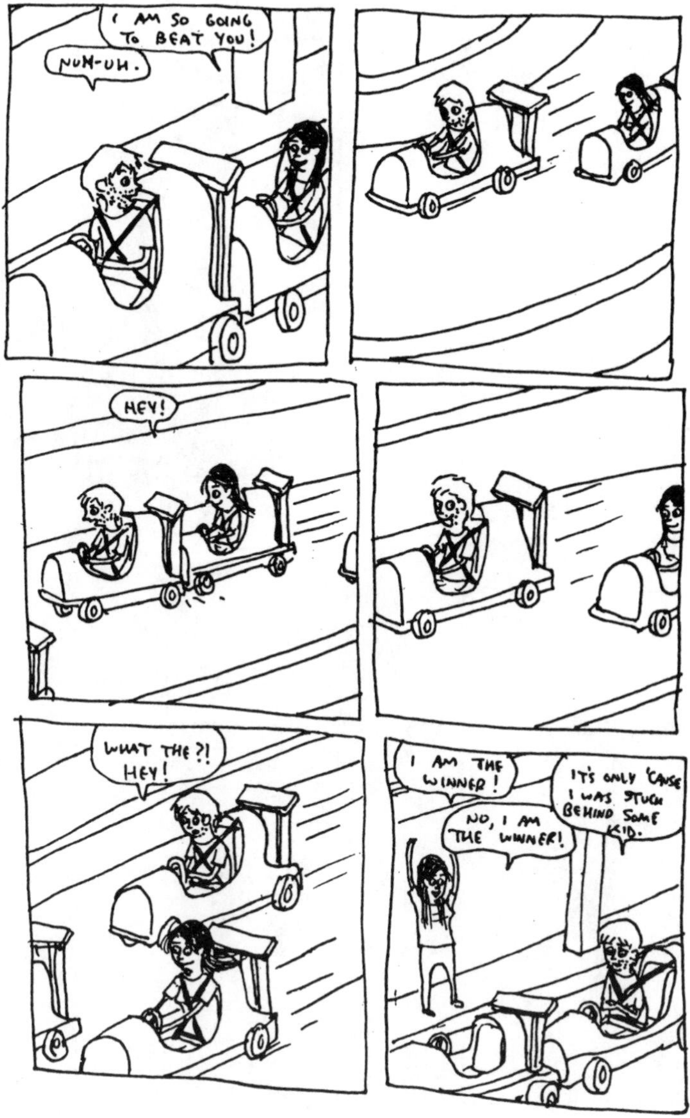
I AM SO GOING TO BEAT YOU!
NUH-UH.
HEY!
WHAT THE?! HEY!
I AM THE WINNER!
NO, I AM THE WINNER!
IT'S ONLY 'CAUSE I WAS STUCK BEHIND SOME KID.

TOENAILS

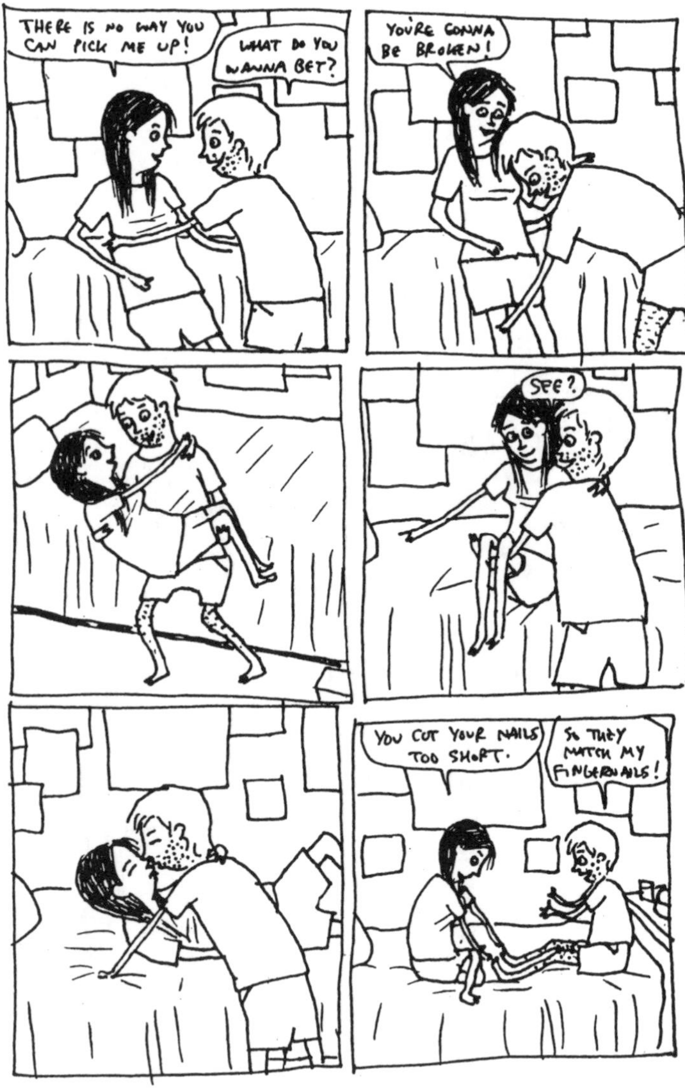
THERE IS NO WAY YOU CAN PICK ME UP!
WHAT DO YOU WANNA BET?
YOU'RE GONNA BE BROKEN!
SEE?
YOU CUT YOUR NAILS TOO SHORT.
SO THEY MATCH MY FINGERNAILS!

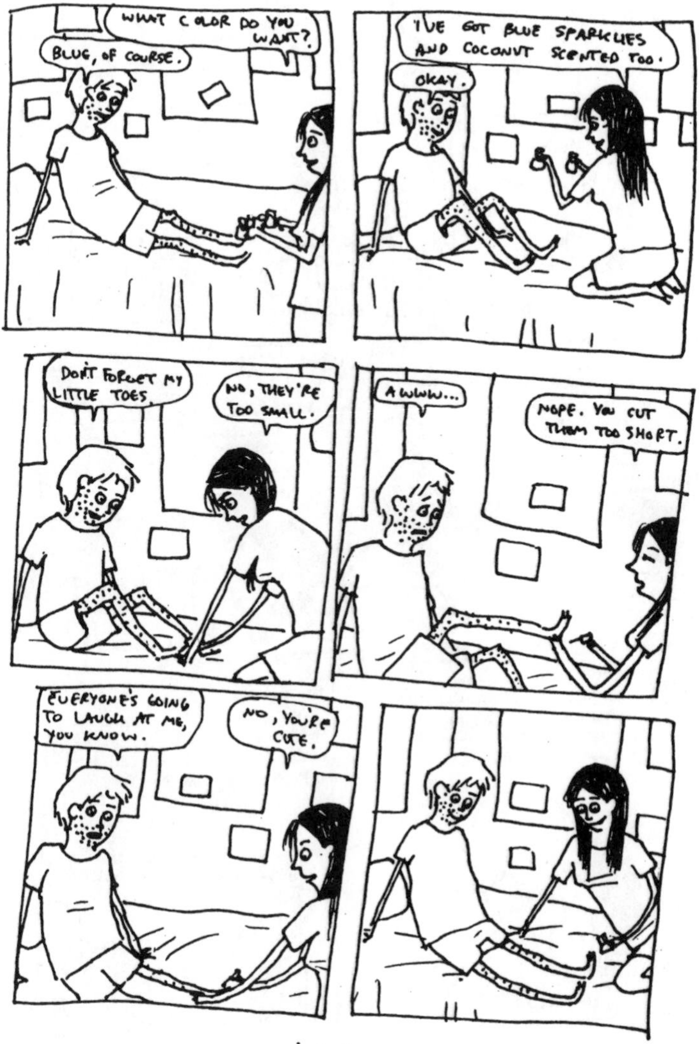
WHAT COLOR DO YOU WANT?
BLUE, OF COURSE.
I'VE GOT BLUE SPARKLIES AND COCONUT SCENTED TOO.
OKAY.
DON'T FORGET MY LITTLE TOES.
NO, THEY'RE TOO SMALL.
AWWW...
NOPE. YOU CUT THEM TOO SHORT.
EVERYONE'S GOING TO LAUGH AT ME, YOU KNOW.
NO, YOU'RE CUTE.

TEA

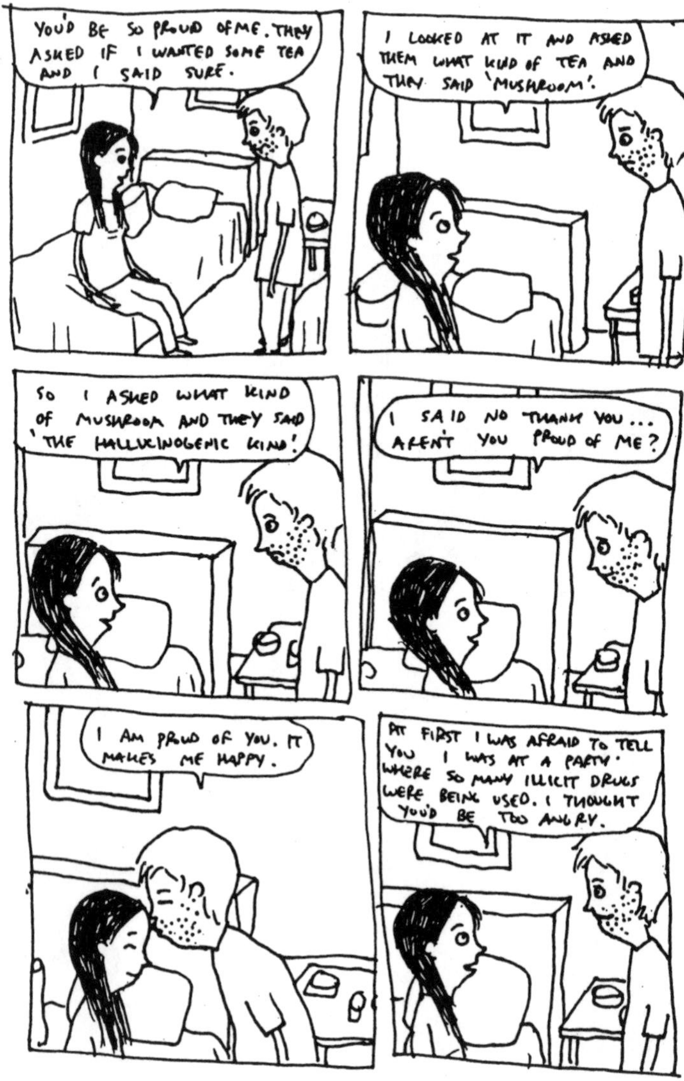
YOU'D BE SO PROUD OF ME. THEY ASKED IF I WANTED SOME TEA AND I SAID SURE.
I LOOKED AT IT AND ASKED THEM WHAT KIND OF TEA AND THEY SAID 'MUSHROOM'.
SO I ASKED WHAT KIND OF MUSHROOM AND THEY SAID 'THE HALLUCINOGENIC KIND'.
I SAID NO THANK YOU... AREN'T YOU PROUD OF ME?
I AM PROUD OF YOU. IT MAKES ME HAPPY.
AT FIRST I WAS AFRAID TO TELL YOU I WAS AT A PARTY WHERE SO MANY ILLICIT DRUGS WERE BEING USED. I THOUGHT YOU'D BE TOO ANGRY.

STUTTERING

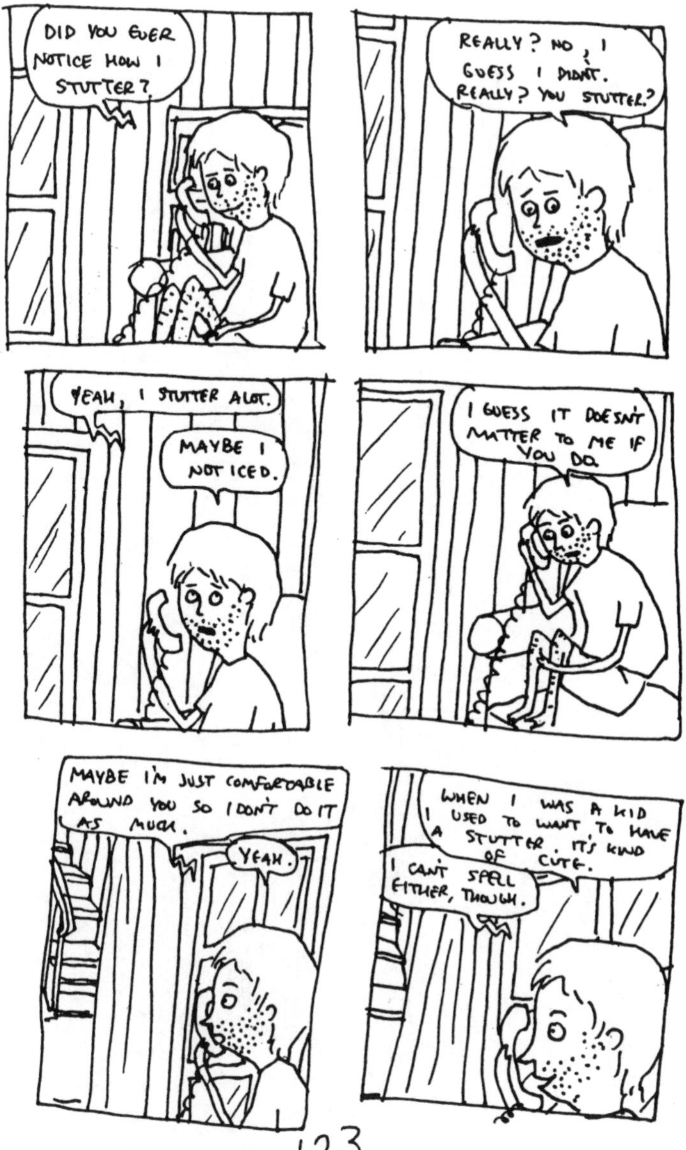
DID YOU EVER NOTICE HOW I STUTTER?
REALLY? NO, I GUESS I DIDN'T. REALLY? YOU STUTTER?
YEAH, I STUTTER ALOT.
MAYBE I NOTICED.
I GUESS IT DOESN'T MATTER TO ME IF YOU DO.
MAYBE I'M JUST COMFORTABLE AROUND YOU SO I DON'T DO IT AS MUCH.
YEAH.
WHEN I WAS A KID I USED TO WANT TO HAVE A STUTTER. IT'S KIND OF CUTE.
I CAN'T SPELL EITHER, THOUGH.

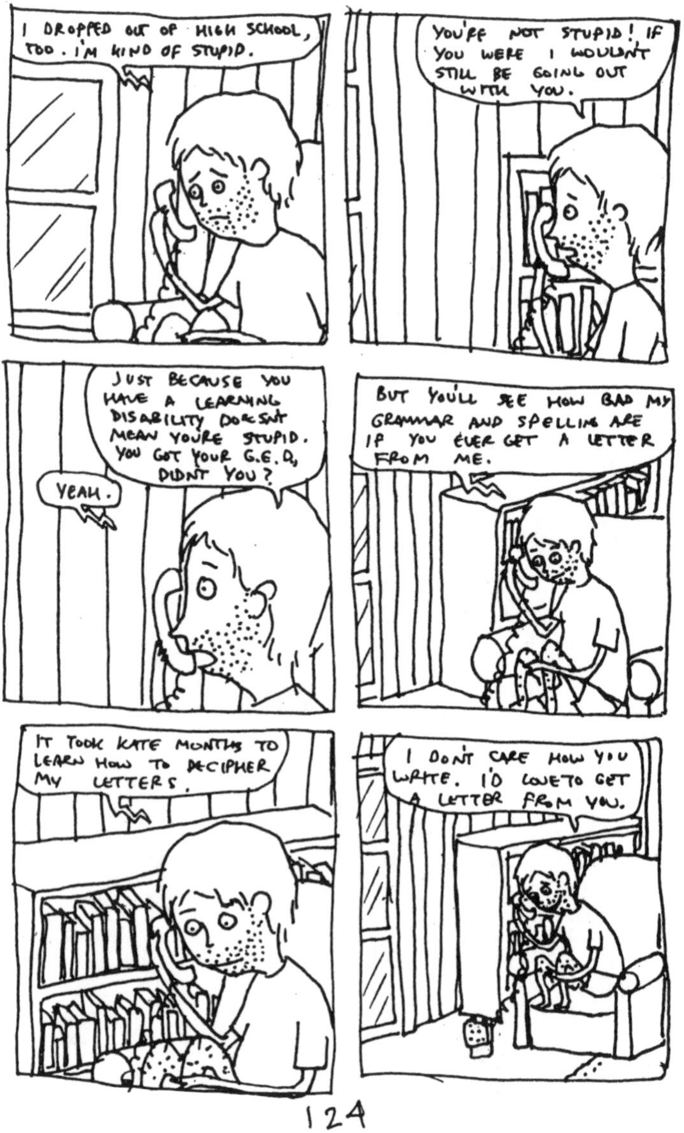
I DROPPED OUT OF HIGH SCHOOL, TOO. I'M KIND OF STUPID.
YOU'RE NOT STUPID! IF YOU WERE I WOULDN'T STILL BE GOING OUT WITH YOU.
JUST BECAUSE YOU HAVE A LEARNING DISABILITY DOESN'T MEAN YOU'RE STUPID. YOU GOT YOUR G.E.D, DIDN'T YOU?
YEAH.
BUT YOU'LL SEE HOW BAD MY GRAMMAR AND SPELLING ARE IF YOU EVER GET A LETTER FROM ME.
IT TOOK KATE MONTHS TO LEARN HOW TO DECIPHER MY LETTERS.
I DON'T CARE HOW YOU WRITE. I'D LOVE TO GET A LETTER FROM YOU.

UNEXPECTED

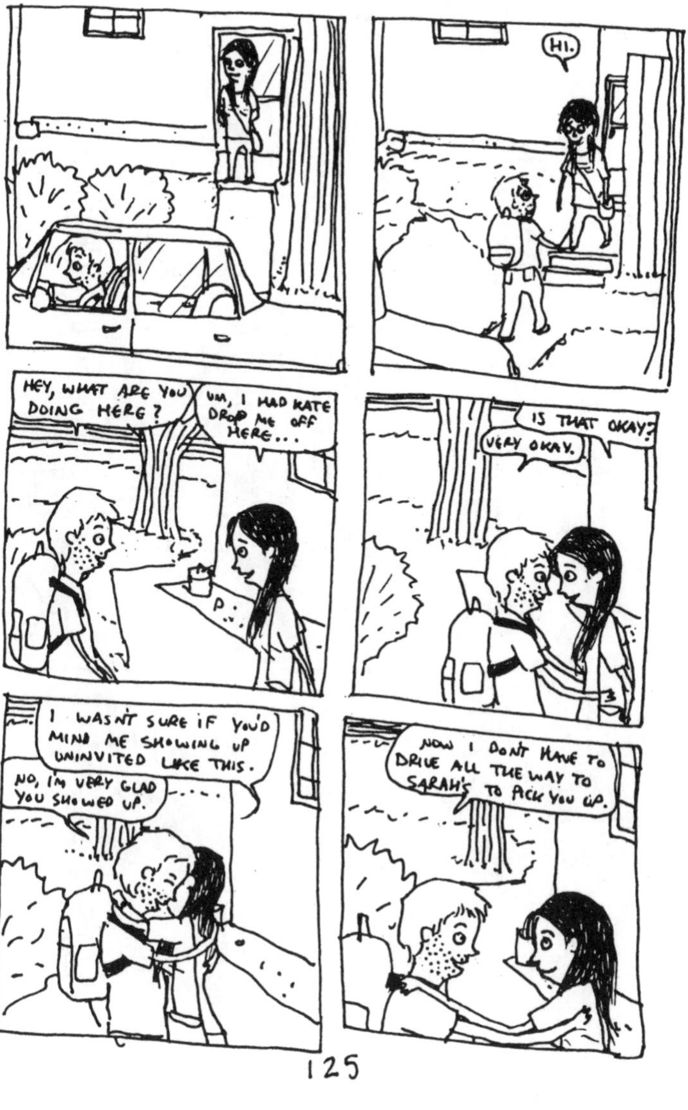
HI.
HEY, WHAT ARE YOU DOING HERE?
UM, I HAD KATE DROP ME OFF HERE...
IS THAT OKAY?
VERY OKAY.
I WASN'T SURE IF YOU'D MIND ME SHOWING UP UNINVITED LIKE THIS.
NO, I'M VERY GLAD YOU SHOWED UP.
NOW I DON'T HAVE TO DRIVE ALL THE WAY TO SARAH'S TO PICK YOU UP.

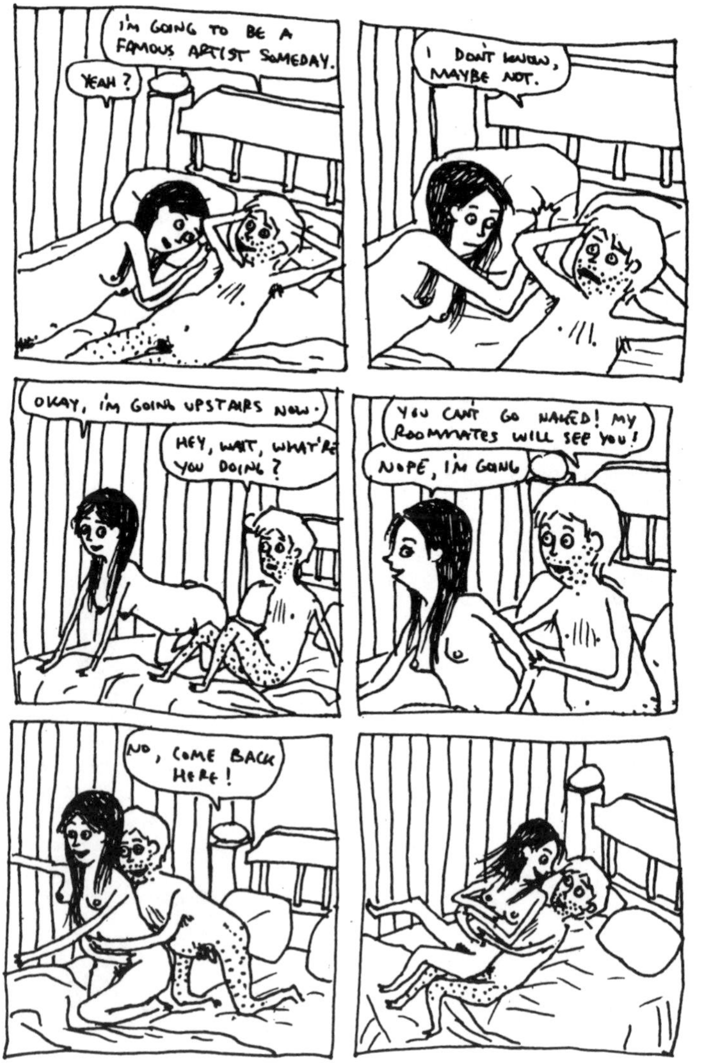
I'M GOING TO BE A FAMOUS ARTIST SOMEDAY.
YEAH?
I DON'T KNOW, MAYBE NOT.
OKAY, I'M GOING UPSTAIRS NOW.
HEY, WAIT, WHAT'RE YOU DOING?
YOU CAN'T GO NAKED! MY ROOMMATES WILL SEE YOU!
NOPE, I'M GOING
NO, COME BACK HERE!

MORNING SHOWER

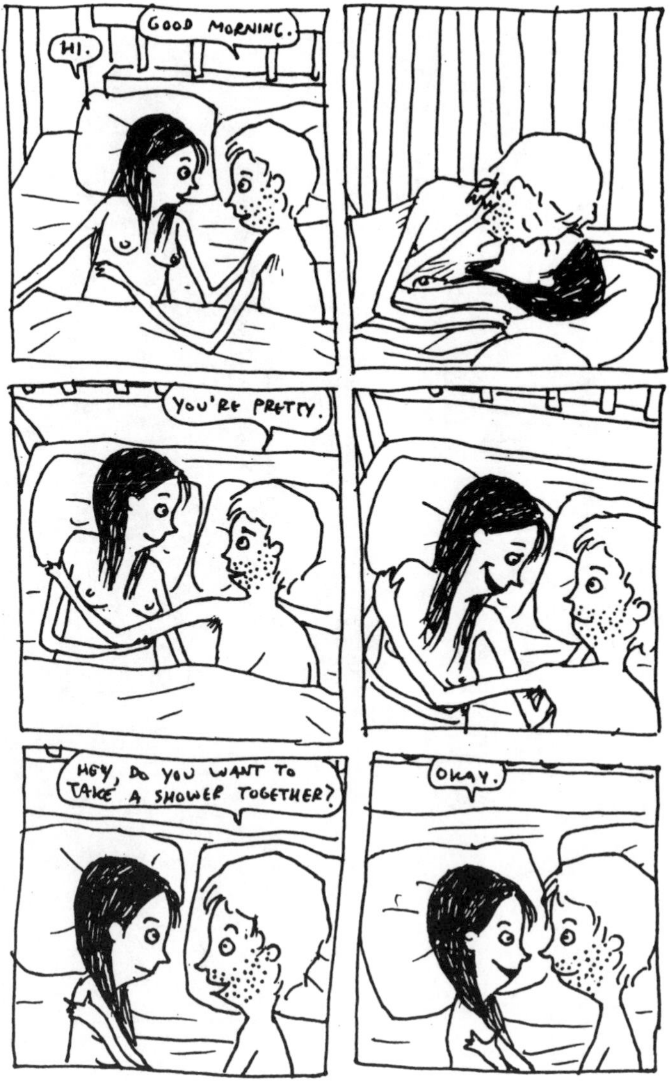
HI.
GOOD MORNING.
YOU'RE PRETTY.
HEY, DO YOU WANT TO TAKE A SHOWER TOGETHER?
OKAY.

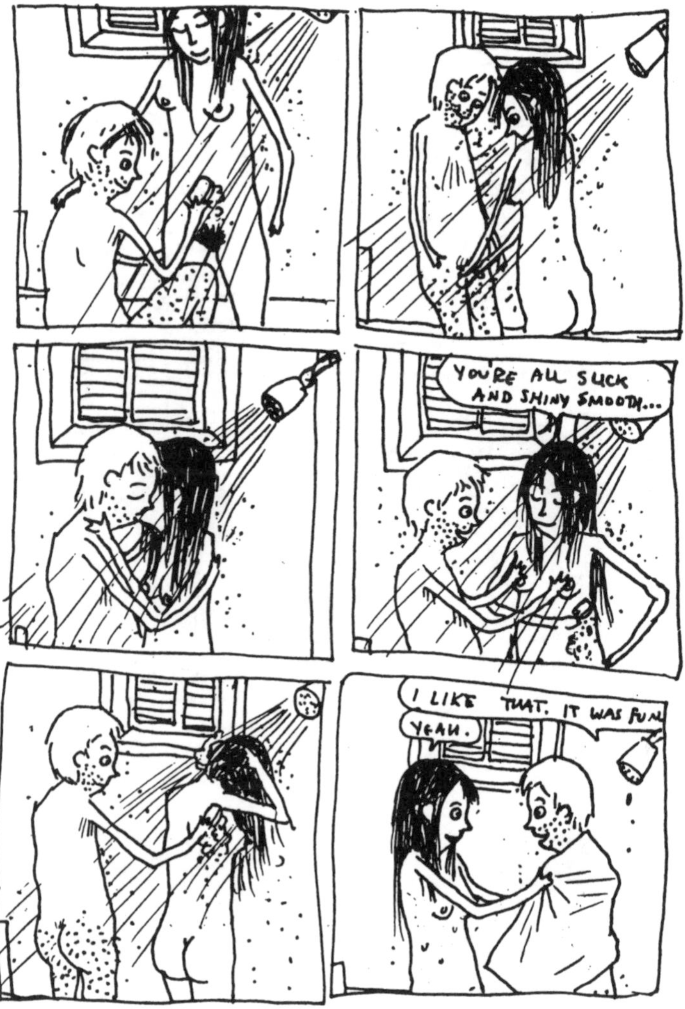
YOU'RE ALL SLICK AND SHINY SMOOTH...
I LIKE THAT. IT WAS FUN
YEAH.

SEPARATE ROOMS

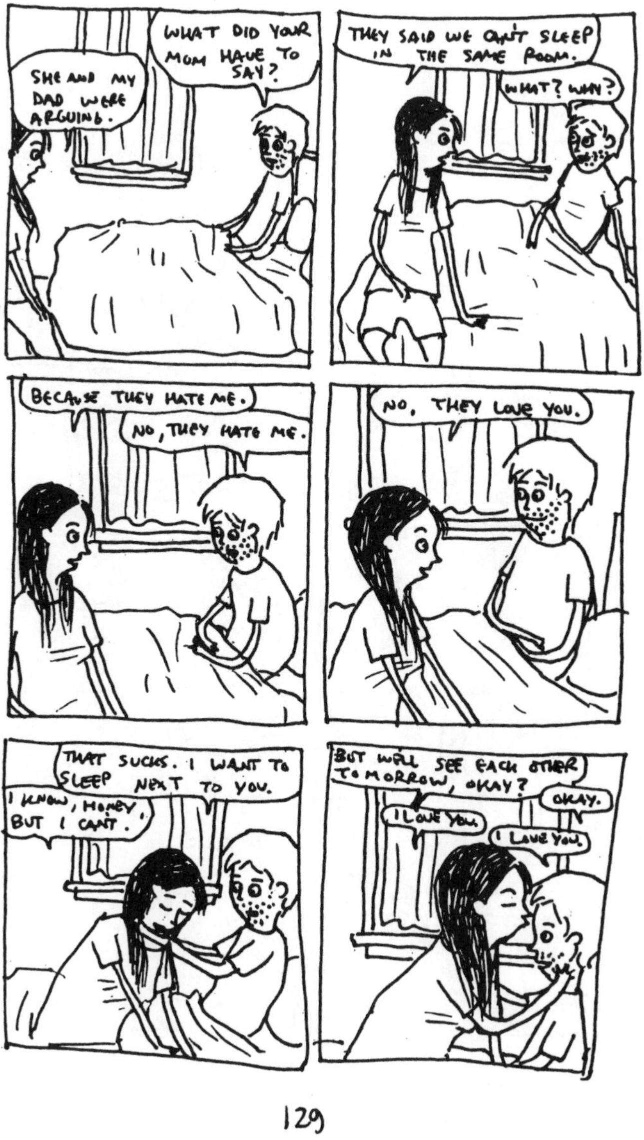
WHAT DID YOUR MOM HAVE TO SAY?
SHE AND MY DAD WERE ARGUING.
THEY SAID WE CAN'T SLEEP IN THE SAME ROOM.
WHAT? WHY?
BECAUSE THEY HATE ME.
NO, THEY HATE ME.
NO, THEY LOVE YOU.
THAT SUCKS. I WANT TO SLEEP NEXT TO YOU.
I KNOW, HONEY. BUT I CAN'T.
BUT WE'LL SEE EACH OTHER TOMORROW, OKAY?
OKAY.
I LOVE YOU.
I LOVE YOU.

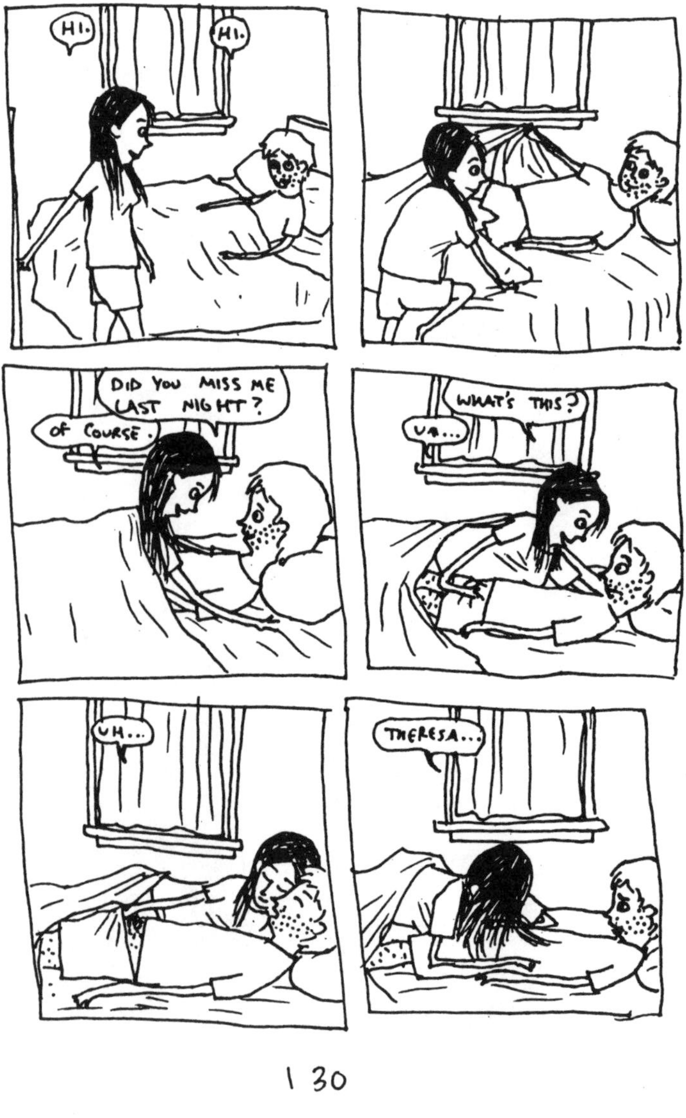
HI.
HI.
DID YOU MISS ME LAST NIGHT?
OF COURSE.
WHAT'S THIS?
UH...
UH...
THERESA...

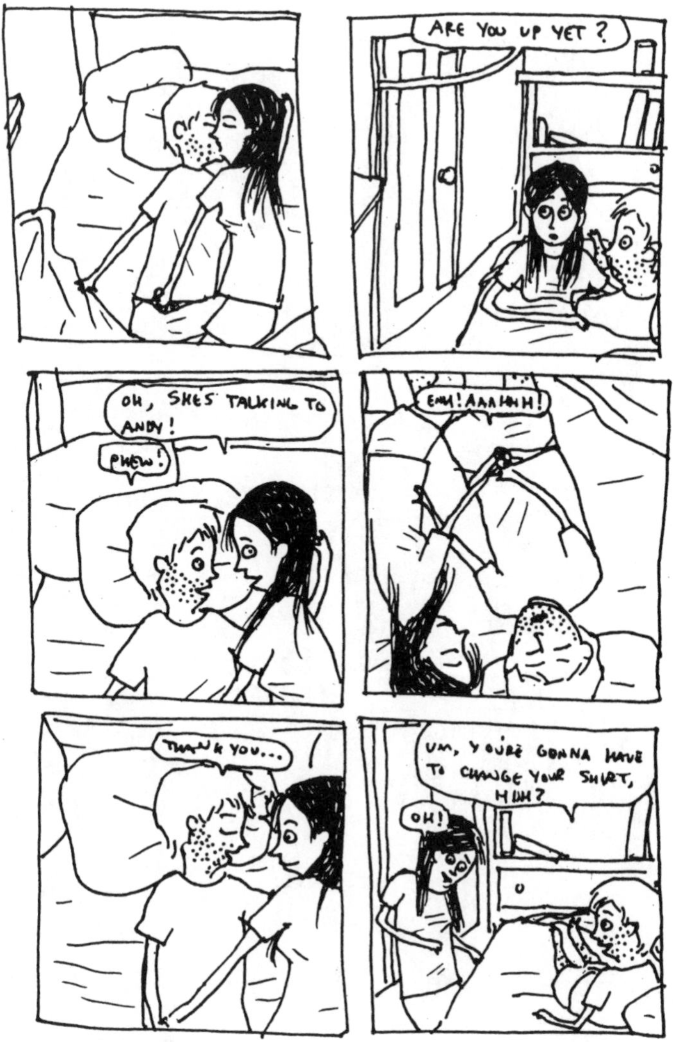
ARE YOU UP YET?
OH, SHES TALKING TO ANDY!
PHEW!
EMM! AAAHHH!
THANK YOU...
UM, YOU'RE GONNA HAVE TO CHANGE YOUR SHIRT, HUH?
OH!

LAUNDRY

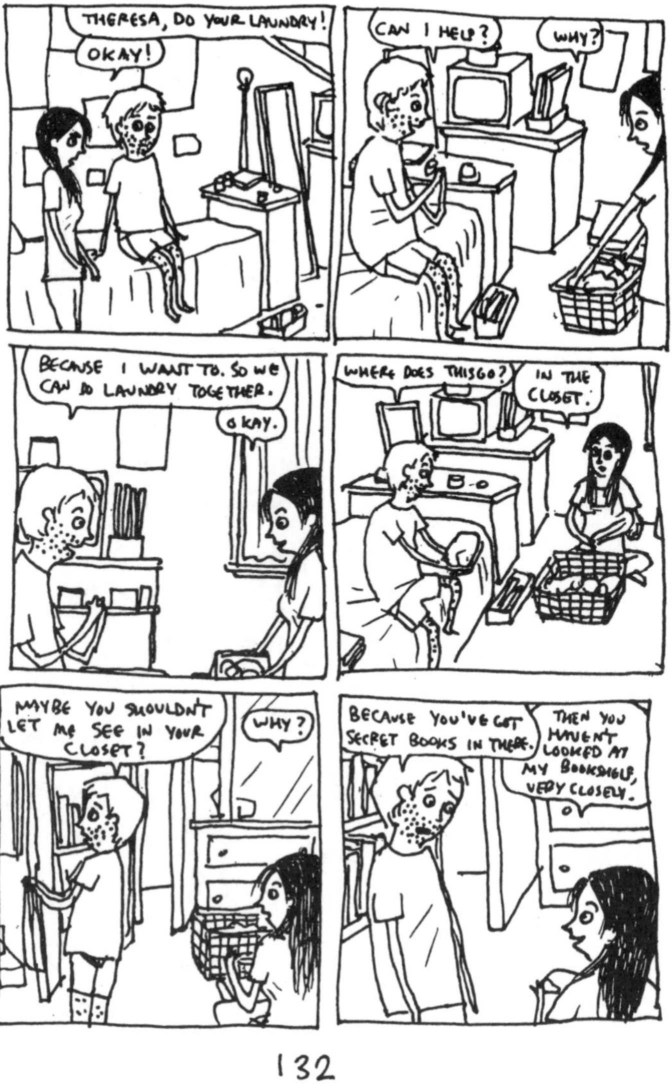
THERESA, DO YOUR LAUNDRY!
OKAY!
CAN I HELP?
WHY?
BECAUSE I WANT TO. SO WE CAN DO LAUNDRY TOGETHER.
OKAY.
WHERE DOES THIS GO?
IN THE CLOSET.
MAYBE YOU SHOULDN'T LET ME SEE IN YOUR CLOSET?
WHY?
BECAUSE YOU'VE GOT SECRET BOOKS IN THERE.
THEN YOU HAVEN'T LOOKED AT MY BOOKSHELF, VERY CLOSELY.

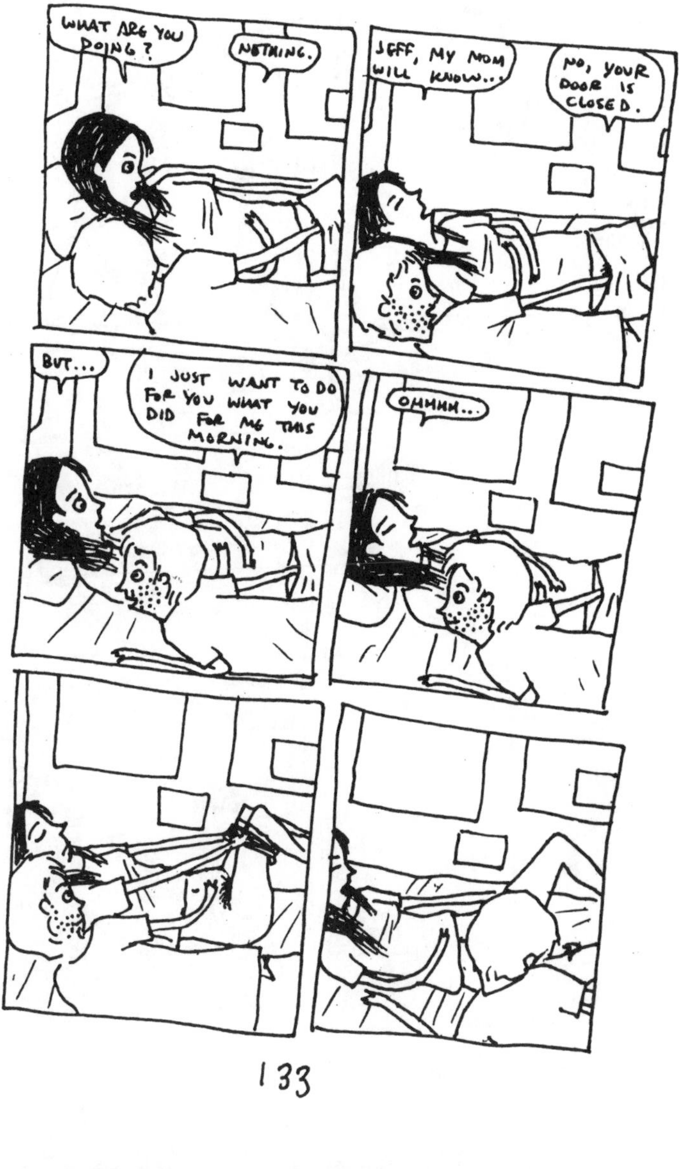
WHAT ARE YOU DOING?
NOTHING.
JEFF, MY MOM WILL KNOW...
NO, YOUR DOOR IS CLOSED.
BUT...
I JUST WANT TO DO FOR YOU WHAT YOU DID FOR ME THIS MORNING.
OHMMM...

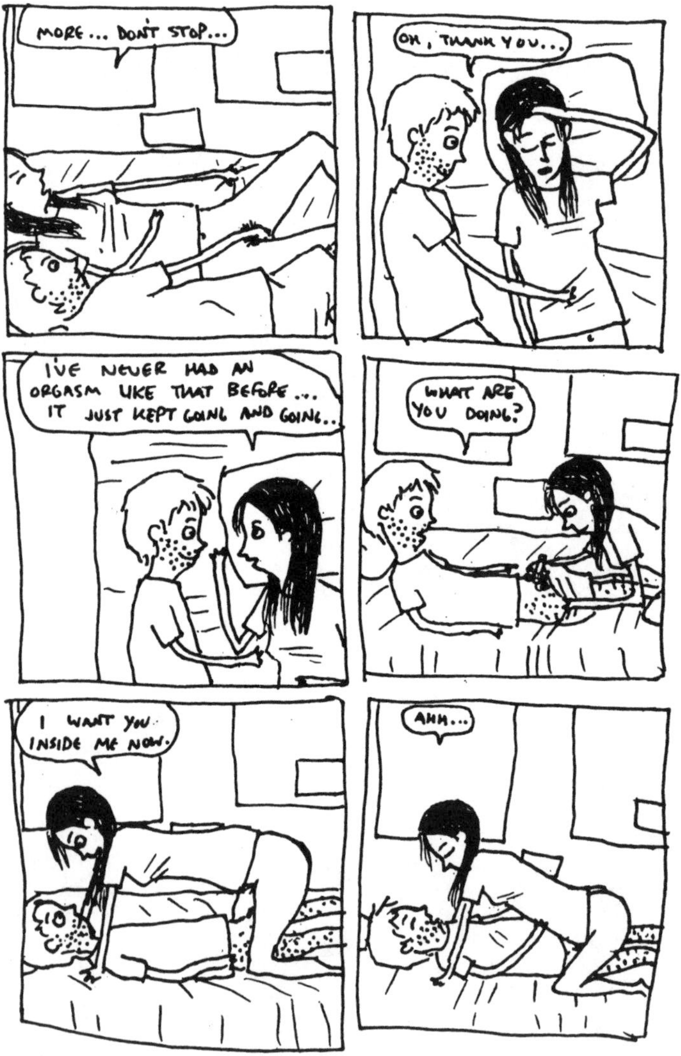
MORE... DON'T STOP...
OH, THANK YOU...
I'VE NEVER HAD AN ORGASM LIKE THAT BEFORE... IT JUST KEPT GOING AND GOING...
WHAT ARE YOU DOING?
I WANT YOU INSIDE ME NOW.
AHH...

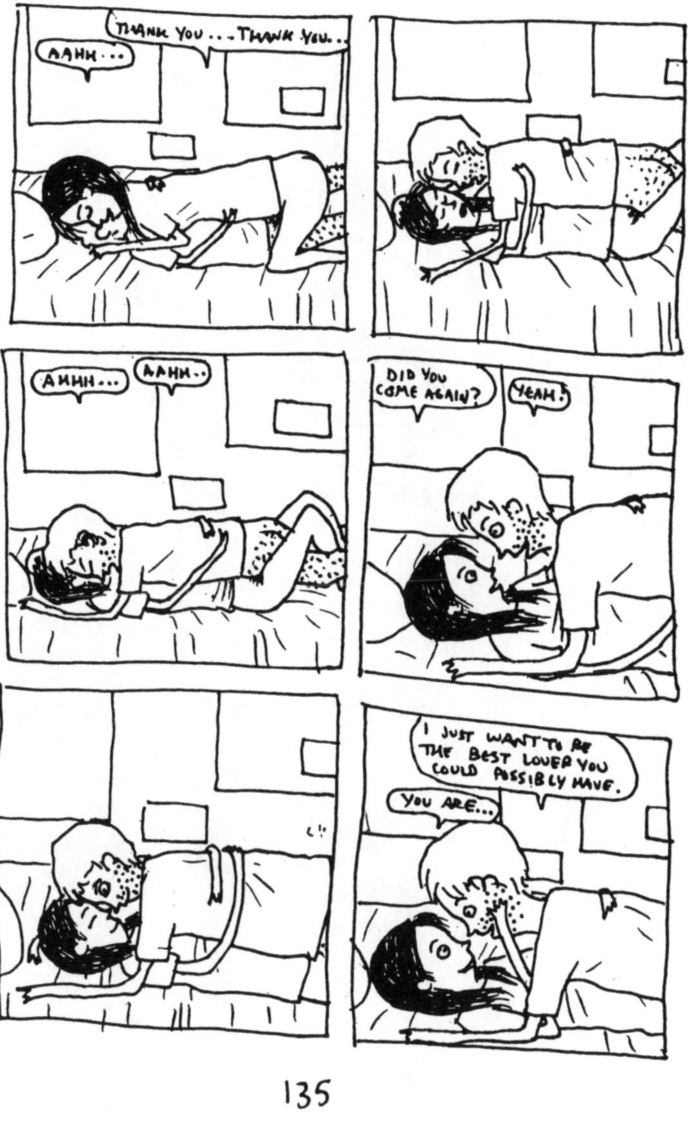
AAHH...
THANK YOU... THANK YOU...
AHHH...
AAHH...
DID YOU COME AGAIN?
YEAH!
I JUST WANT TO BE THE BEST LOVER YOU COULD POSSIBLY HAVE.
YOU ARE...

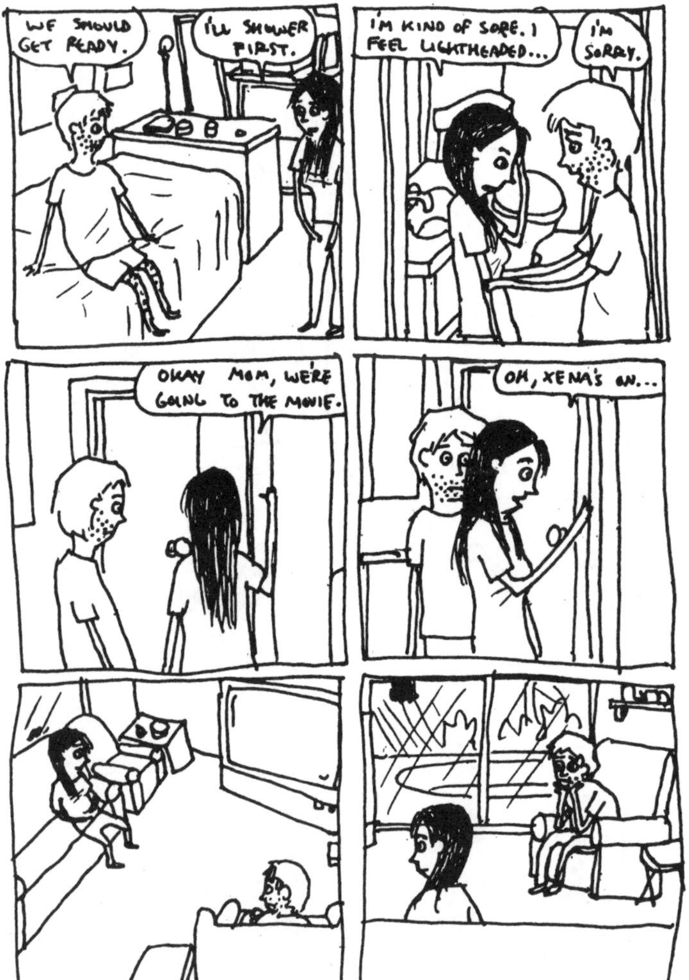
WE SHOULD GET READY.
I'LL SHOWER FIRST.
I'M KIND OF SORE. I FEEL LIGHTHEADED...
I'M SORRY.
OKAY MOM, WE'RE GOING TO THE MOVIE.
OH, XENA'S ON...

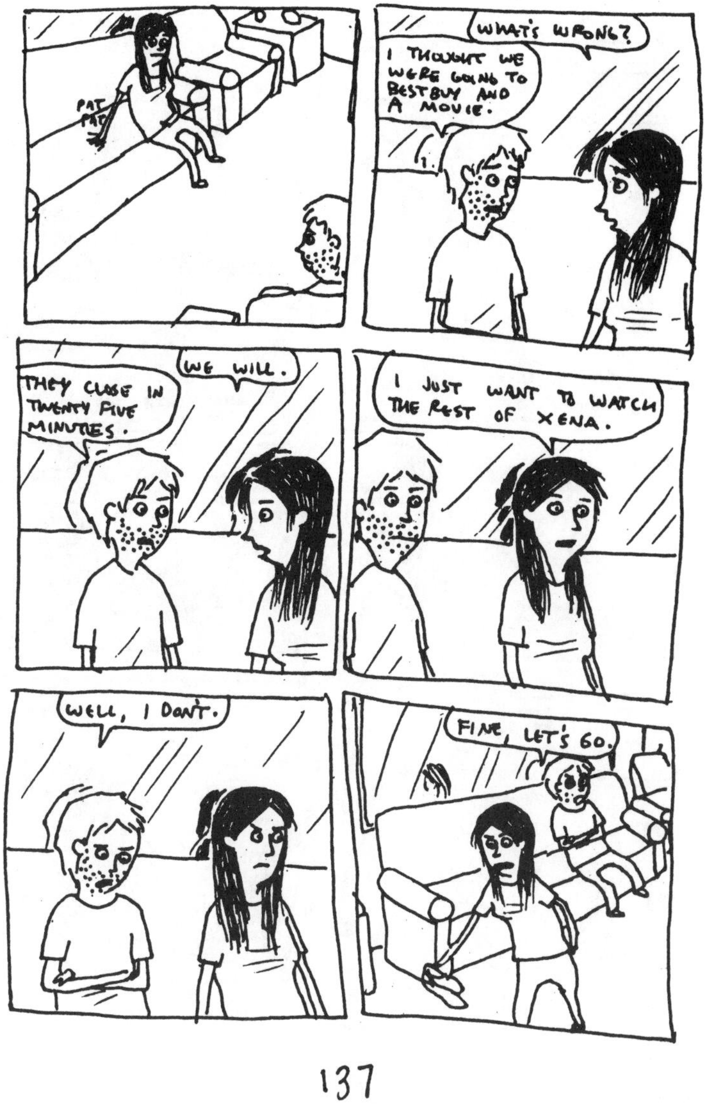
PAT PAT
WHAT'S WRONG?
I THOUGHT WE WERE GOING TO BESTBUY AND A MOVIE.
WE WILL.
THEY CLOSE IN TWENTY FIVE MINUTES.
I JUST WANT TO WATCH THE REST OF XENA.
WELL, I DON'T.
FINE, LET'S GO.

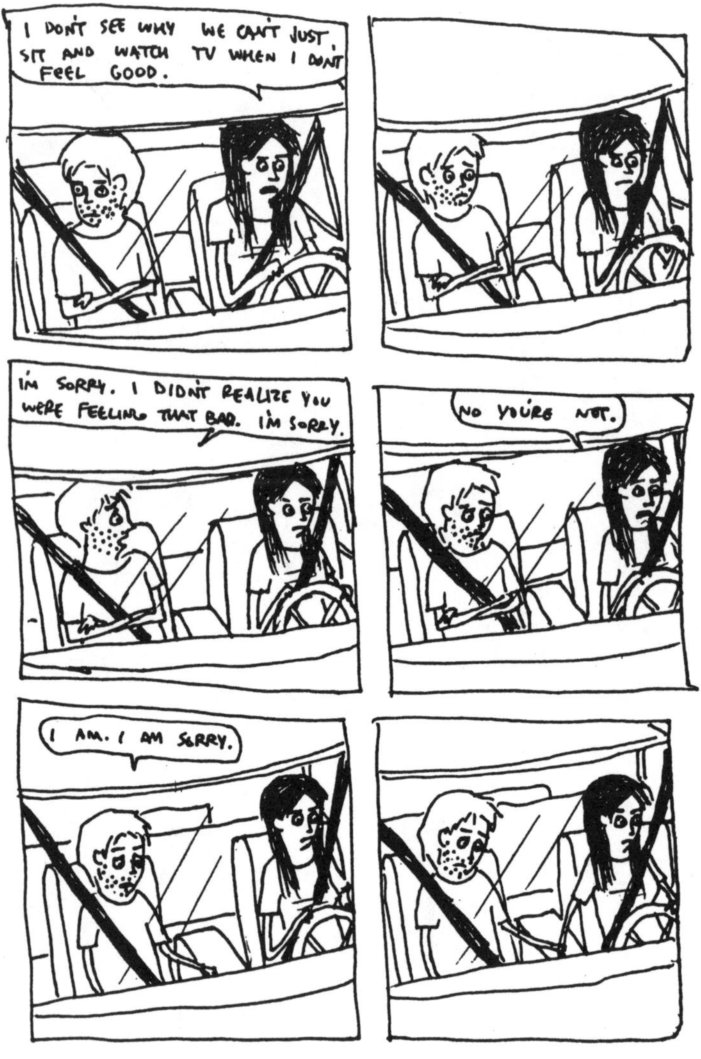
I DON'T SEE WHY WE CAN'T JUST SIT AND WATCH TV WHEN I DON'T FEEL GOOD.
I'M SORRY. I DIDN'T REALIZE YOU WERE FEELING THAT BAD. I'M SORRY.
NO YOU'RE NOT.
I AM. I AM SORRY.

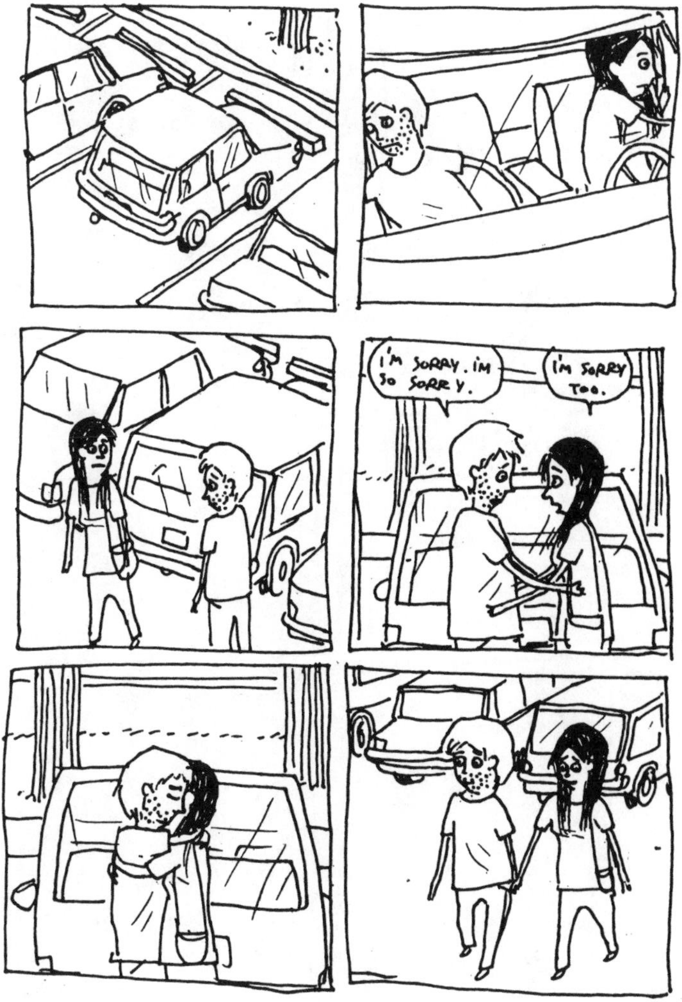
I'M SORRY. IM SO SORRY.
I'M SORRY TOO.

ART INSTITUTE

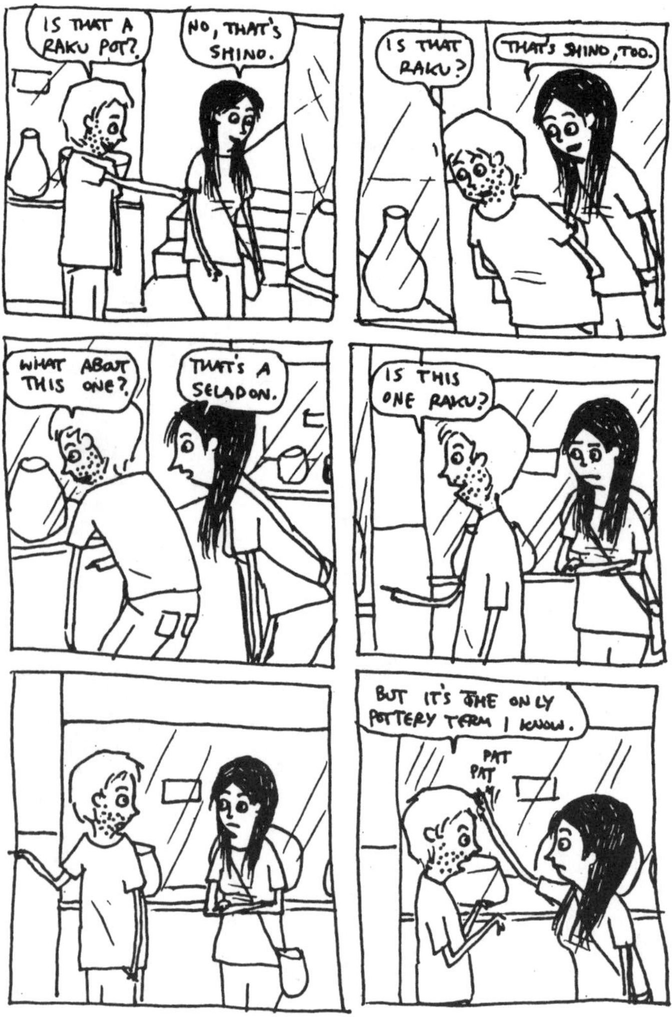
IS THAT A RAKU POT?
NO, THAT'S SHINO.
IS THAT RAKU?
THAT'S SHINO, TOO.
WHAT ABOUT THIS ONE?
THAT'S A SELADON.
IS THIS ONE RAKU?
BUT IT'S THE ONLY POTTERY TERM I KNOW.
PAT PAT

CROHN'S

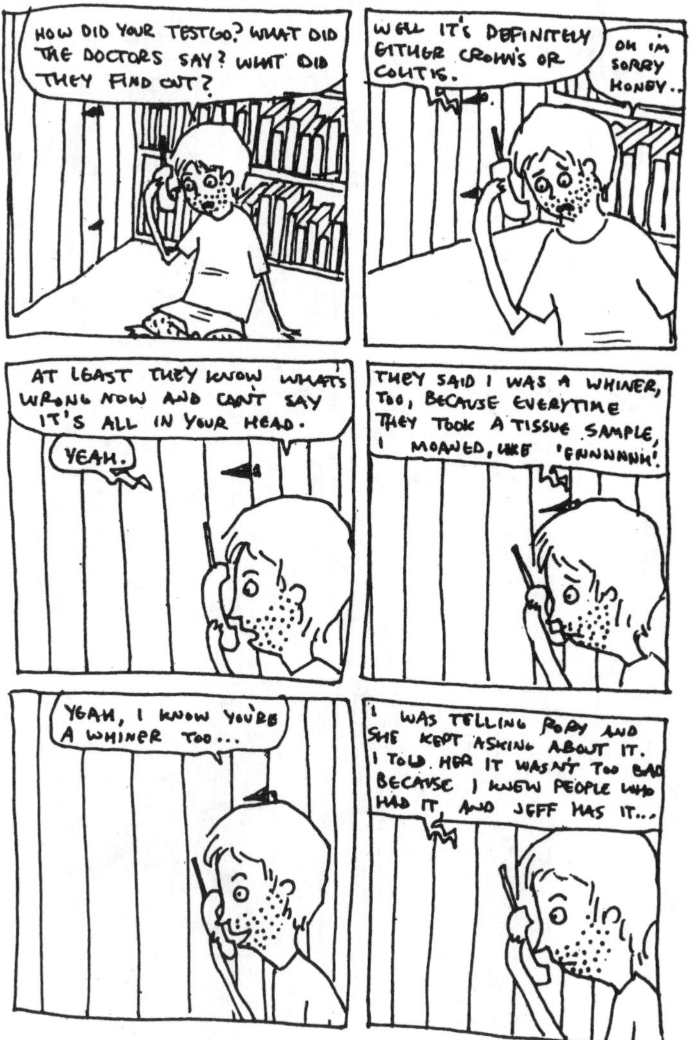
HOW DID YOUR TEST GO? WHAT DID THE DOCTORS SAY? WHAT DID THEY FIND OUT?
WELL IT'S DEFINITELY EITHER CROHN'S OR COLITIS.
OH I'M SORRY HONEY..
AT LEAST THEY KNOW WHAT'S WRONG NOW AND CAN'T SAY IT'S ALL IN YOUR HEAD.
YEAH.
THEY SAID I WAS A WHINER, TOO, BECAUSE EVERYTIME THEY TOOK A TISSUE SAMPLE, I MOANED, LIKE 'GNNNNNH'.
YEAH, I KNOW YOU'RE A WHINER TOO...
I WAS TELLING RORY AND SHE KEPT ASKING ABOUT IT. I TOLD HER IT WASN'T TOO BAD BECAUSE I KNEW PEOPLE WHO HAD IT, AND JEFF HAS IT...

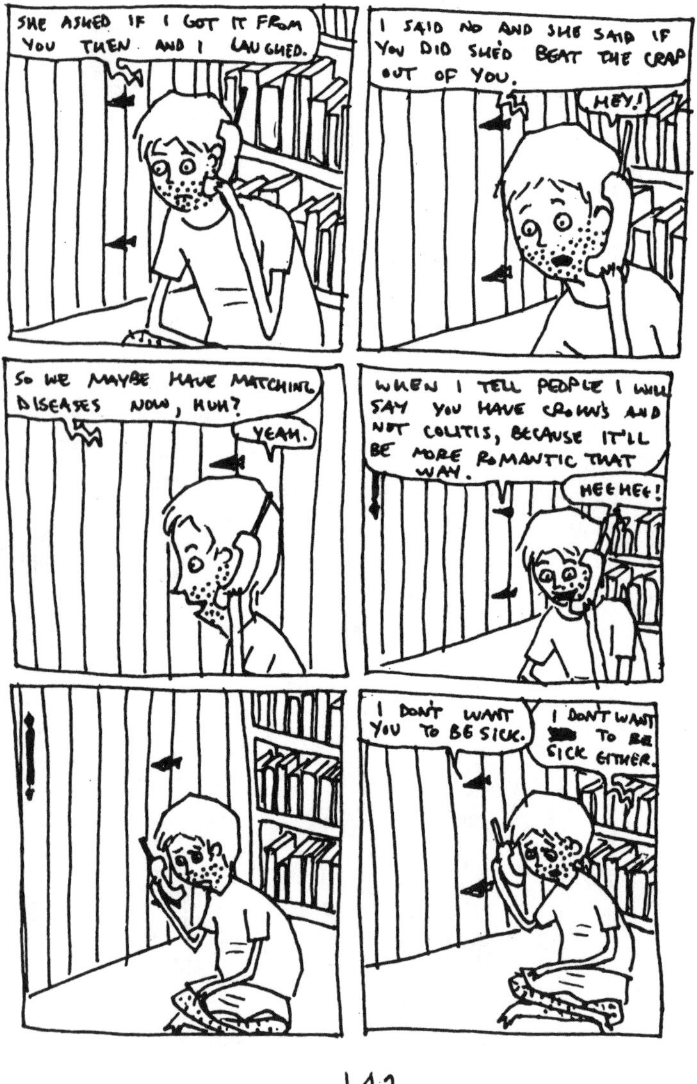
SHE ASKED IF I GOT IT FROM YOU THEN AND I LAUGHED.
I SAID NO AND SHE SAID IF YOU DID SHE'D BEAT THE CRAP OUT OF YOU.
HEY!
SO WE MAYBE HAVE MATCHING DISEASES NOW, HUH?
YEAH.
WHEN I TELL PEOPLE I WILL SAY YOU HAVE CROHN'S AND NOT COLITIS, BECAUSE IT'LL BE MORE ROMANTIC THAT WAY.
HEE HEE!
I DON'T WANT YOU TO BE SICK.
I DON'T WANT [redacted] TO BE SICK EITHER.

SLEEP

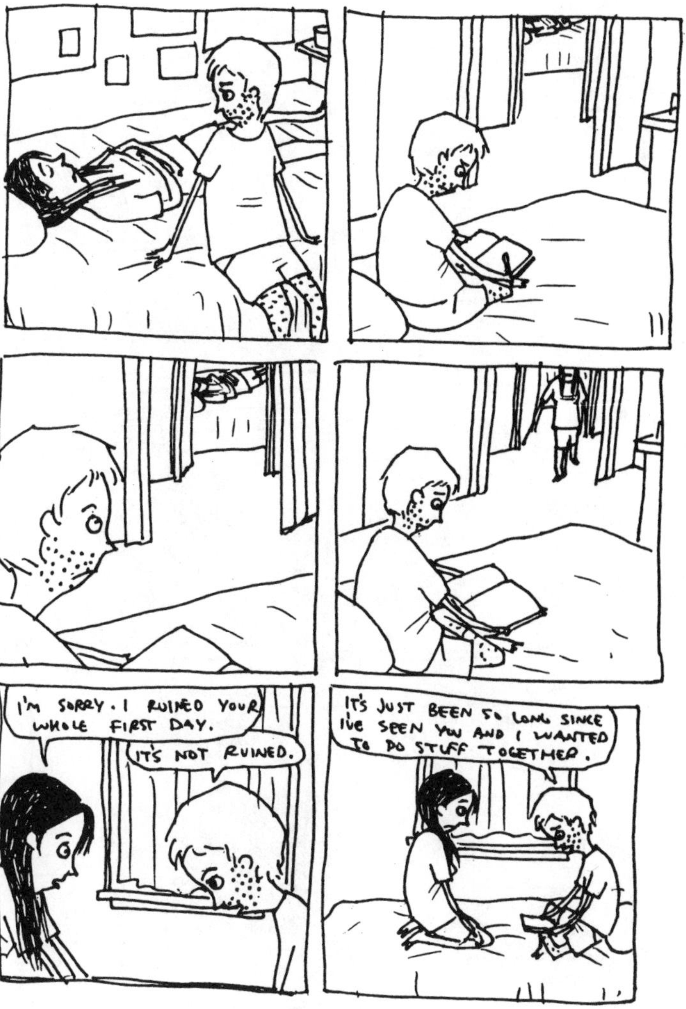
I'M SORRY. I RUINED YOUR WHOLE FIRST DAY.
IT'S NOT RUINED.
IT'S JUST BEEN SO LONG SINCE I'VE SEEN YOU AND I WANTED TO DO STUFF TOGETHER.

CLEAN

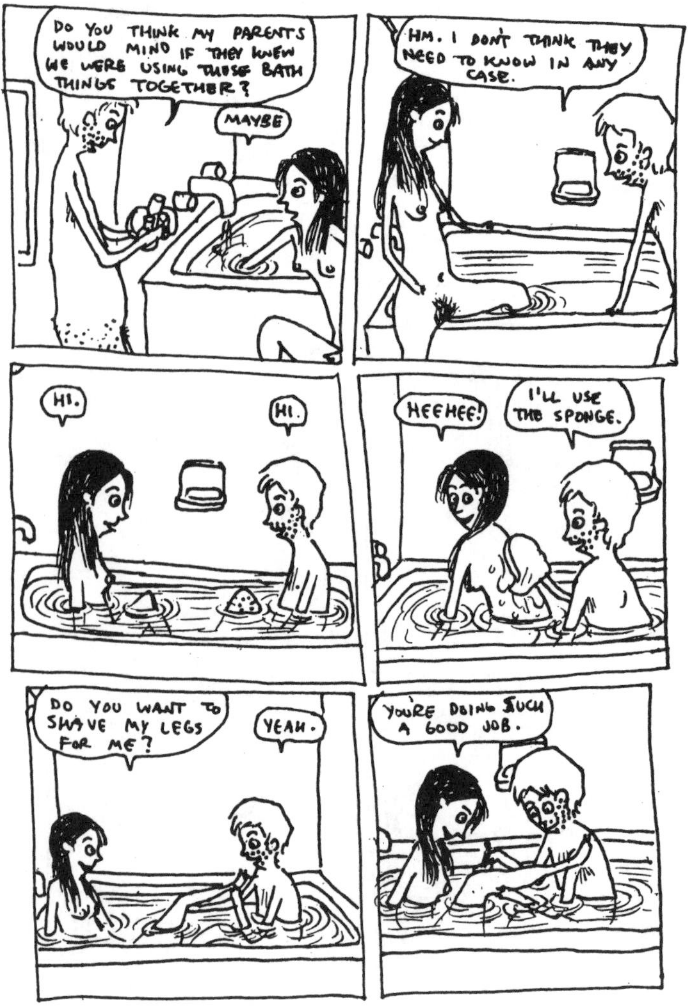
DO YOU THINK MY PARENTS WOULD MIND IF THEY KNEW WE WERE USING THESE BATH THINGS TOGETHER?
MAYBE
HM. I DON'T THINK THEY NEED TO KNOW IN ANY CASE.
HI.
HI.
HEEHEE!
I'LL USE THE SPONGE.
DO YOU WANT TO SHAVE MY LEGS FOR ME?
YEAH.
YOU'RE DOING SUCH A GOOD JOB.

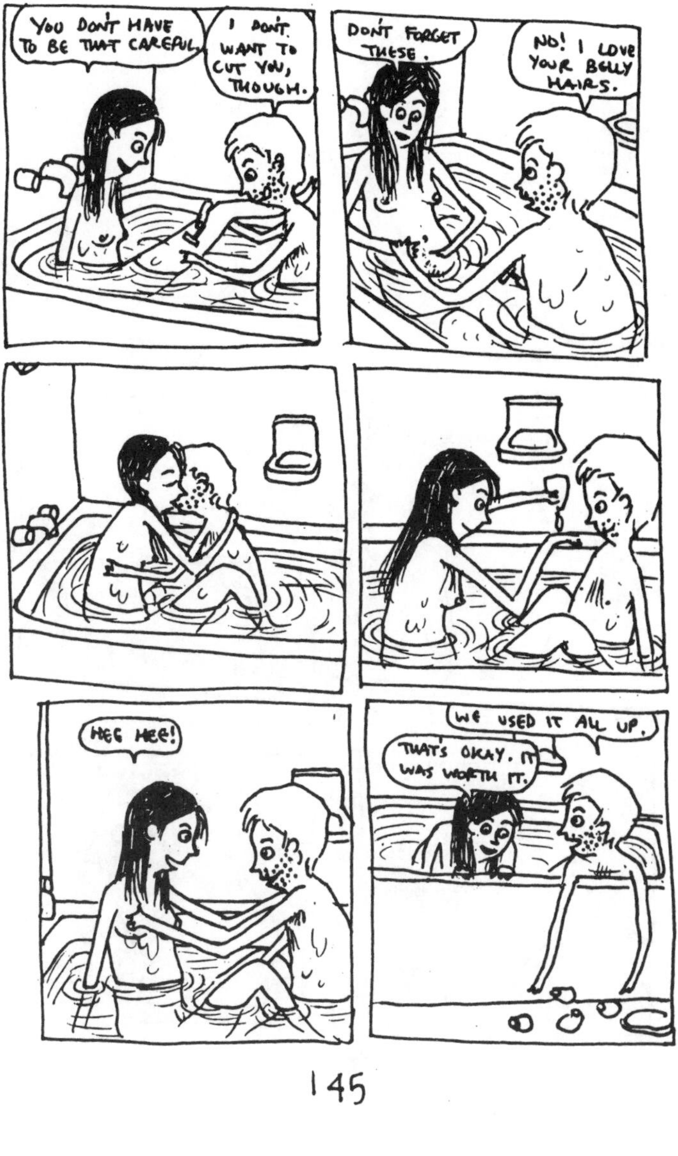
YOU DON'T HAVE TO BE THAT CAREFUL.
I DON'T WANT TO CUT YOU, THOUGH.
DON'T FORGET THESE.
NO! I LOVE YOUR BELLY HAIRS.
HEE HEE!
WE USED IT ALL UP.
THAT'S OKAY. IT WAS WORTH IT.

SICK

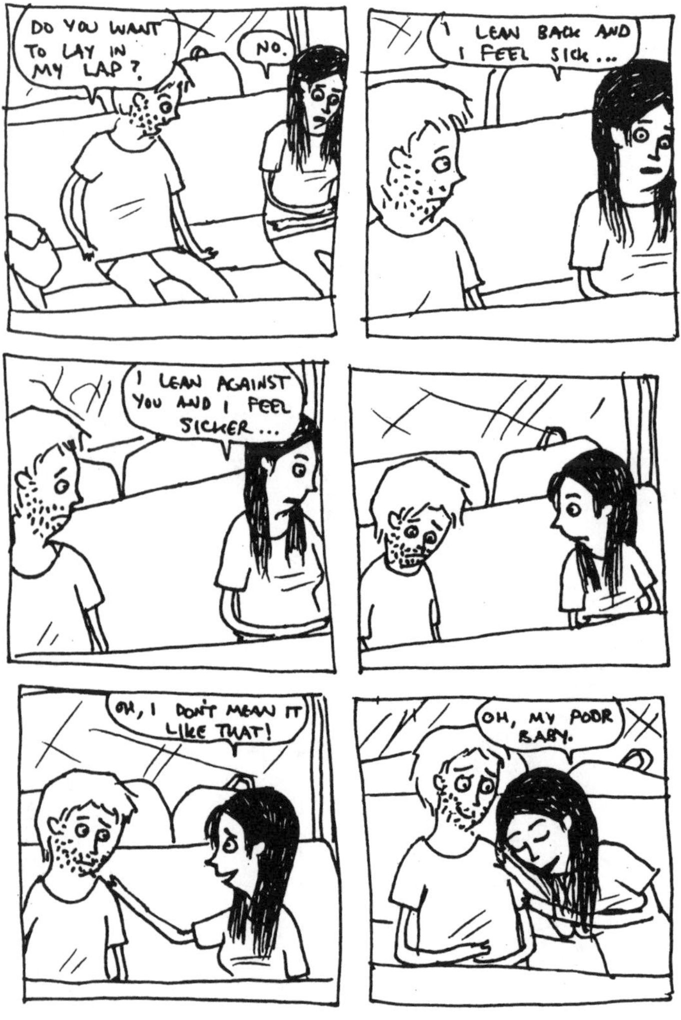
DO YOU WANT TO LAY IN MY LAP?
NO.
I LEAN BACK AND I FEEL SICK...
I LEAN AGAINST YOU AND I FEEL SICKER...
OH, I DON'T MEAN IT LIKE THAT!
OH, MY POOR BABY.

KISSES

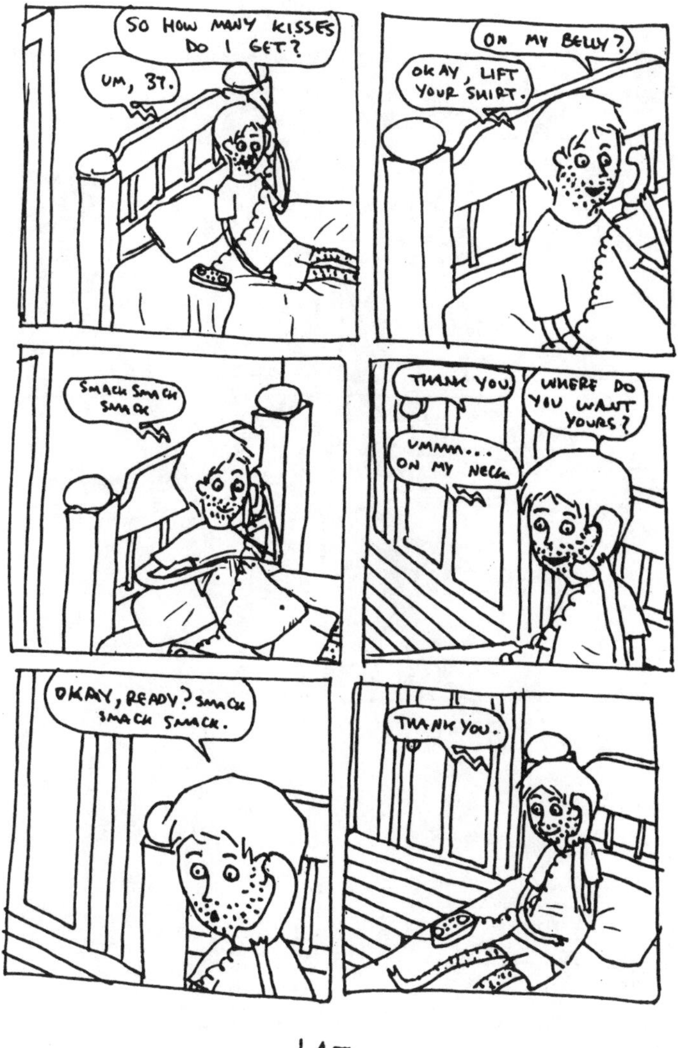
SO HOW MANY KISSES DO I GET?
UM, 37.
ON MY BELLY?
OKAY, LIFT YOUR SHIRT.
SMACK SMACK SMACK
THANK YOU.
WHERE DO YOU WANT YOURS?
UMMM... ON MY NECK
OKAY, READY? SMACK SMACK SMACK.
THANK YOU.

MINIATURE GOLFING

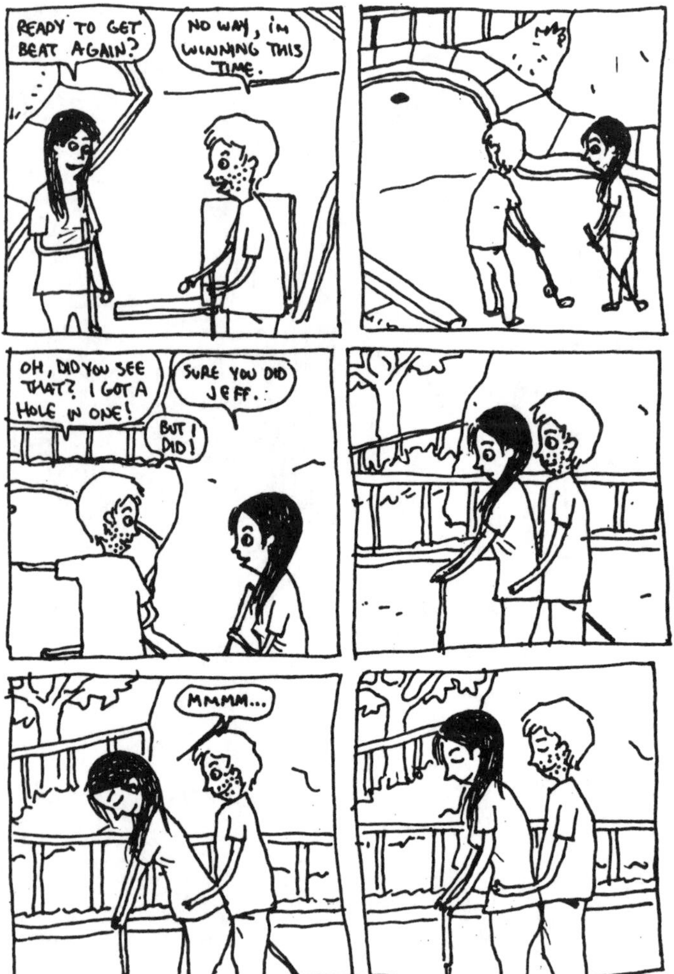
READY TO GET BEAT AGAIN?
NO WAY, IM WINNING THIS TIME.
OH, DID YOU SEE THAT? I GOT A HOLE IN ONE!
SURE YOU DID JEFF.
BUT I DID!
MMMM...

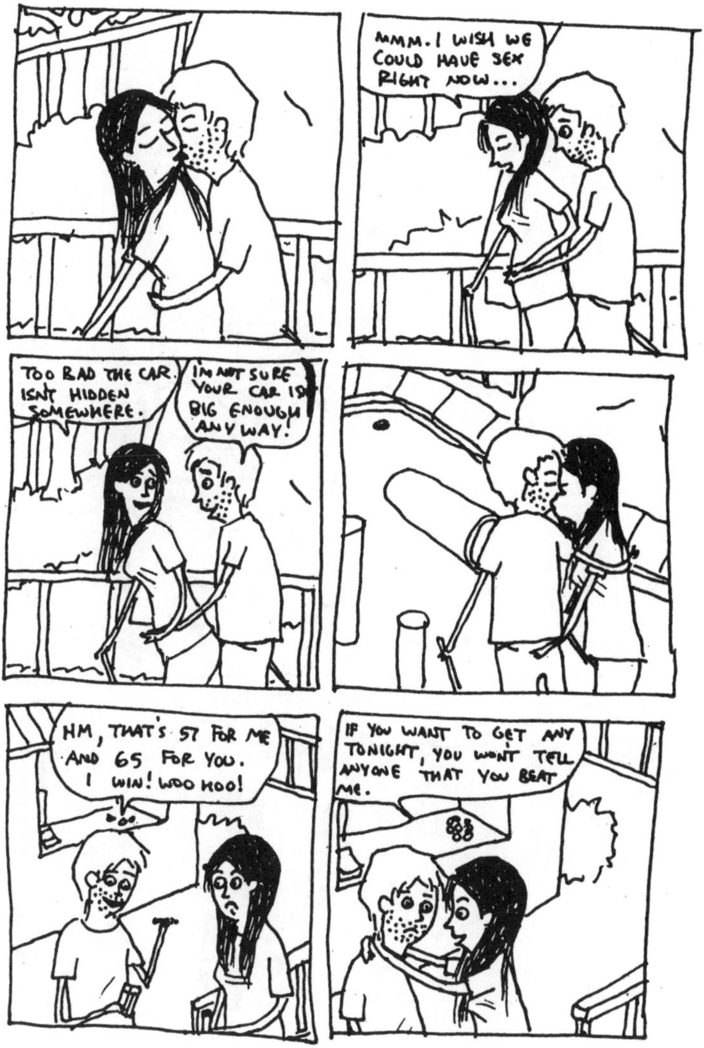
MMM. I WISH WE COULD HAVE SEX RIGHT NOW...
TOO BAD THE CAR ISN'T HIDDEN SOMEWHERE.
I'M NOT SURE YOUR CAR IS BIG ENOUGH ANYWAY!
HM, THAT'S 57 FOR ME AND 65 FOR YOU. I WIN! WOO HOO!
IF YOU WANT TO GET ANY TONIGHT, YOU WON'T TELL ANYONE THAT YOU BEAT ME.

PRIZE

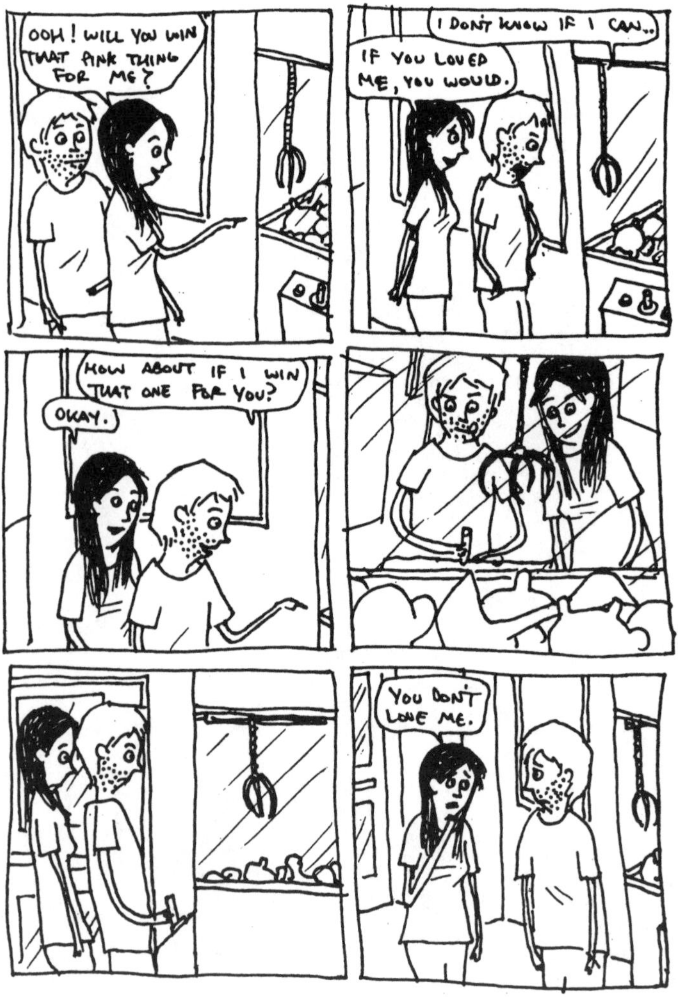
OOH! WILL YOU WIN THAT PINK THING FOR ME?
I DON'T KNOW IF I CAN..
IF YOU LOVED ME, YOU WOULD.
HOW ABOUT IF I WIN THAT ONE FOR YOU?
OKAY.
YOU DON'T LOVE ME.

NAP

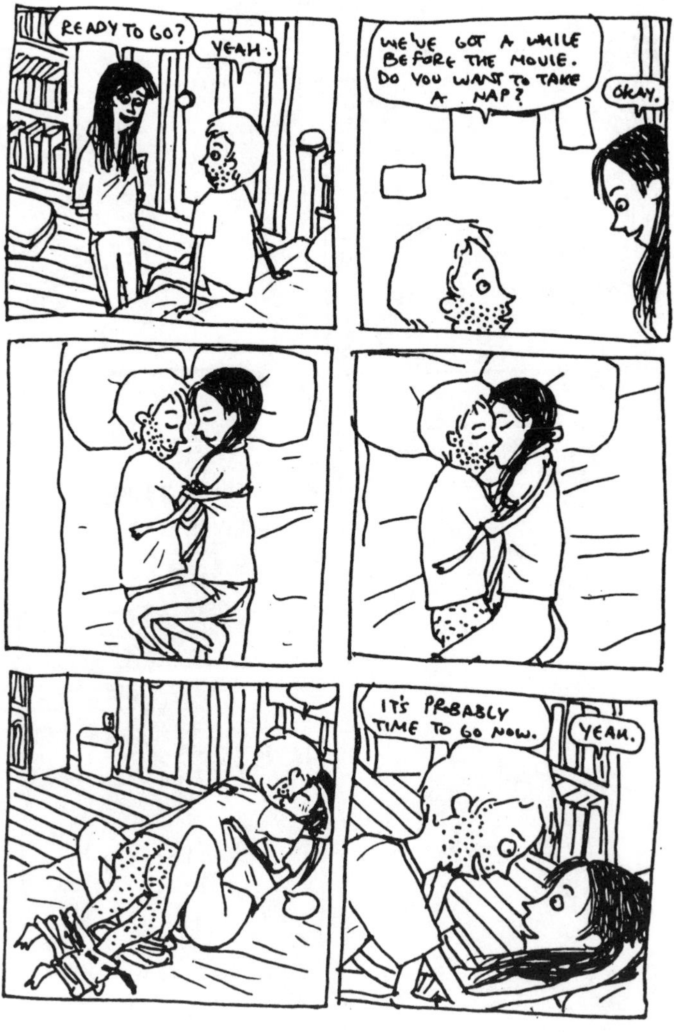
READY TO GO?
YEAH.
WE'VE GOT A WHILE BEFORE THE MOVIE. DO YOU WANT TO TAKE A NAP?
OKAY.
IT'S PROBABLY TIME TO GO NOW.
YEAH.

TAN

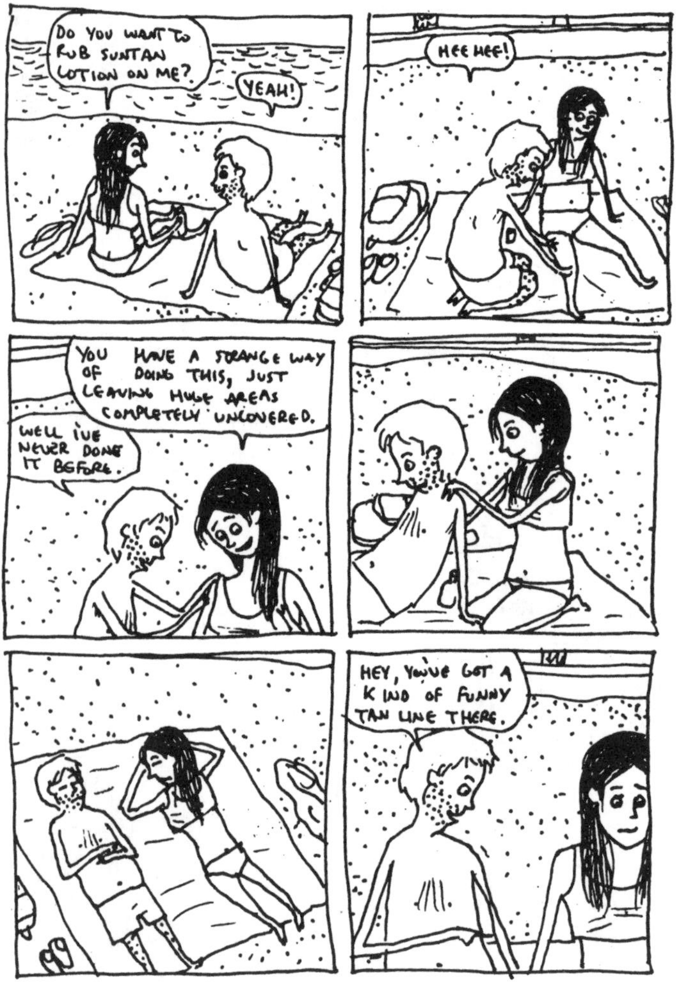
DO YOU WANT TO RUB SUNTAN LOTION ON ME?
YEAH!
HEE HEE!
YOU HAVE A STRANGE WAY OF DOING THIS, JUST LEAVING HUGE AREAS COMPLETELY UNCOVERED.
WELL I'VE NEVER DONE IT BEFORE.
HEY, YOU'VE GOT A KIND OF FUNNY TAN LINE THERE.

AMAZING

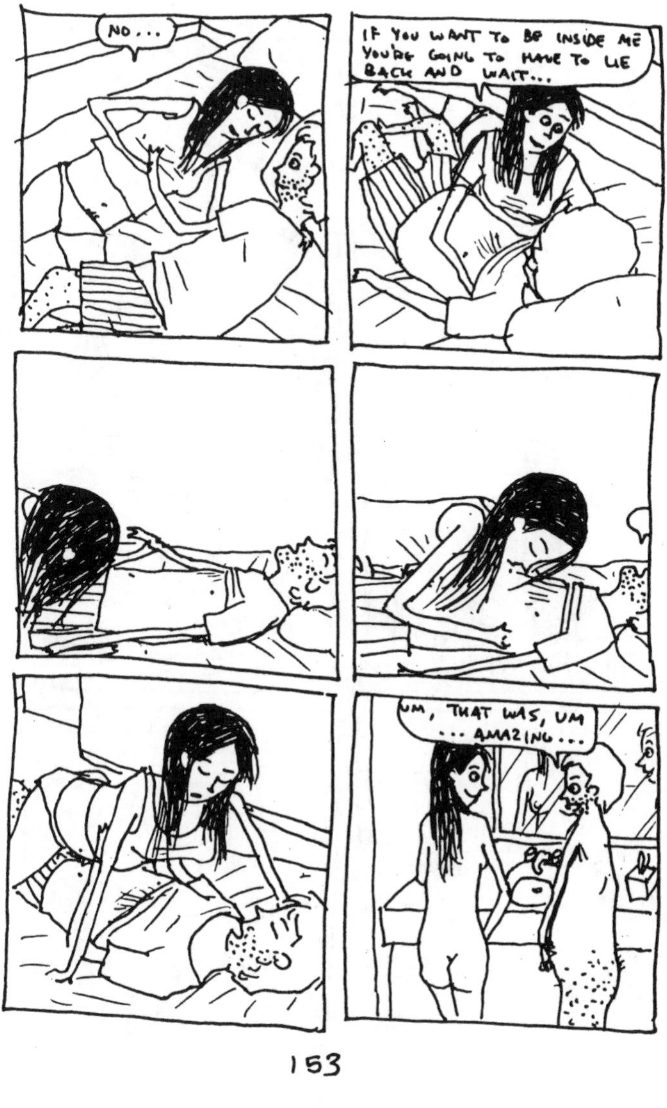
NO...
IF YOU WANT TO BE INSIDE ME YOU'RE GOING TO HAVE TO LIE BACK AND WAIT...
UM, THAT WAS, UM ... AMAZING...

LAS OLAS

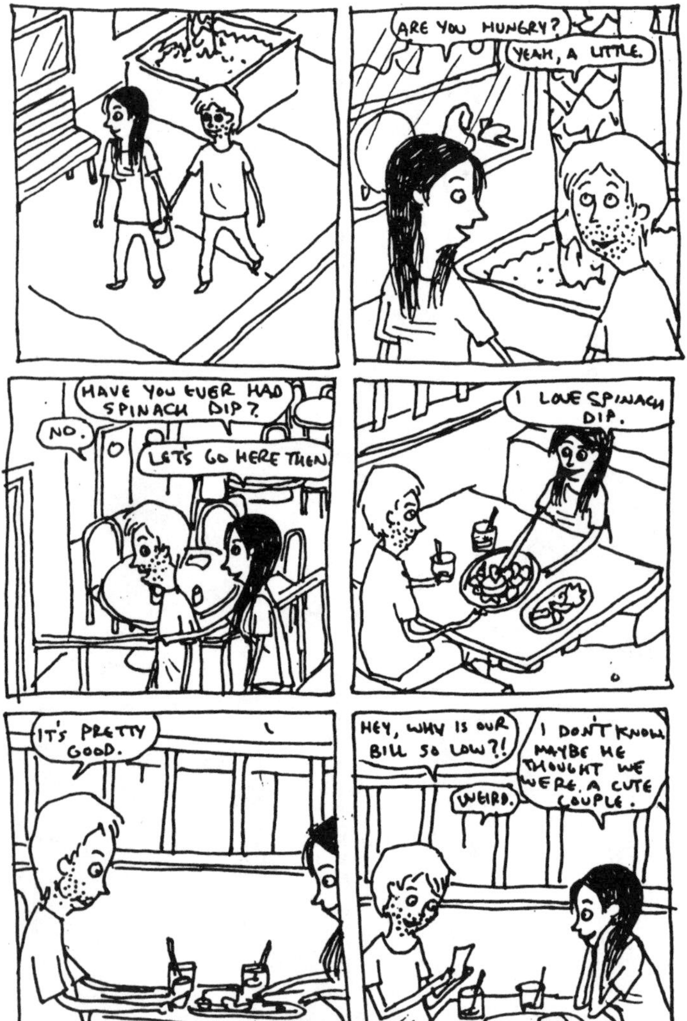
ARE YOU HUNGRY?
YEAH, A LITTLE.
HAVE YOU EVER HAD SPINACH DIP?
NO.
LETS GO HERE THEN.
I LOVE SPINACH DIP.
IT'S PRETTY GOOD.
HEY, WHY IS OUR BILL SO LOW?!
I DON'T KNOW MAYBE HE THOUGHT WE WERE A CUTE COUPLE.
WEIRD.

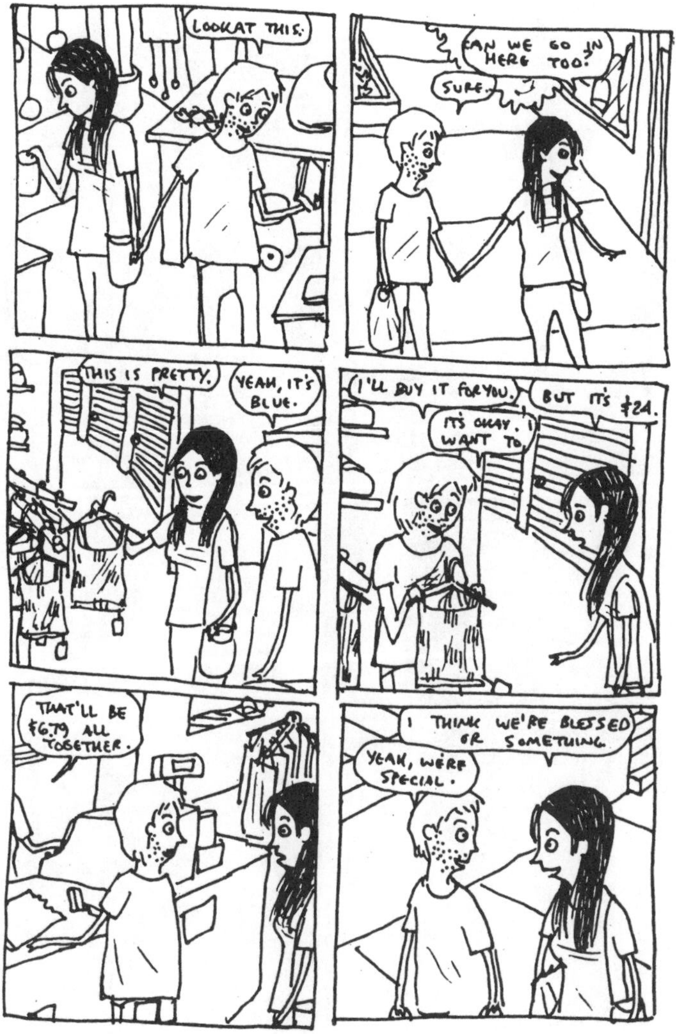
LOOKAT THIS.
CAN WE GO IN HERE TOO?
SURE.
THIS IS PRETTY.
YEAH, IT'S BLUE.
I'LL BUY IT FOR YOU.
BUT IT'S $24.
IT'S OKAY. I WANT TO.
THAT'LL BE $6.79 ALL TOGETHER.
I THINK WE'RE BLESSED OR SOMETHING.
YEAH, WE'RE SPECIAL.

VALENTINE'S DAY

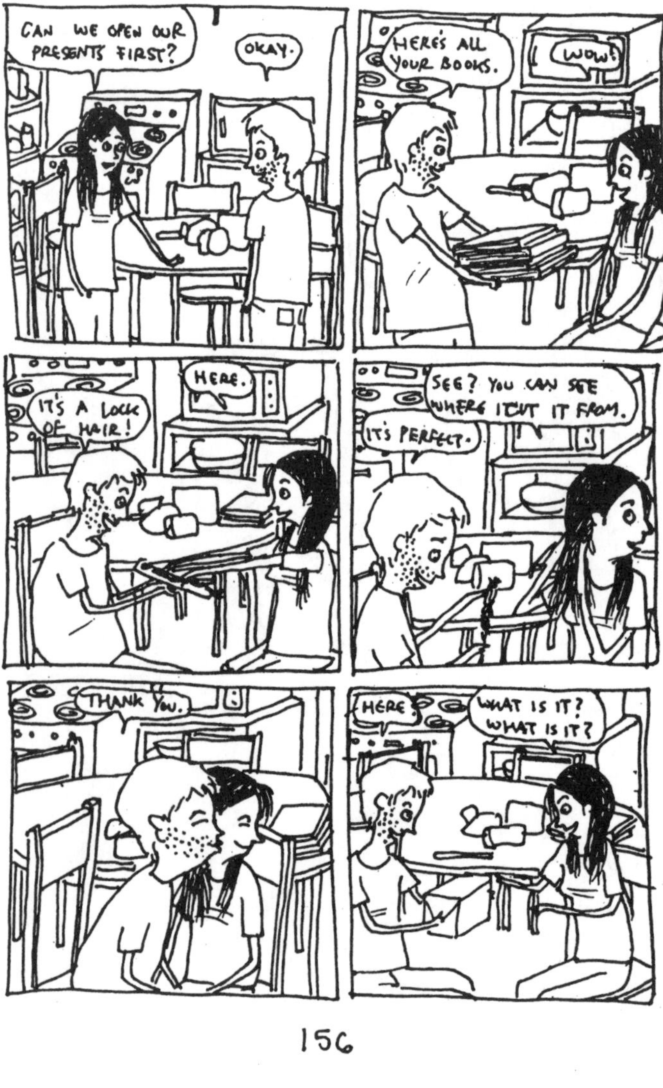
CAN WE OPEN OUR PRESENTS FIRST?
OKAY.
HERE'S ALL YOUR BOOKS.
WOW!
HERE.
IT'S A LOCK OF HAIR!
SEE? YOU CAN SEE WHERE I CUT IT FROM.
IT'S PERFECT.
THANK YOU.
HERE.
WHAT IS IT? WHAT IS IT?

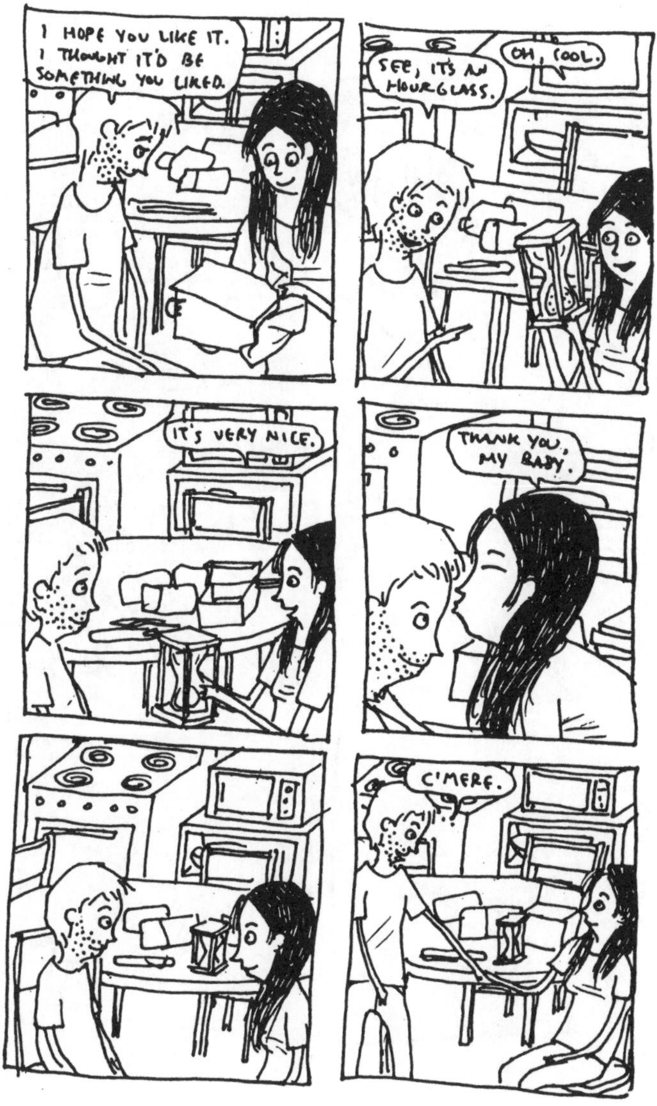
I HOPE YOU LIKE IT. I THOUGHT IT'D BE SOMETHING YOU LIKED.
SEE, IT'S AN HOURGLASS.
OH, COOL.
IT'S VERY NICE.
THANK YOU, MY BABY.
C'MERE.

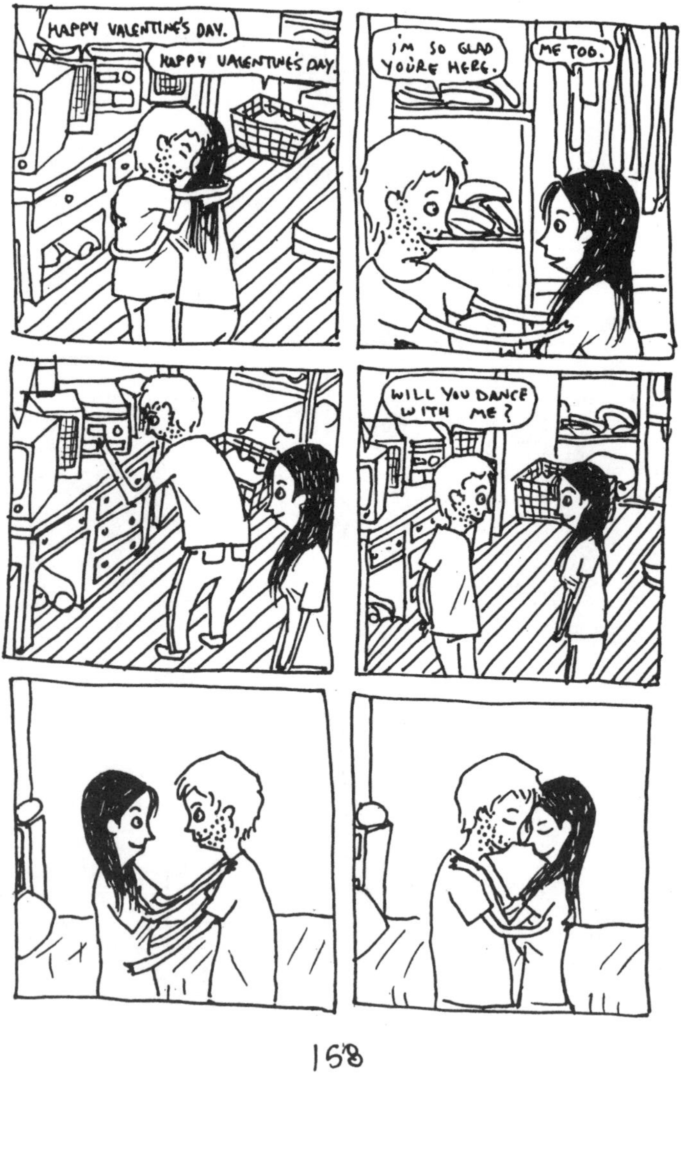
HAPPY VALENTINE'S DAY.
HAPPY VALENTINE'S DAY.
I'M SO GLAD YOU'RE HERE.
ME TOO.
WILL YOU DANCE WITH ME?

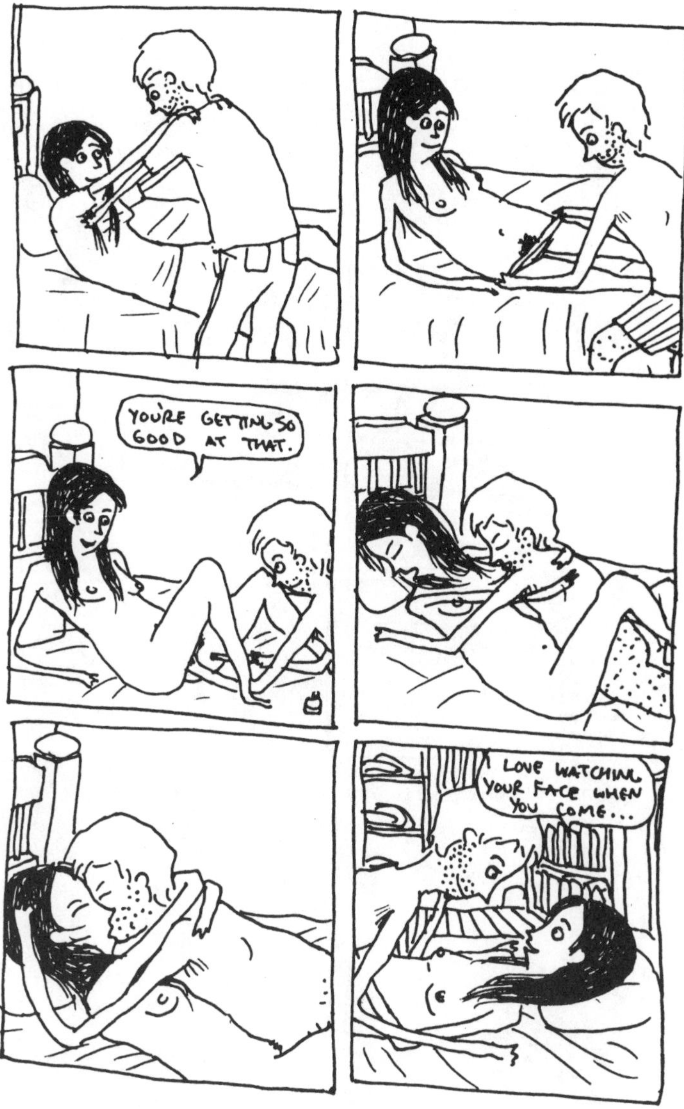
YOU'RE GETTING SO GOOD AT THAT.
LOVE WATCHING YOUR FACE WHEN YOU COME...

LONG DISTANCE

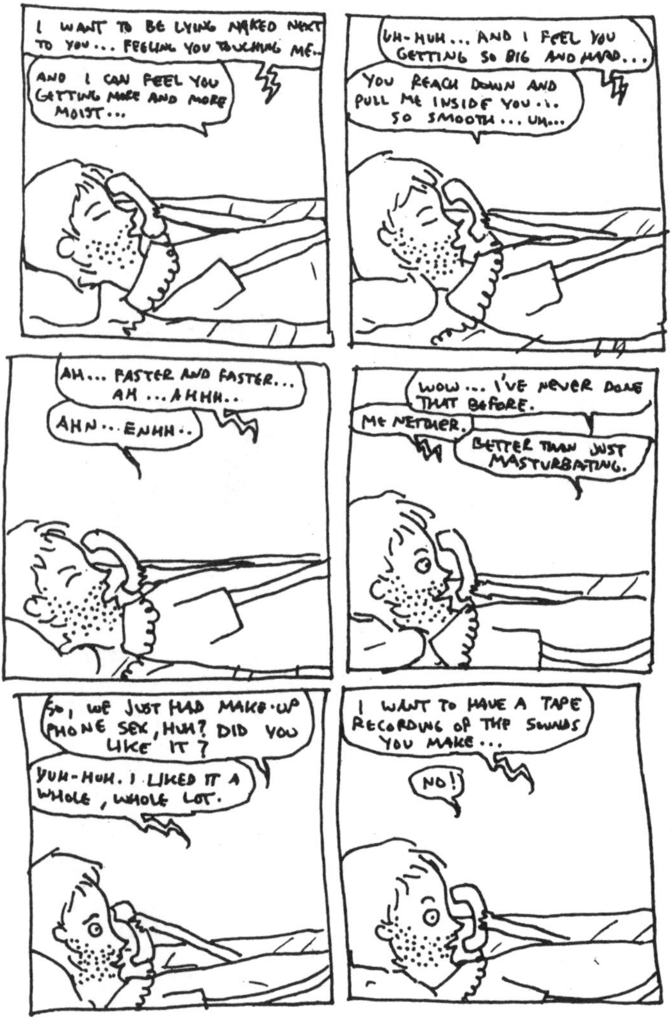

I WANT TO BE LYING NAKED NEXT TO YOU... FEELING YOU TOUCHING ME..
AND I CAN FEEL YOU GETTING MORE AND MORE MOIST...
UH-HUH... AND I FEEL YOU GETTING SO BIG AND HARD...
YOU REACH DOWN AND PULL ME INSIDE YOU... SO SMOOTH... UH...
AH... FASTER AND FASTER... AH ...AHHH..
AHN... ENHH..
WOW... I'VE NEVER DONE THAT BEFORE.
ME NEITHER.
BETTER THAN JUST MASTURBATING.
SO, WE JUST HAD MAKE-UP PHONE SEX, HUH? DID YOU LIKE IT?
YUH-HUH. I LIKED IT A WHOLE, WHOLE LOT.
I WANT TO HAVE A TAPE RECORDING OF THE SOUNDS YOU MAKE...
NO!

SLOW DANCE

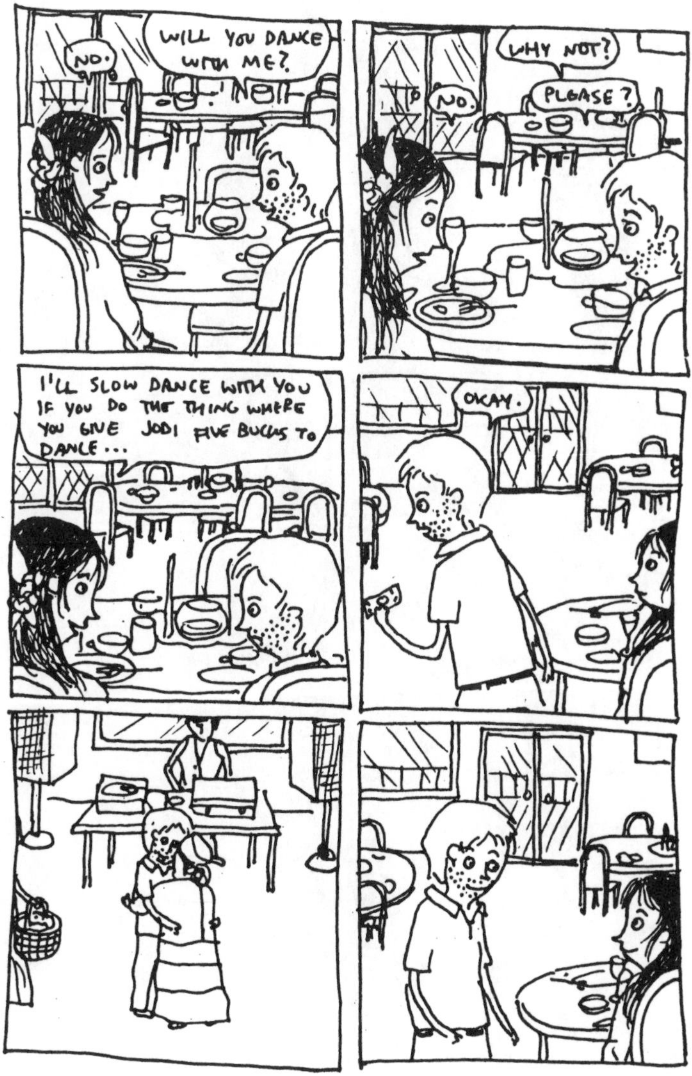
WILL YOU DANCE WITH ME?
NO.
WHY NOT?
NO.
PLEASE?
I'LL SLOW DANCE WITH YOU IF YOU DO THE THING WHERE YOU GIVE JODI FIVE BUCKS TO DANCE...
OKAY.

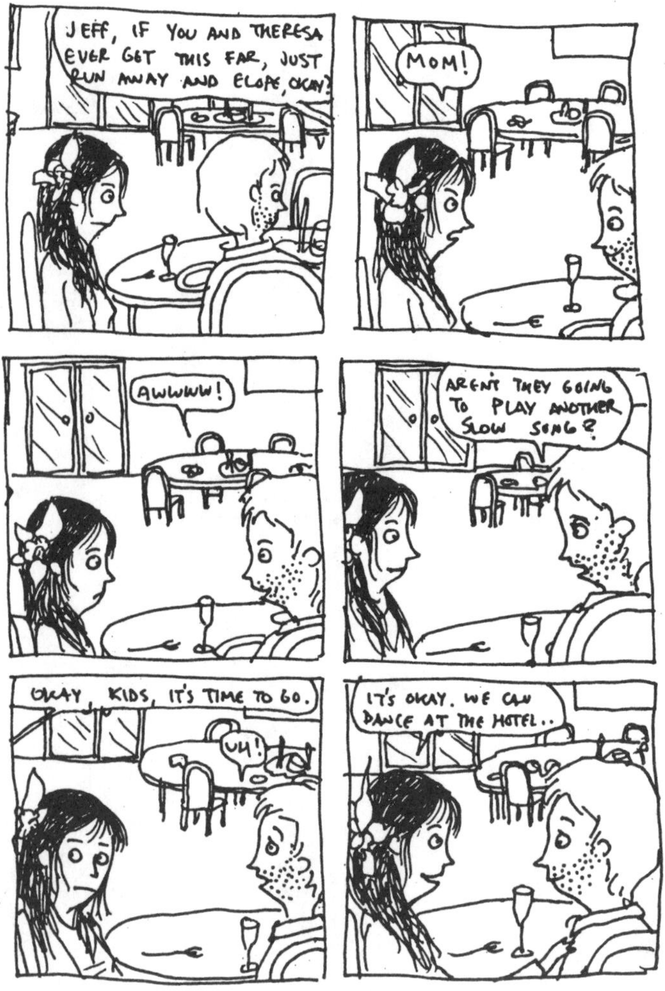
JEFF, IF YOU AND THERESA EVER GET THIS FAR, JUST RUN AWAY AND ELOPE, OKAY?
MOM!
AWWWW!
AREN'T THEY GOING TO PLAY ANOTHER SLOW SONG?
OKAY, KIDS, IT'S TIME TO GO.
UH!
IT'S OKAY. WE CAN DANCE AT THE HOTEL..

REUNITED

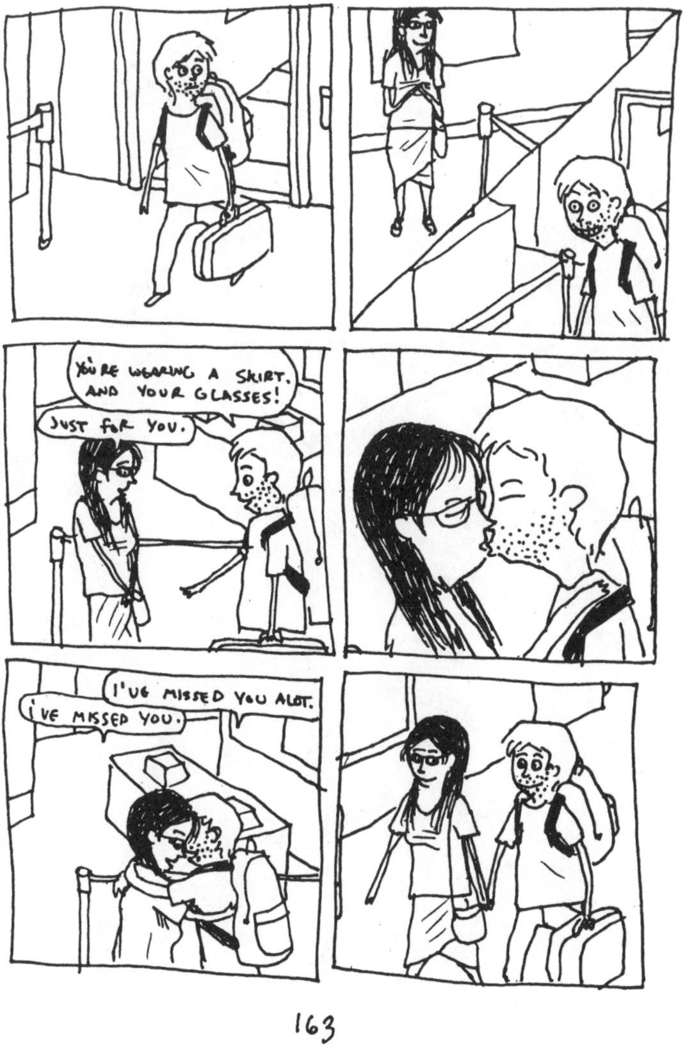
YOU'RE WEARING A SKIRT. AND YOUR GLASSES!
JUST FOR YOU.
I'VE MISSED YOU.
I'VE MISSED YOU ALOT.

COOKIES

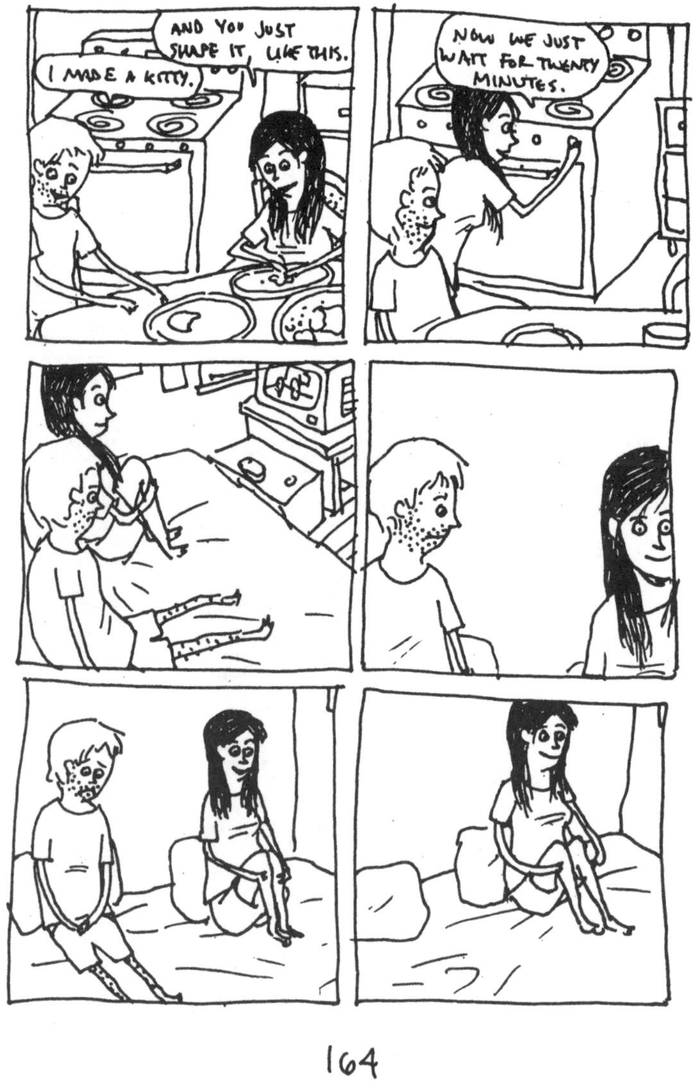
AND YOU JUST SHAPE IT, LIKE THIS.
I MADE A KITTY.
NOW WE JUST WAIT FOR TWENTY MINUTES.

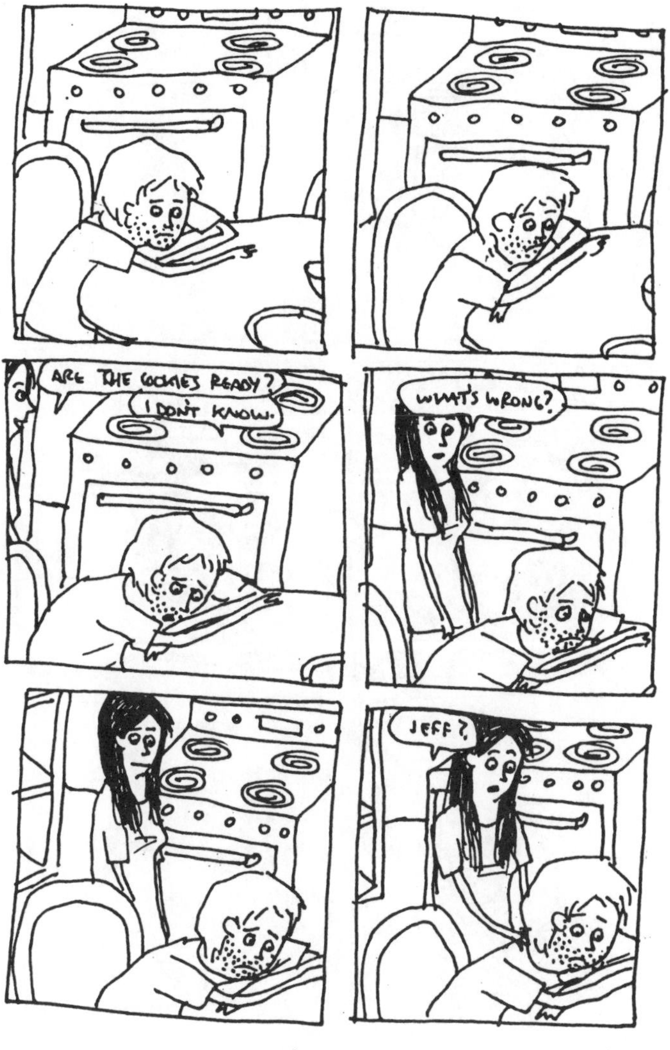
ARE THE COOKIES READY?
I DON'T KNOW.
WHAT'S WRONG?
JEFF?

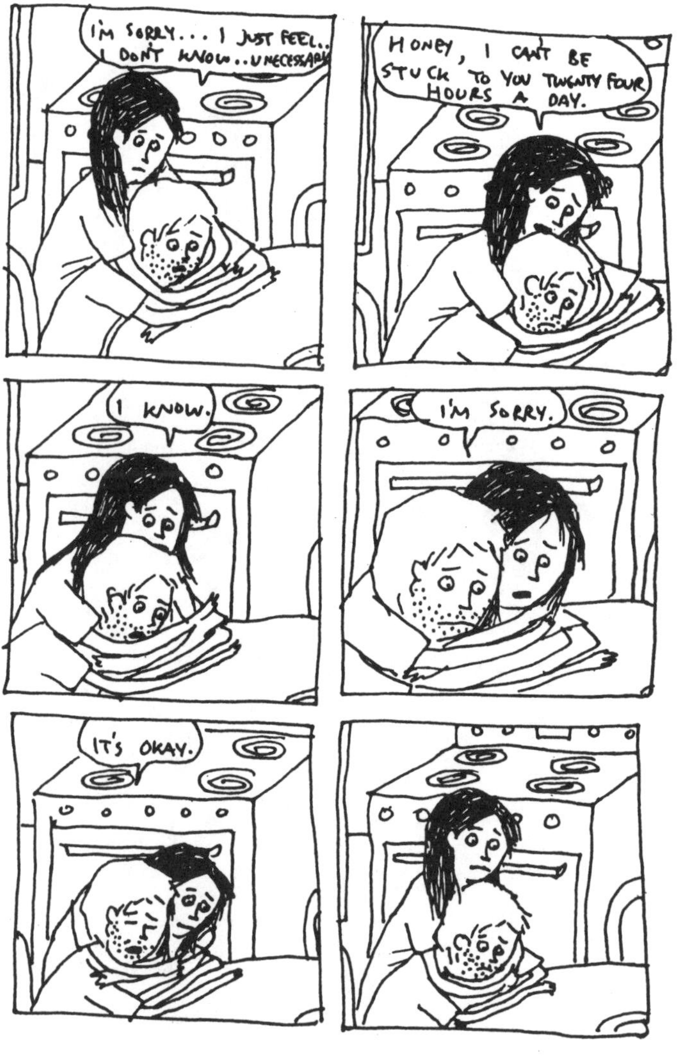
I'M SORRY... I JUST FEEL.. I DON'T KNOW..UNECESSARI
HONEY, I CAN'T BE STUCK TO YOU TWENTY FOUR HOURS A DAY.
I KNOW.
I'M SORRY.
IT'S OKAY.

SICK QUICK GOODBYE

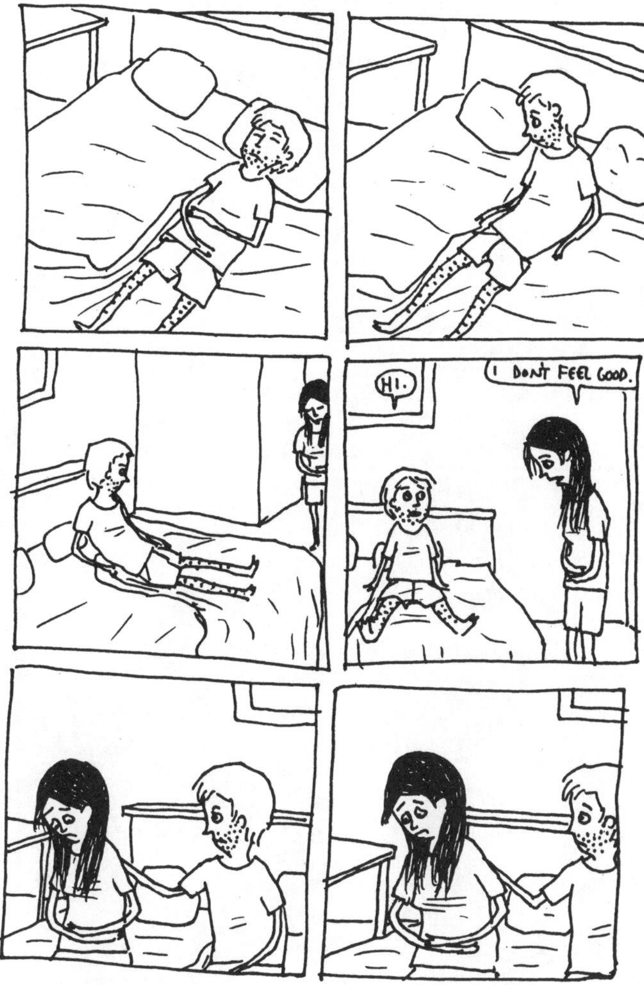
HI.
I DON'T FEEL GOOD.

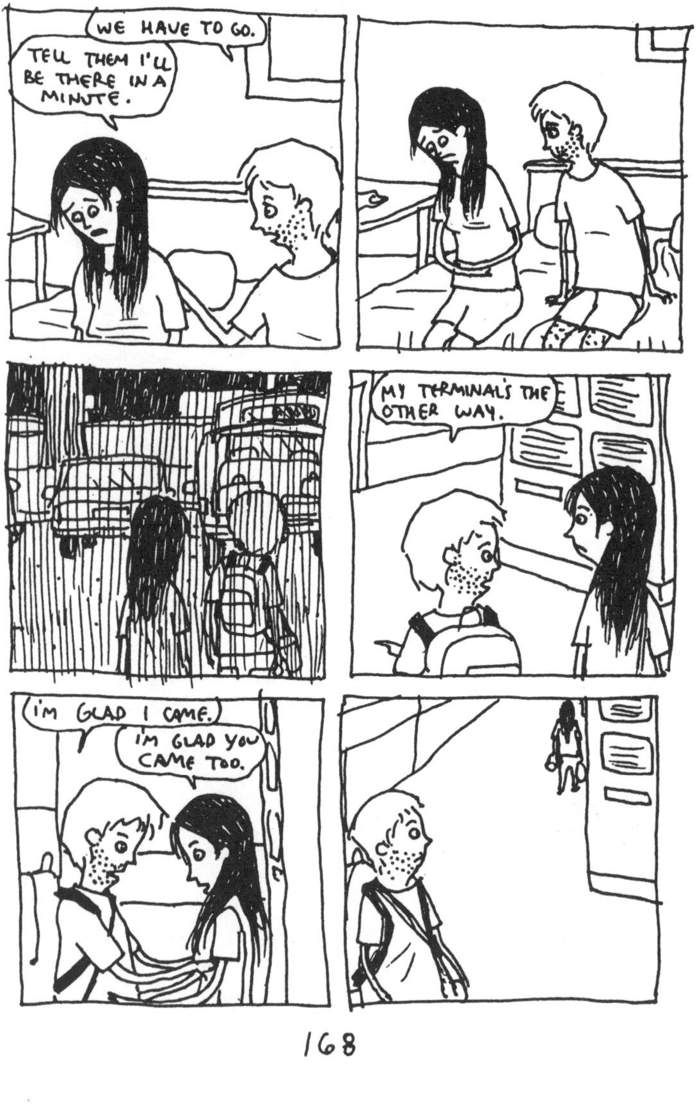
WE HAVE TO GO.
TELL THEM I'LL BE THERE IN A MINUTE.
MY TERMINAL'S THE OTHER WAY.
I'M GLAD I CAME.
I'M GLAD YOU CAME TOO.

KITTY POTS

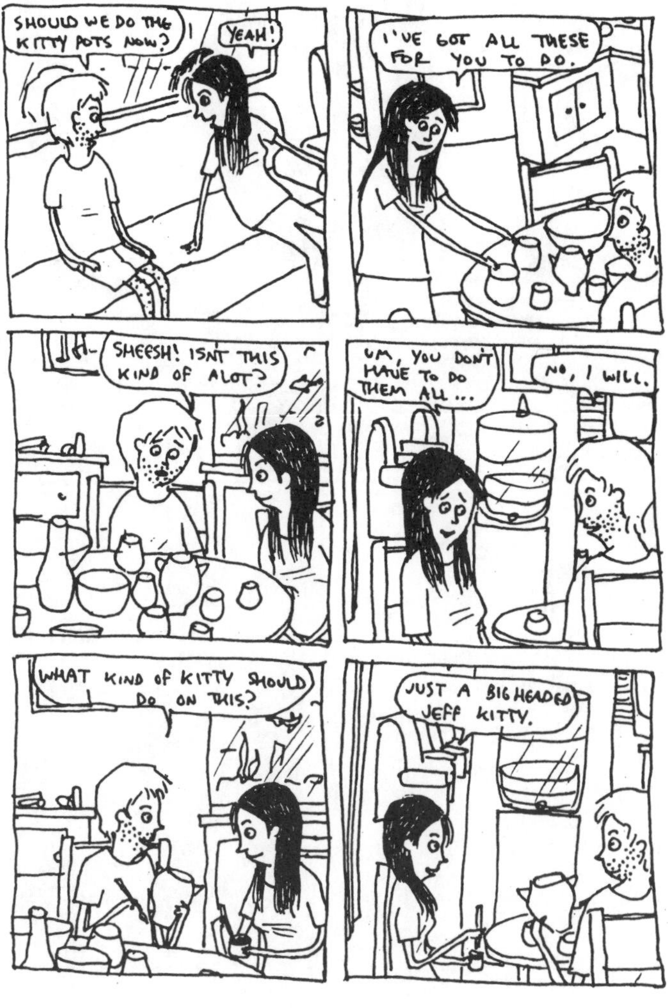
SHOULD WE DO THE KITTY POTS NOW?
YEAH!
I'VE GOT ALL THESE FOR YOU TO DO.
SHEESH! ISN'T THIS KIND OF ALOT?
UM, YOU DON'T HAVE TO DO THEM ALL...
NO, I WILL.
WHAT KIND OF KITTY SHOULD I DO ON THIS?
JUST A BIG HEADED JEFF KITTY.

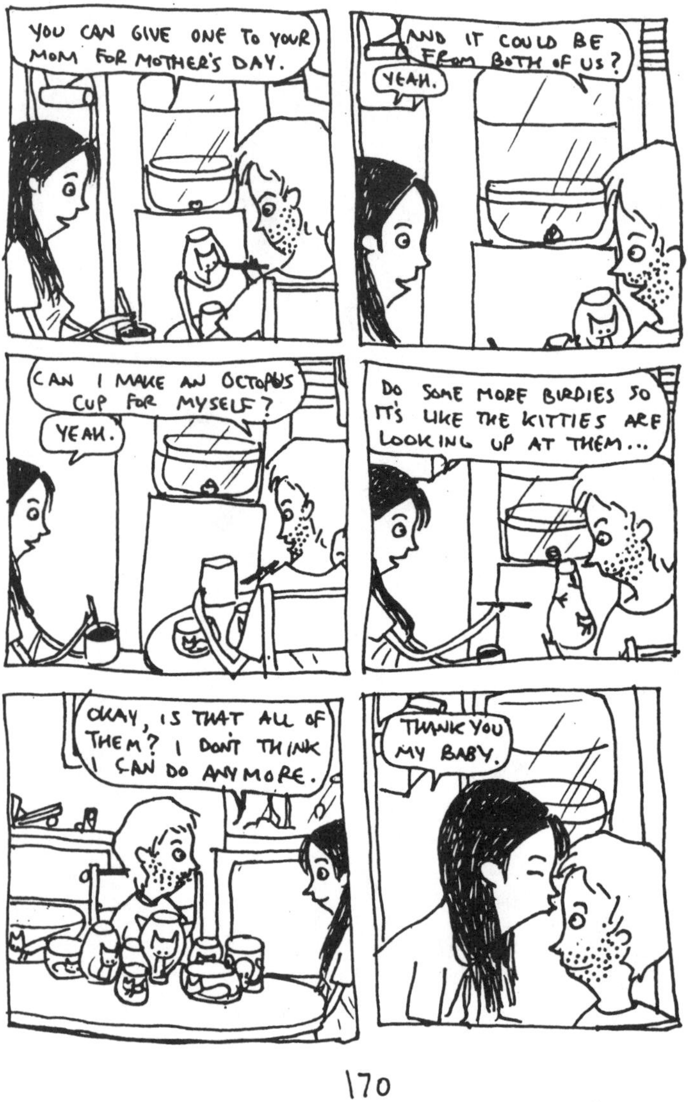
YOU CAN GIVE ONE TO YOUR MOM FOR MOTHER'S DAY.
AND IT COULD BE FROM BOTH OF US?
YEAH.
CAN I MAKE AN OCTOPUS CUP FOR MYSELF?
YEAH.
DO SOME MORE BIRDIES SO IT'S LIKE THE KITTIES ARE LOOKING UP AT THEM...
OKAY, IS THAT ALL OF THEM? I DON'T THINK I CAN DO ANYMORE.
THANK YOU MY BABY.

WEDDING

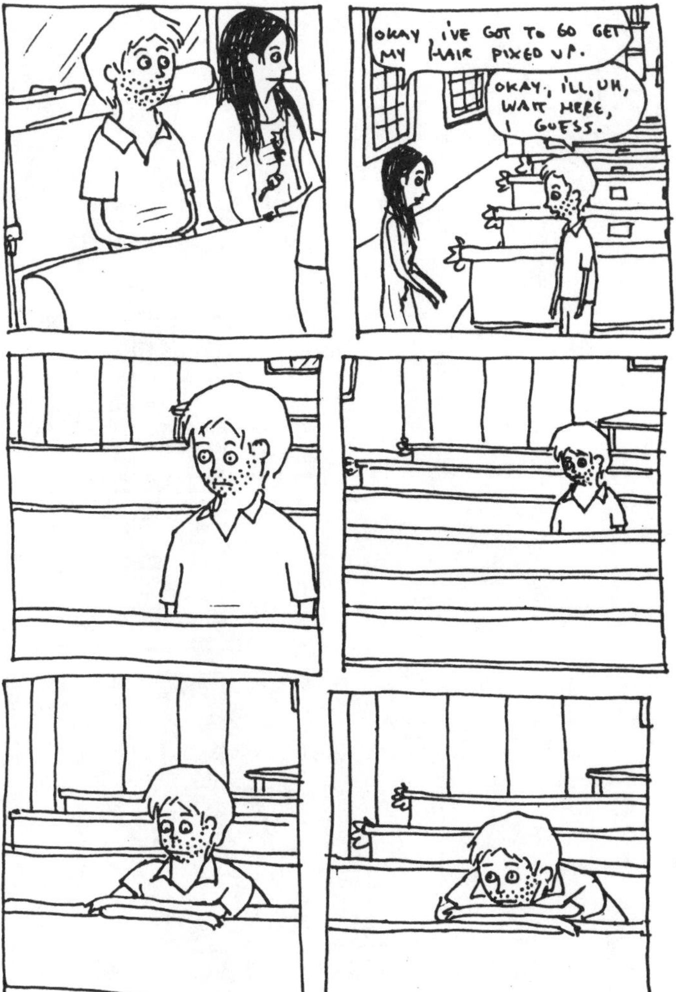

OKAY, I'VE GOT TO GO GET MY HAIR FIXED UP.
OKAY, I'LL, UH, WAIT HERE, I GUESS.

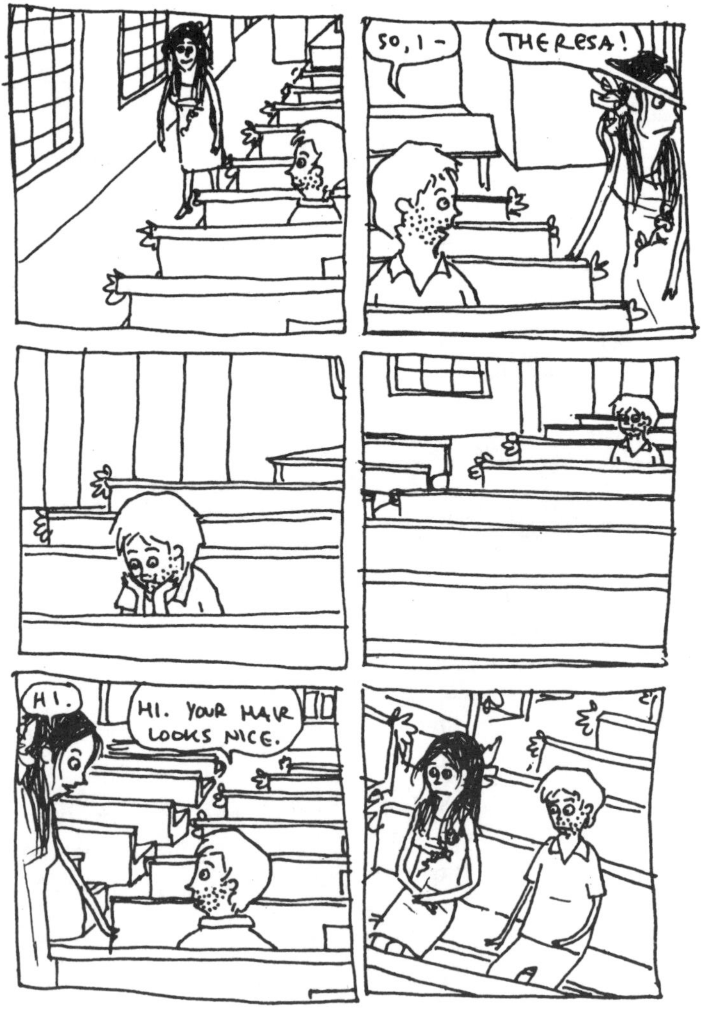
SO, I -
THERESA!
HI.
HI. YOUR HAIR LOOKS NICE.

SPRINGER

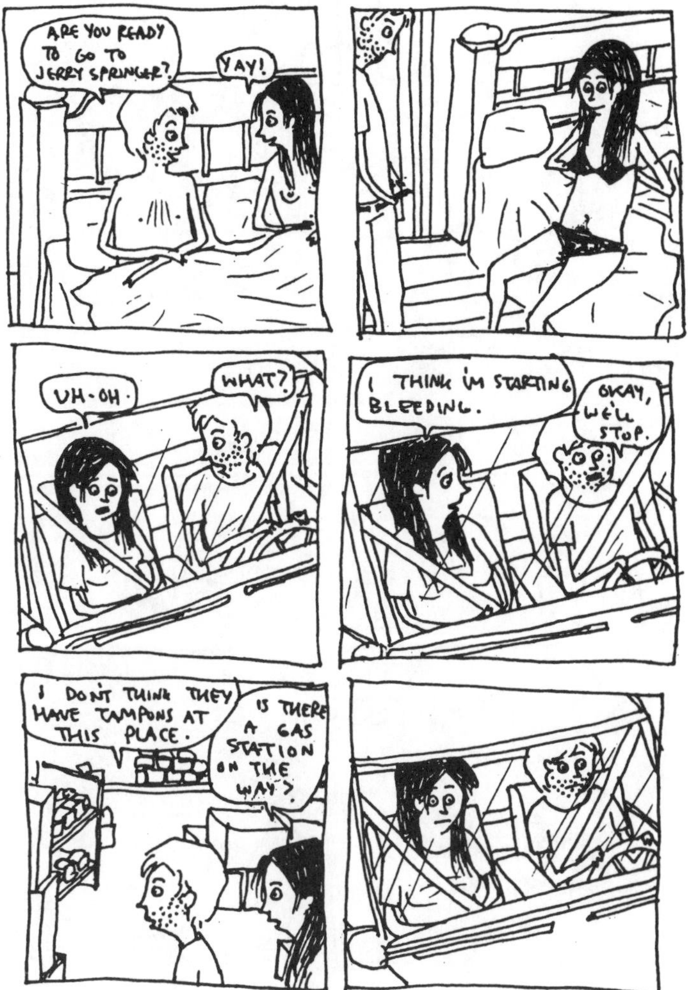
ARE YOU READY TO GO TO JERRY SPRINGER?
YAY!
UH-OH.
WHAT?
I THINK I'M STARTING BLEEDING.
OKAY, WE'LL STOP.
I DON'T THINK THEY HAVE TAMPONS AT THIS PLACE.
IS THERE A GAS STATION ON THE WAY?

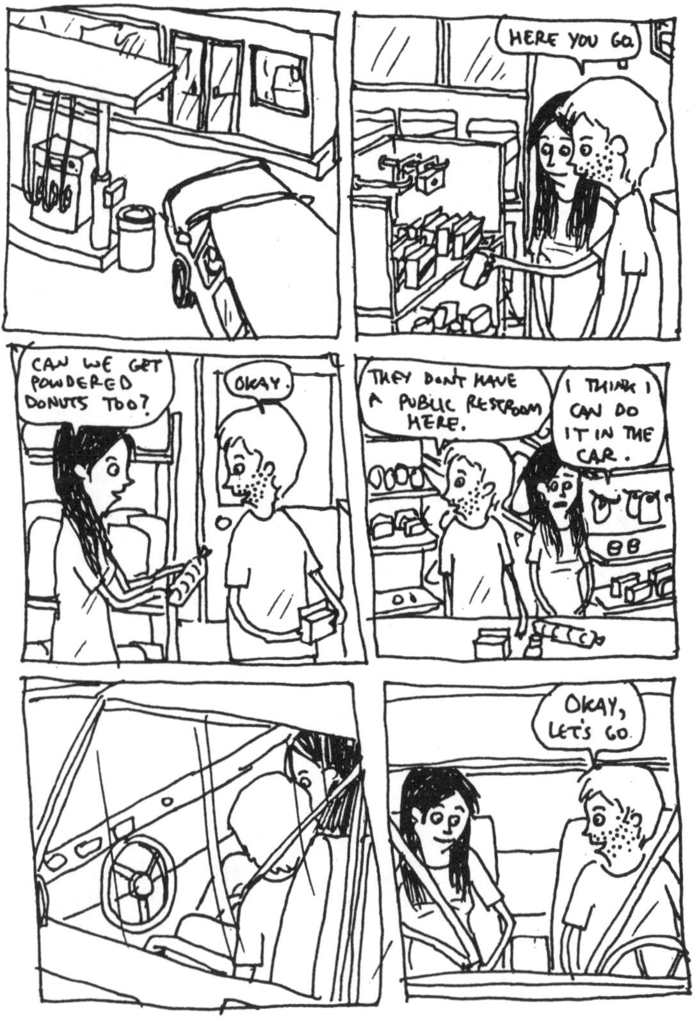
HERE YOU GO.
CAN WE GET POWDERED DONUTS TOO?
OKAY.
THEY DON'T HAVE A PUBLIC RESTROOM HERE.
I THINK I CAN DO IT IN THE CAR.
OKAY, LET'S GO.

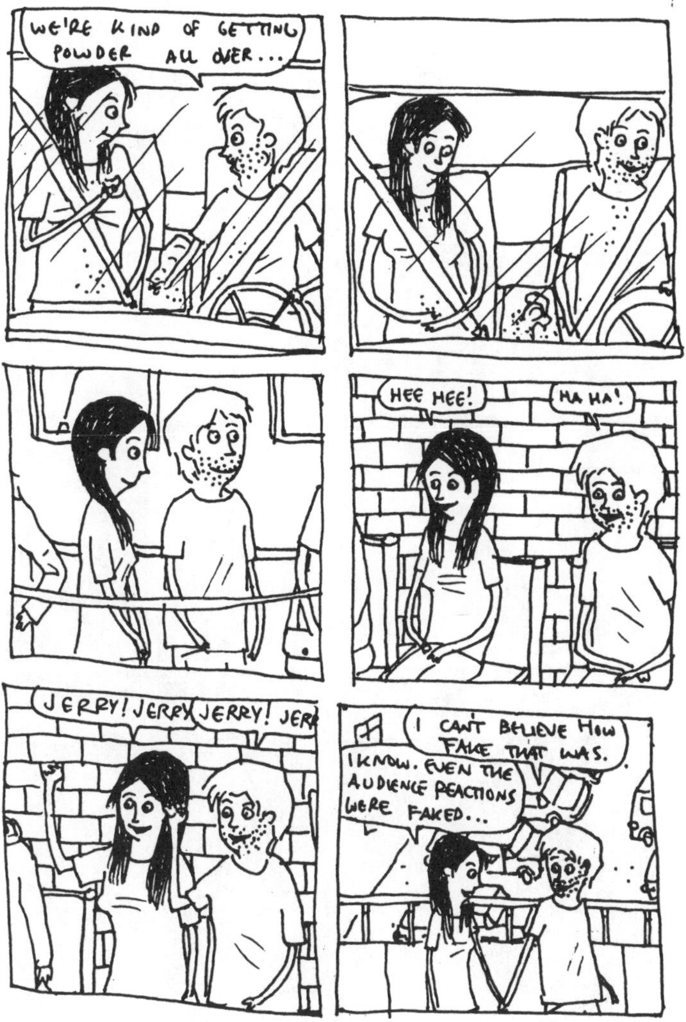
WE'RE KIND OF GETTING POWDER ALL OVER...
HEE HEE!
HA HA!
JERRY! JERRY
JERRY! JER
I CAN'T BELIEVE HOW FAKE THAT WAS.
I KNOW. EVEN THE AUDIENCE REACTIONS WERE FAKED...

THE BEACH AT NIGHT

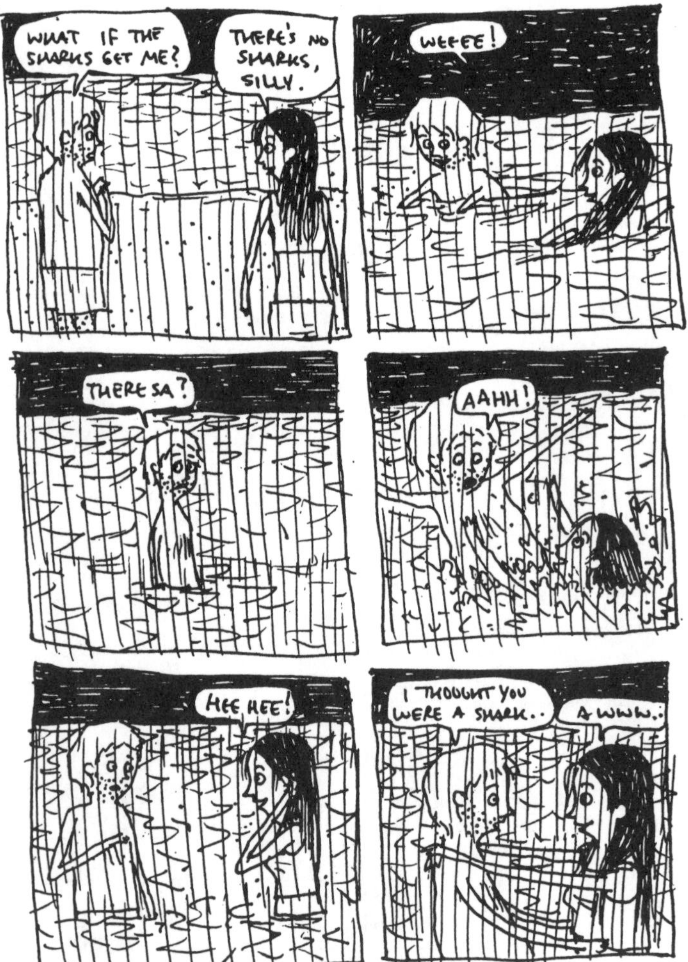
WHAT IF THE SHARKS GET ME?
THERE'S NO SHARKS, SILLY.
WEEEE!
THERESA?
AAHH!
HEE HEE!
I THOUGHT YOU WERE A SHARK..
AWWW..

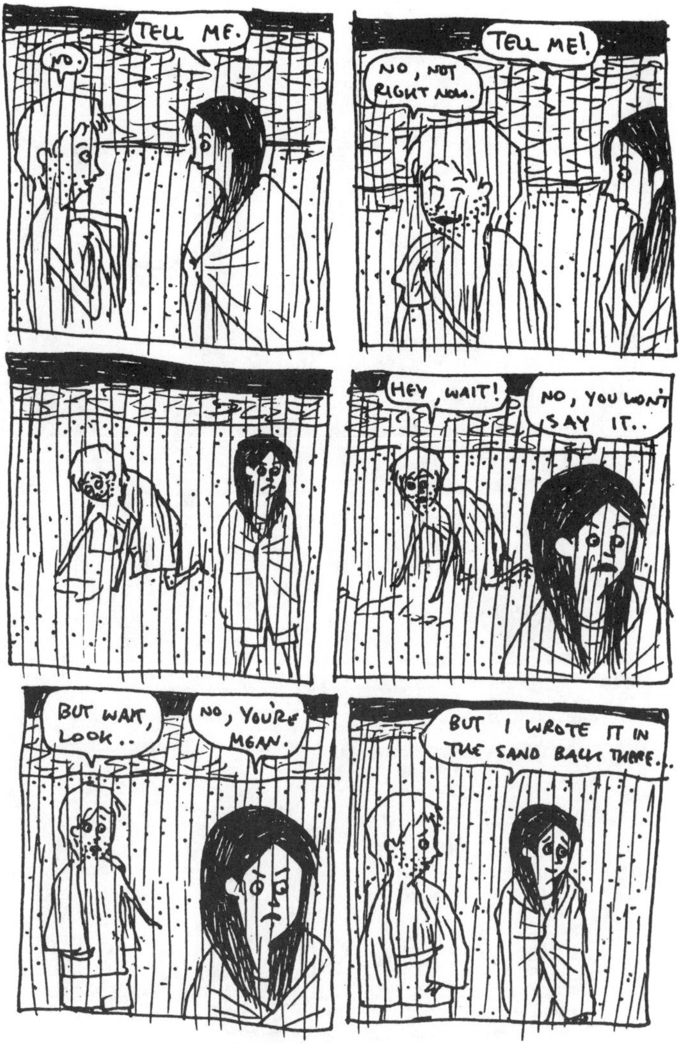
NO.
TELL ME.
NO, NOT RIGHT NOW.
TELL ME!
HEY, WAIT!
NO, YOU WON'T SAY IT..
BUT WAIT, LOOK..
NO, YOU'RE MEAN.
BUT I WROTE IT IN THE SAND BACK THERE...

BUG BITE

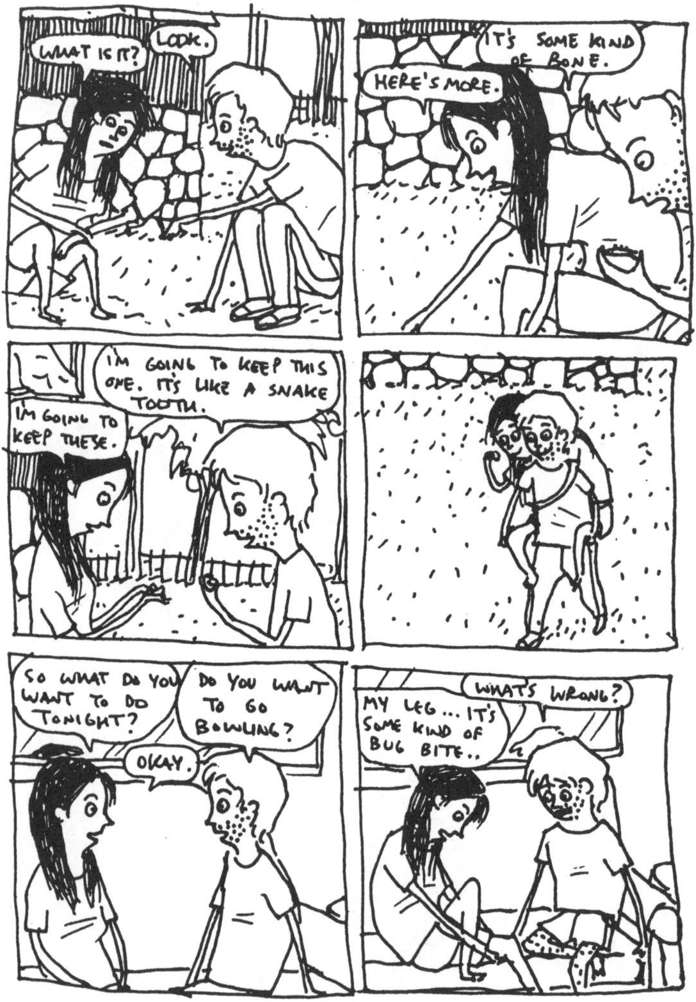

LOOK.
WHAT IS IT?
IT'S SOME KIND OF BONE.
HERE'S MORE.
I'M GOING TO KEEP THIS ONE. IT'S LIKE A SNAKE TOOTH.
I'M GOING TO KEEP THESE.
SO WHAT DO YOU WANT TO DO TONIGHT?
DO YOU WANT TO GO BOWLING?
OKAY.
WHAT'S WRONG?
MY LEG... IT'S SOME KIND OF BUG BITE..

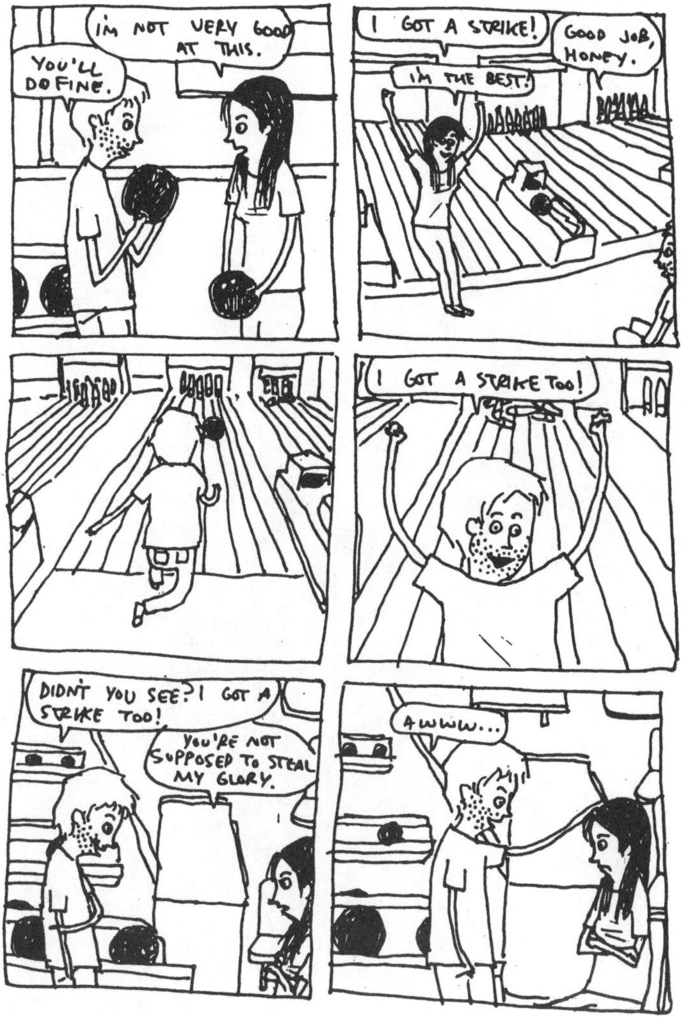
I'M NOT VERY GOOD AT THIS.
YOU'LL DO FINE.
I GOT A STRIKE!
GOOD JOB, HONEY.
I'M THE BEST!
I GOT A STRIKE TOO!
DIDN'T YOU SEE? I GOT A STRIKE TOO!
YOU'RE NOT SUPPOSED TO STEAL MY GLORY.
AWWW...

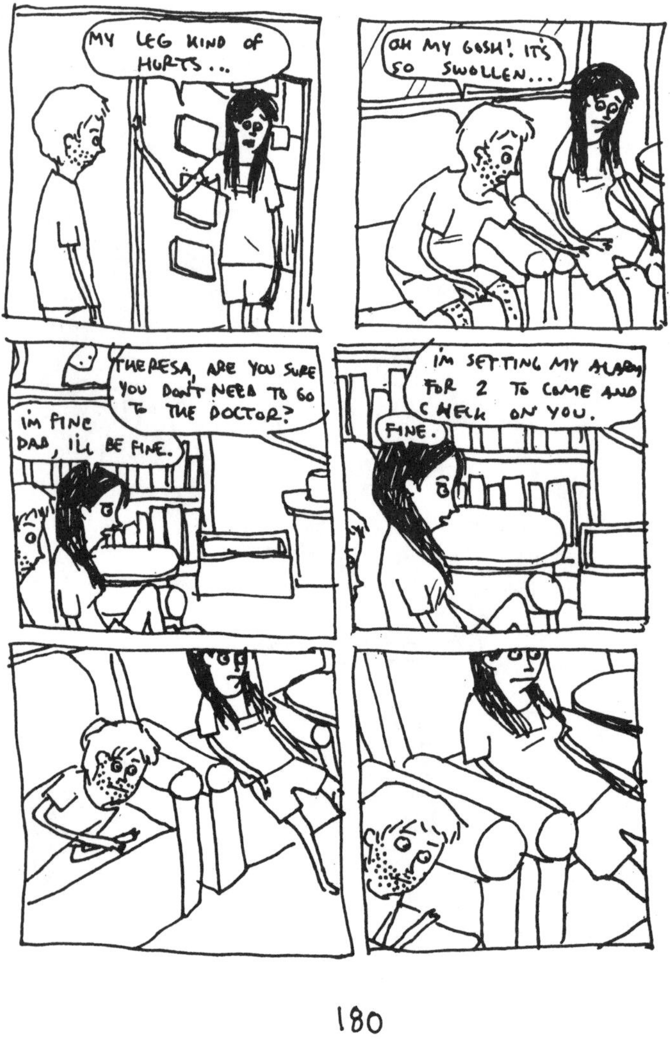
MY LEG KIND OF HURTS...
OH MY GOSH! IT'S SO SWOLLEN...
THERESA, ARE YOU SURE YOU DON'T NEED TO GO TO THE DOCTOR?
IM FINE DAD, ILL BE FINE.
IM SETTING MY ALARM FOR 2 TO COME AND CHECK ON YOU.
FINE.

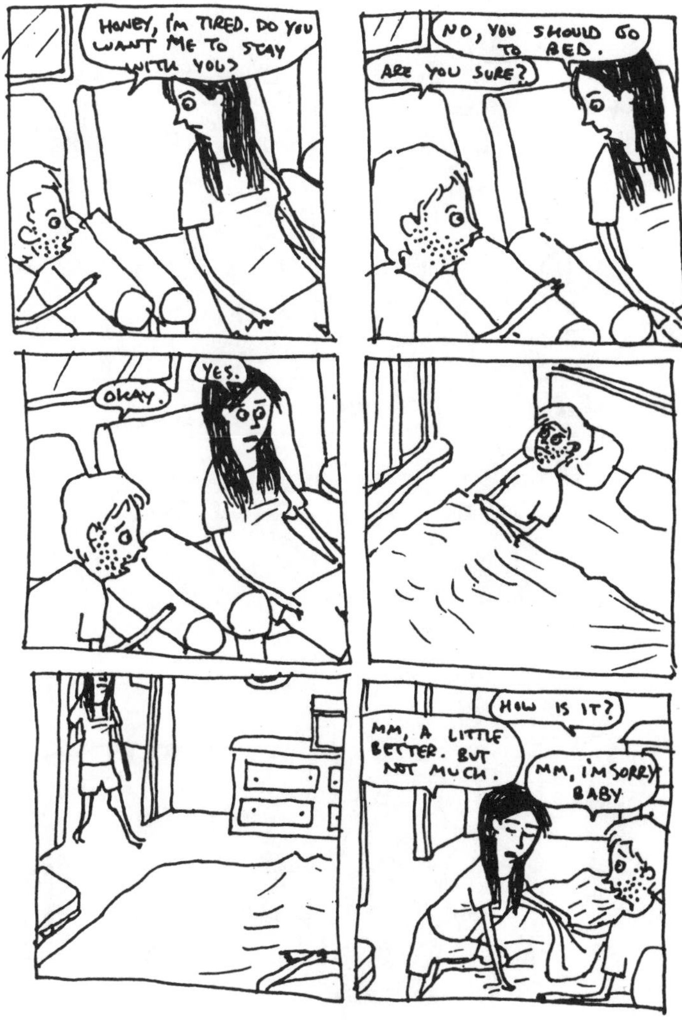
HONEY, I'M TIRED. DO YOU WANT ME TO STAY WITH YOU?
NO, YOU SHOULD GO TO BED.
ARE YOU SURE?
YES.
OKAY.
HOW IS IT?
MM, A LITTLE BETTER. BUT NOT MUCH.
MM, I'M SORRY BABY.

CHRISTMAS 2000

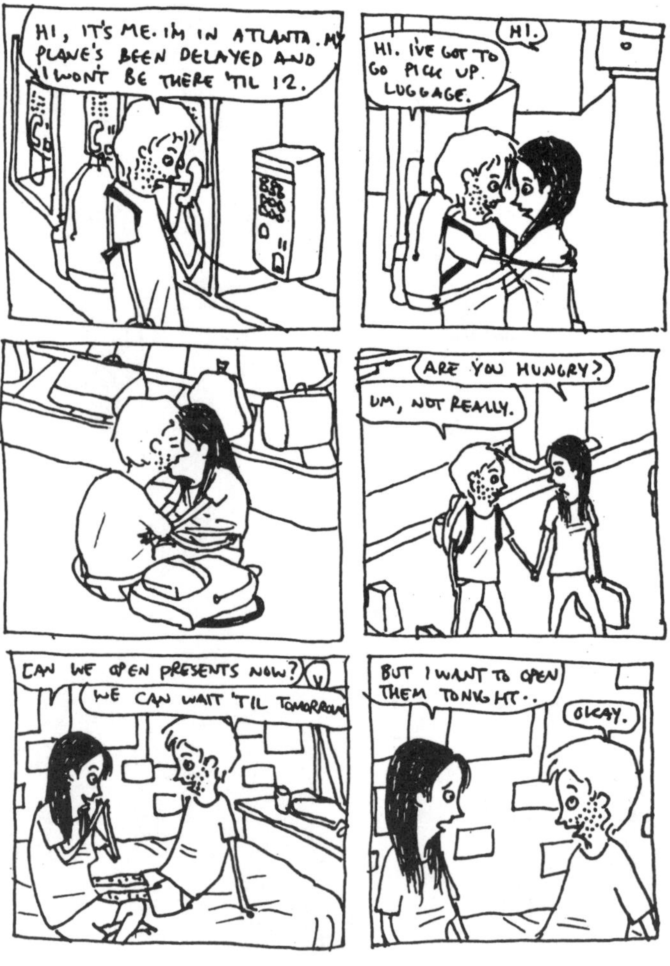
HI, IT'S ME. I'M IN ATLANTA. MY PLANE'S BEEN DELAYED AND I WON'T BE THERE 'TIL 12.
HI.
HI. I'VE GOT TO GO PICK UP LUGGAGE.
ARE YOU HUNGRY?
UM, NOT REALLY.
CAN WE OPEN PRESENTS NOW?
WE CAN WAIT 'TIL TOMORROW
BUT I WANT TO OPEN THEM TONIGHT..
OKAY.

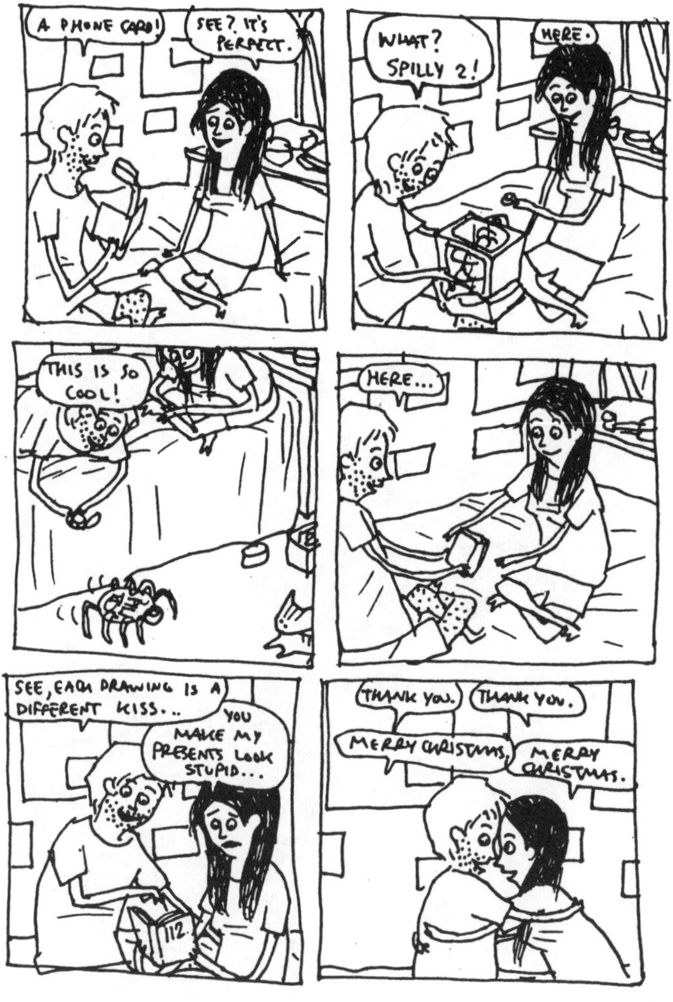
A PHONE CARD!
SEE? IT'S PERFECT.
WHAT? SPILLY 2!
HERE.
THIS IS SO COOL!
HERE...
SEE, EACH DRAWING IS A DIFFERENT KISS...
YOU MAKE MY PRESENTS LOOK STUPID...
112
THANK YOU.
THANK YOU.
MERRY CHRISTMAS.
MERRY CHRISTMAS.

WENDY'S

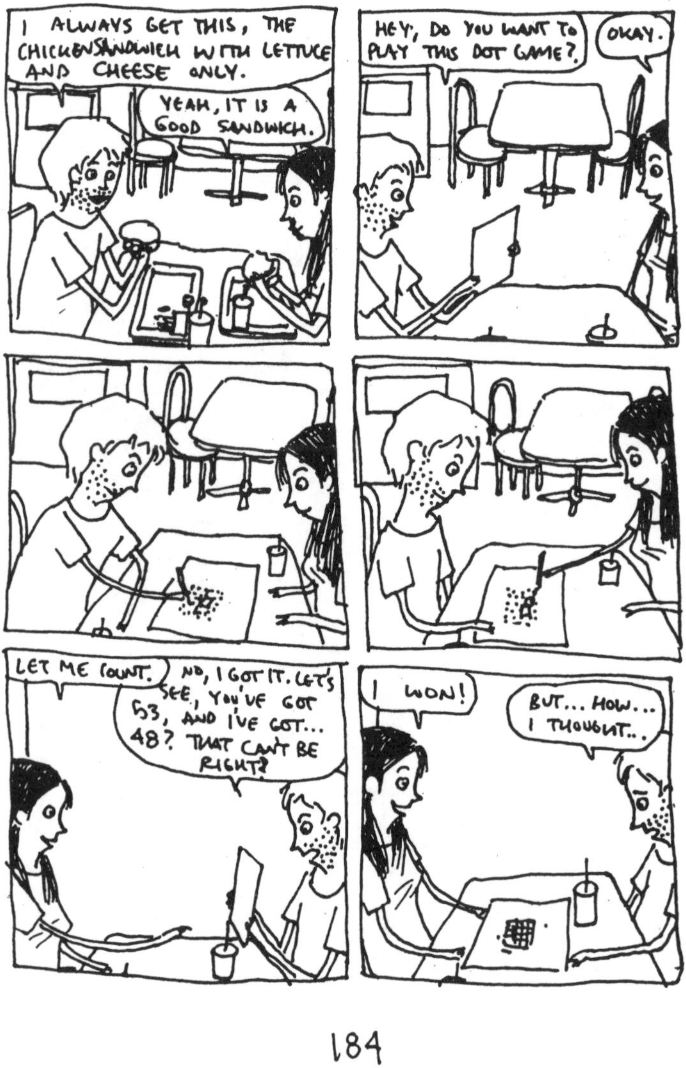

I ALWAYS GET THIS, THE CHICKEN SANDWICH WITH LETTUCE AND CHEESE ONLY.
YEAH, IT IS A GOOD SANDWICH.
HEY, DO YOU WANT TO PLAY THIS DOT GAME?
OKAY.
LET ME COUNT.
NO, I GOT IT. LET'S SEE, YOU'VE GOT 53, AND I'VE GOT... 48? THAT CAN'T BE RIGHT?
I WON!
BUT... HOW... I THOUGHT...

PACKAGE

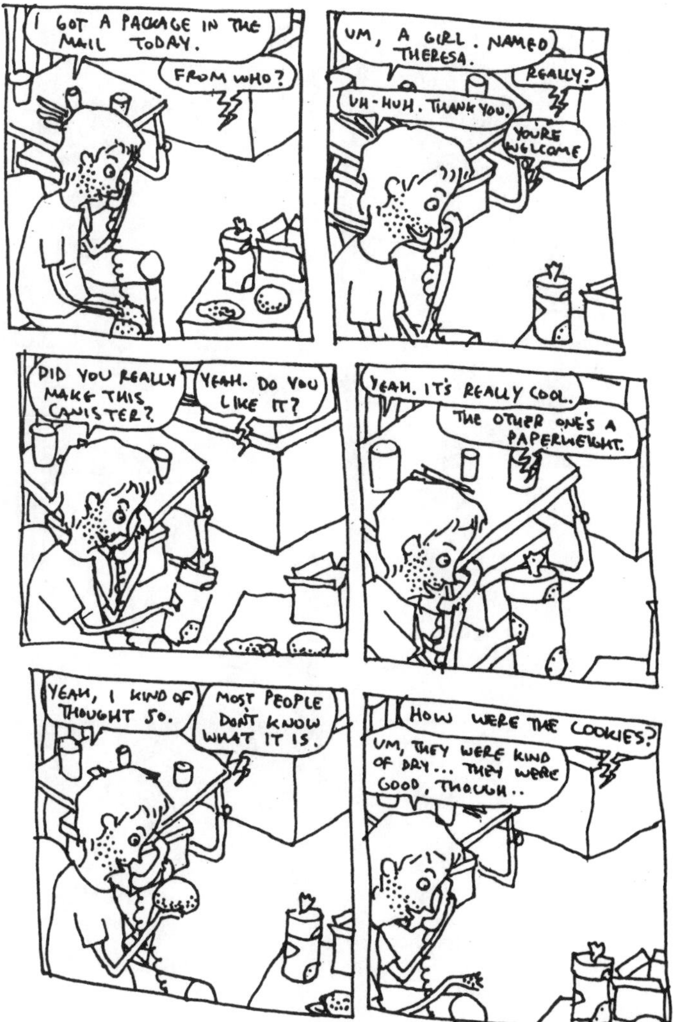

I GOT A PACKAGE IN THE MAIL TODAY.
FROM WHO?
UM, A GIRL. NAMED THERESA.
REALLY?
UH-HUH. THANK YOU.
YOU'RE WELCOME
DID YOU REALLY MAKE THIS CANISTER?
YEAH. DO YOU LIKE IT?
YEAH. IT'S REALLY COOL.
THE OTHER ONE'S A PAPERWEIGHT.
YEAH, I KIND OF THOUGHT SO.
MOST PEOPLE DON'T KNOW WHAT IT IS.
HOW WERE THE COOKIES?
UM, THEY WERE KIND OF DRY... THEY WERE GOOD, THOUGH..

STORIES

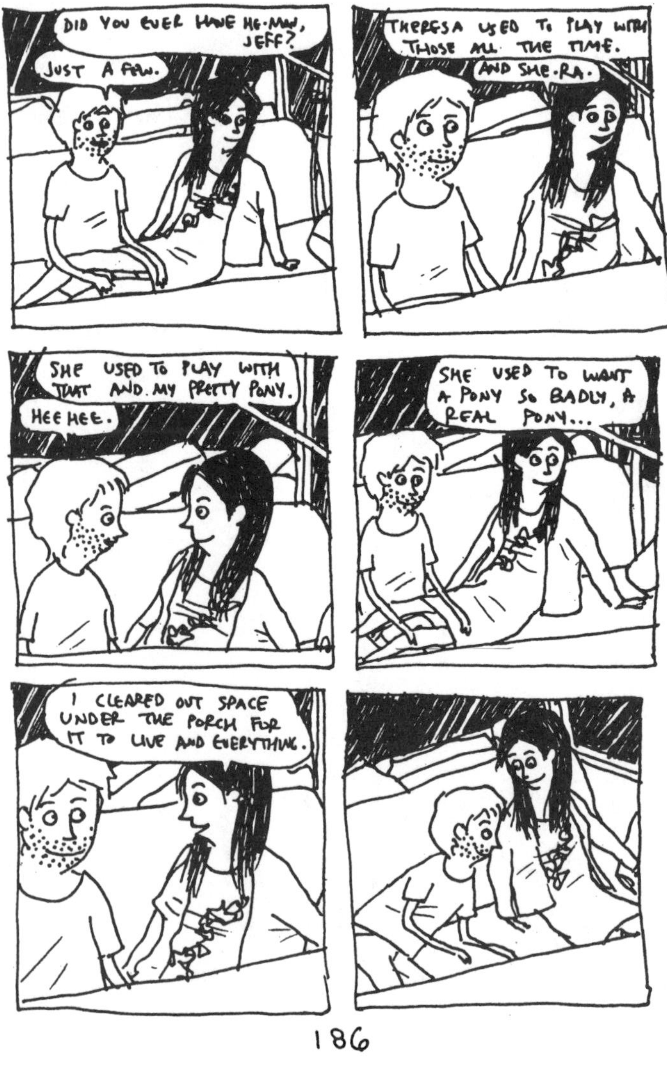
DID YOU EVER HAVE HE-MAN, JEFF?
JUST A FEW.
THERESA USED TO PLAY WITH THOSE ALL THE TIME.
AND SHE-RA.
SHE USED TO PLAY WITH THAT AND MY PRETTY PONY.
HEE HEE.
SHE USED TO WANT A PONY SO BADLY, A REAL PONY...
I CLEARED OUT SPACE UNDER THE PORCH FOR IT TO LIVE AND EVERYTHING.

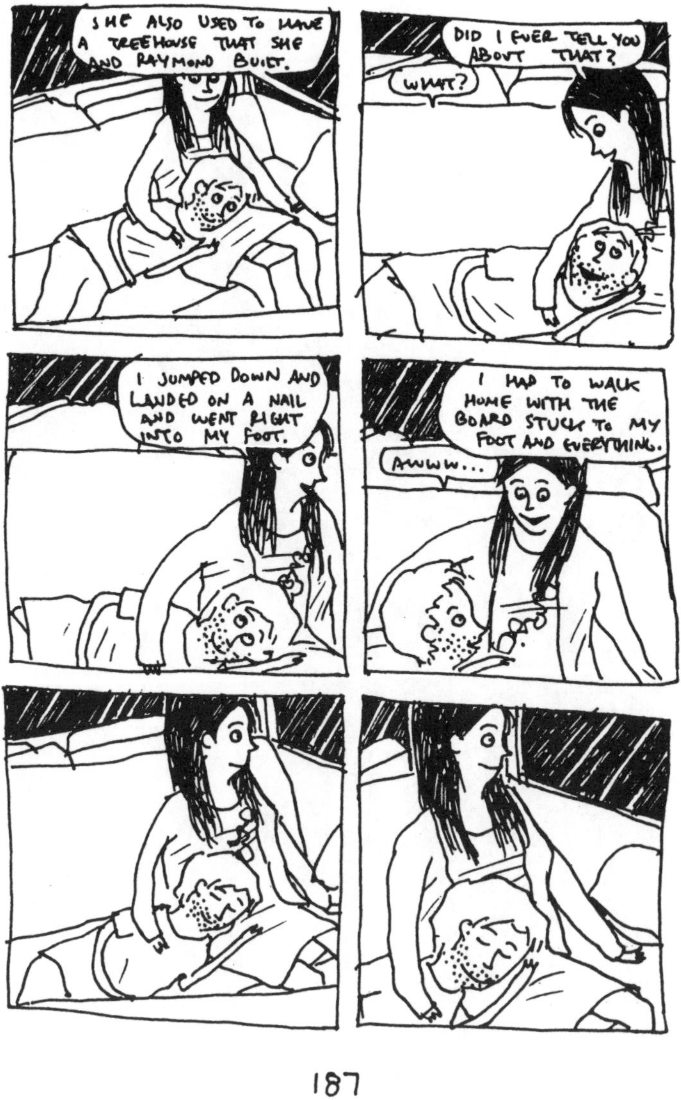
SHE ALSO USED TO HAVE A TREEHOUSE THAT SHE AND RAYMOND BUILT.
DID I EVER TELL YOU ABOUT THAT?
WHAT?
I JUMPED DOWN AND LANDED ON A NAIL AND WENT RIGHT INTO MY FOOT.
I HAD TO WALK HOME WITH THE BOARD STUCK TO MY FOOT AND EVERYTHING.
AWWW...

CREATING

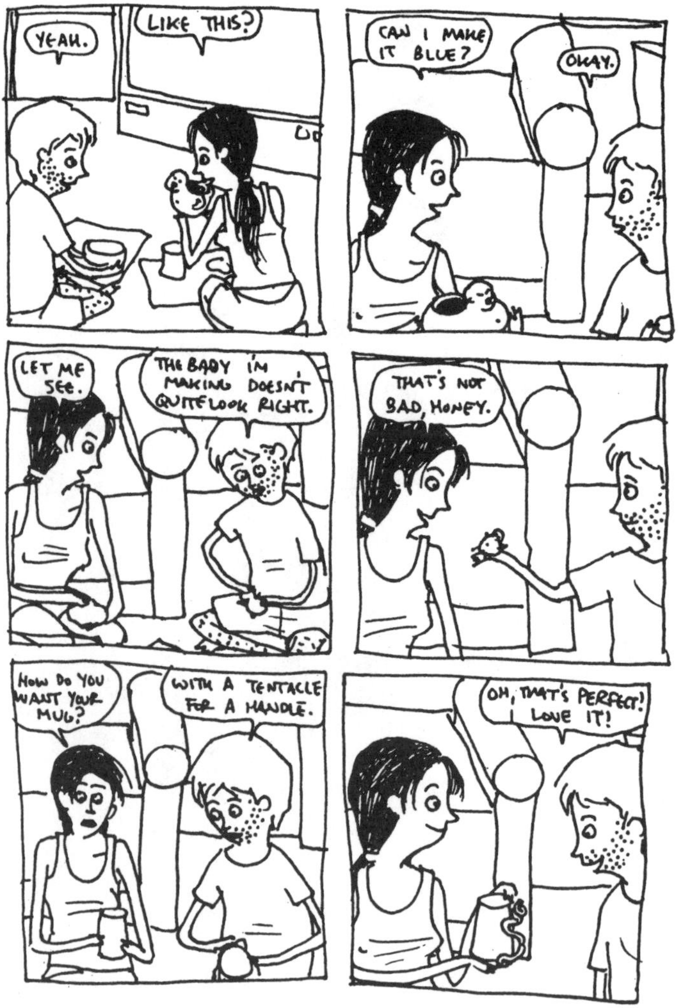

YEAH.
LIKE THIS?
CAN I MAKE IT BLUE?
OKAY.
LET ME SEE.
THE BABY I'M MAKING DOESN'T QUITE LOOK RIGHT.
THAT'S NOT BAD, HONEY.
HOW DO YOU WANT YOUR MUG?
WITH A TENTACLE FOR A HANDLE.
OH, THAT'S PERFECT! LOVE IT!

A NIGHT

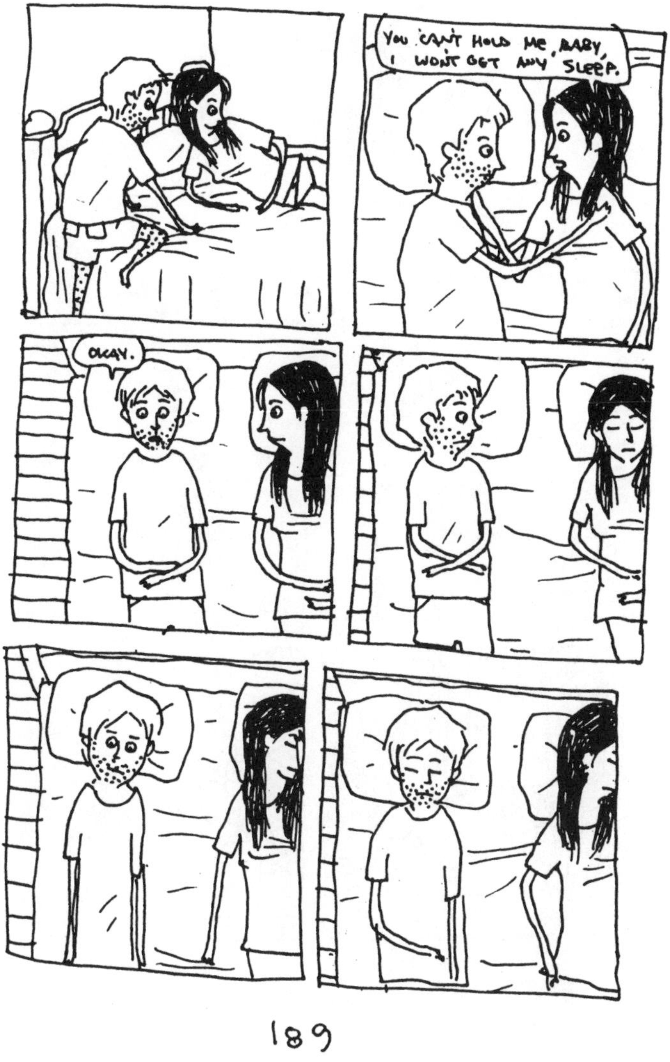
YOU CAN'T HOLD ME, BABY, I WON'T GET ANY SLEEP.
OKAY.

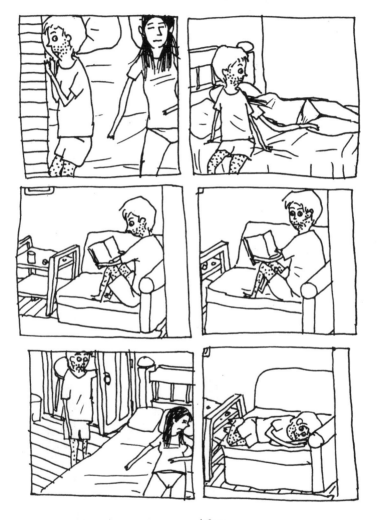

190

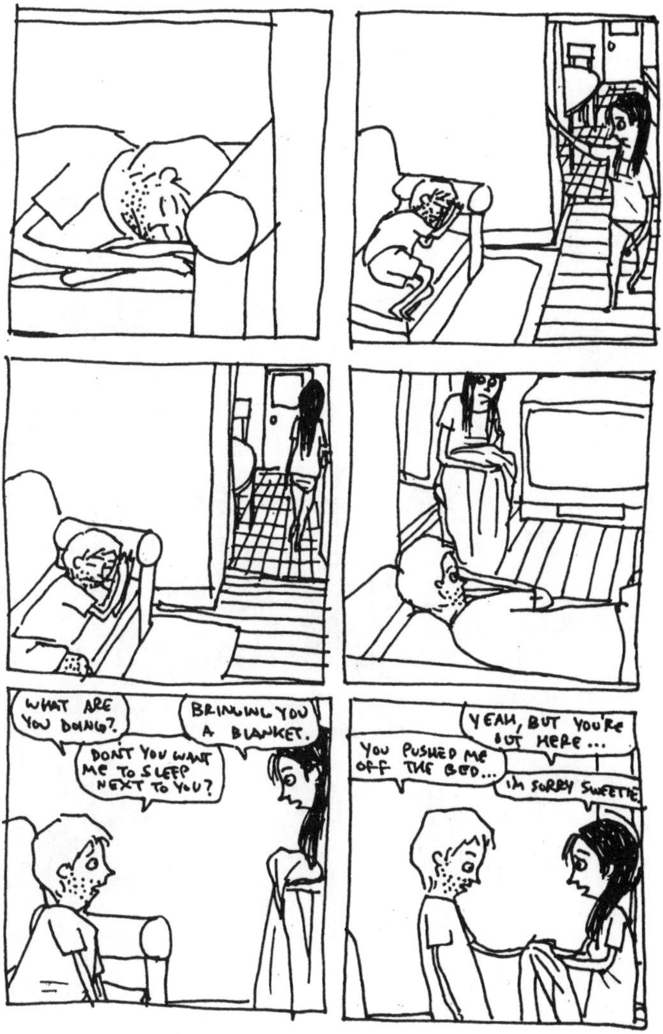
WHAT ARE YOU DOING?
BRINGING YOU A BLANKET.
DON'T YOU WANT ME TO SLEEP NEXT TO YOU?
YEAH, BUT YOU'RE OUT HERE...
YOU PUSHED ME OFF THE BED...
I'M SORRY SWEETIE.

POTTERY SALE

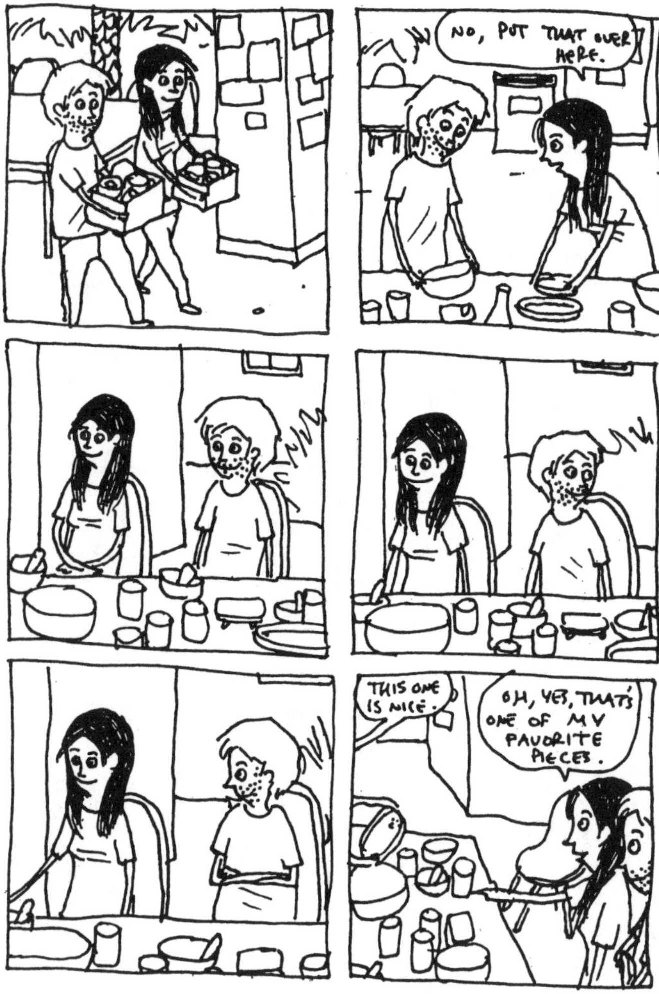
NO, PUT THAT OVER HERE.
THIS ONE IS NICE.
OH, YES, THAT'S ONE OF MY FAVORITE PIECES.

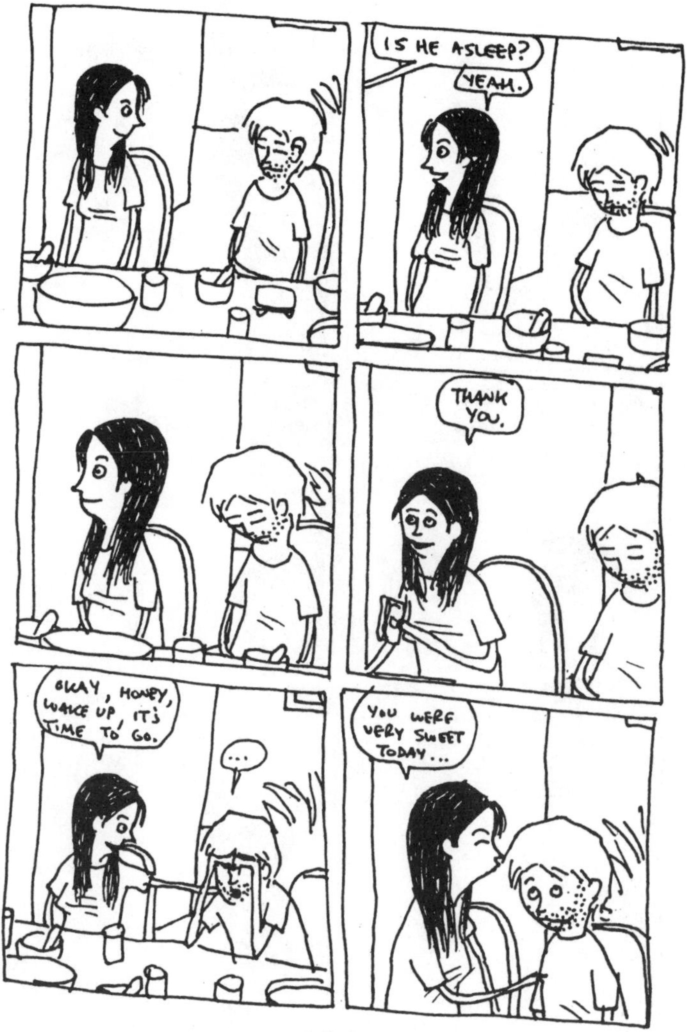
IS HE ASLEEP?
YEAH.
THANK YOU.
OKAY, HONEY, WAKE UP, IT'S TIME TO GO.
...
YOU WERE VERY SWEET TODAY...

CIGARETTE

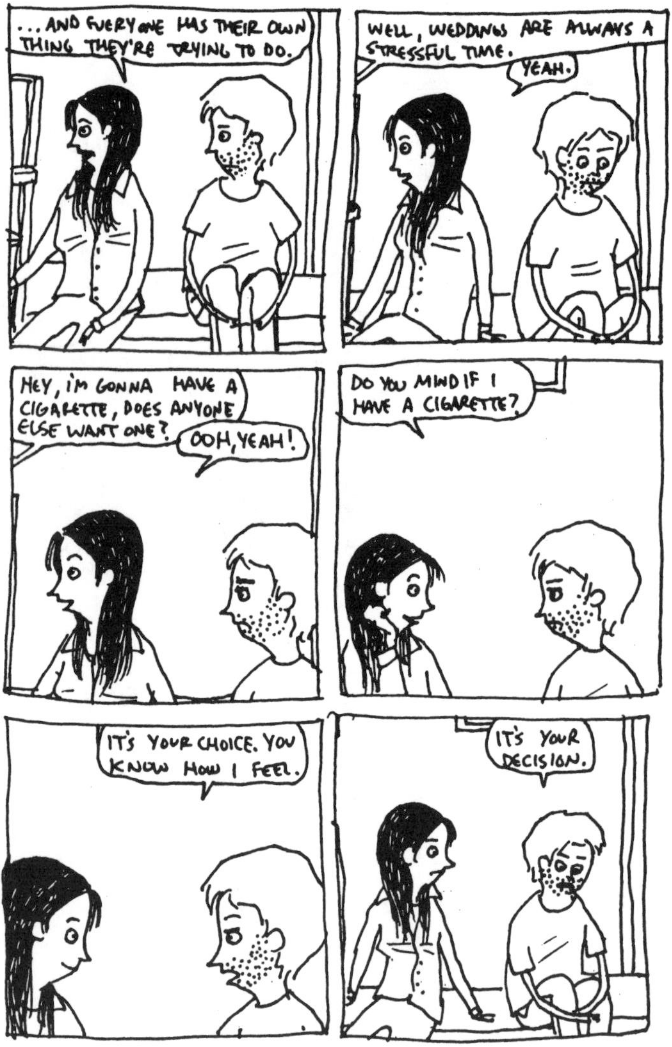

...AND EVERYONE HAS THEIR OWN THING THEY'RE TRYING TO DO.
WELL, WEDDINGS ARE ALWAYS A STRESSFUL TIME.
YEAH.
HEY, I'M GONNA HAVE A CIGARETTE, DOES ANYONE ELSE WANT ONE?
OOH, YEAH!
DO YOU MIND IF I HAVE A CIGARETTE?
IT'S YOUR CHOICE. YOU KNOW HOW I FEEL.
IT'S YOUR DECISION.

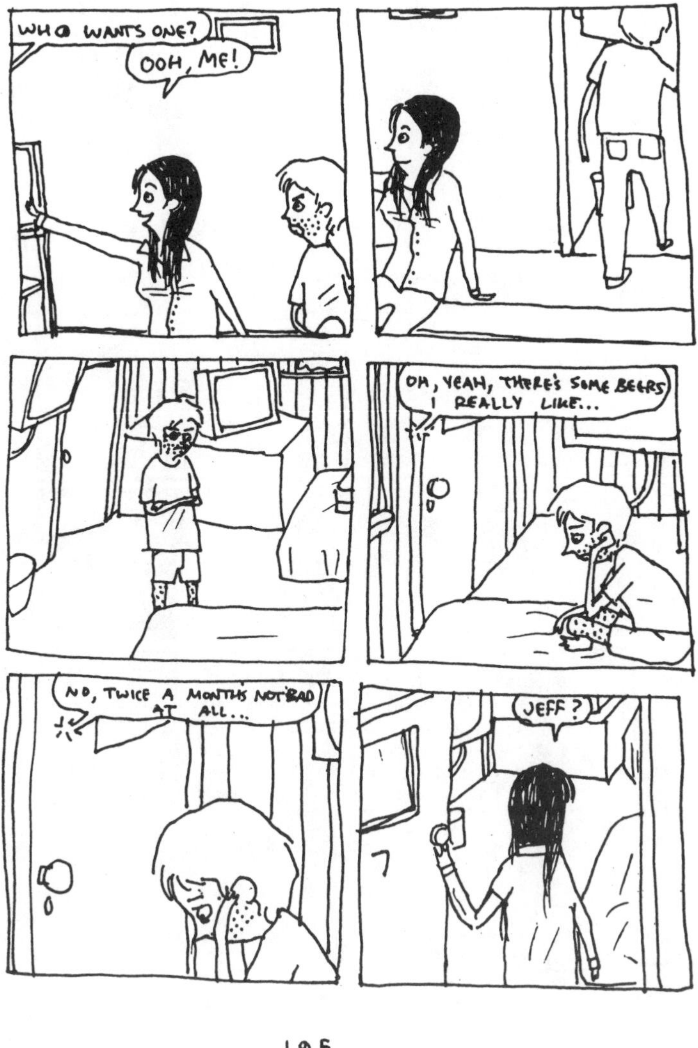
WHO WANTS ONE?
OOH, ME!
OH, YEAH, THERE'S SOME BEERS I REALLY LIKE...
NO, TWICE A MONTH'S NOT BAD AT ALL...
JEFF?

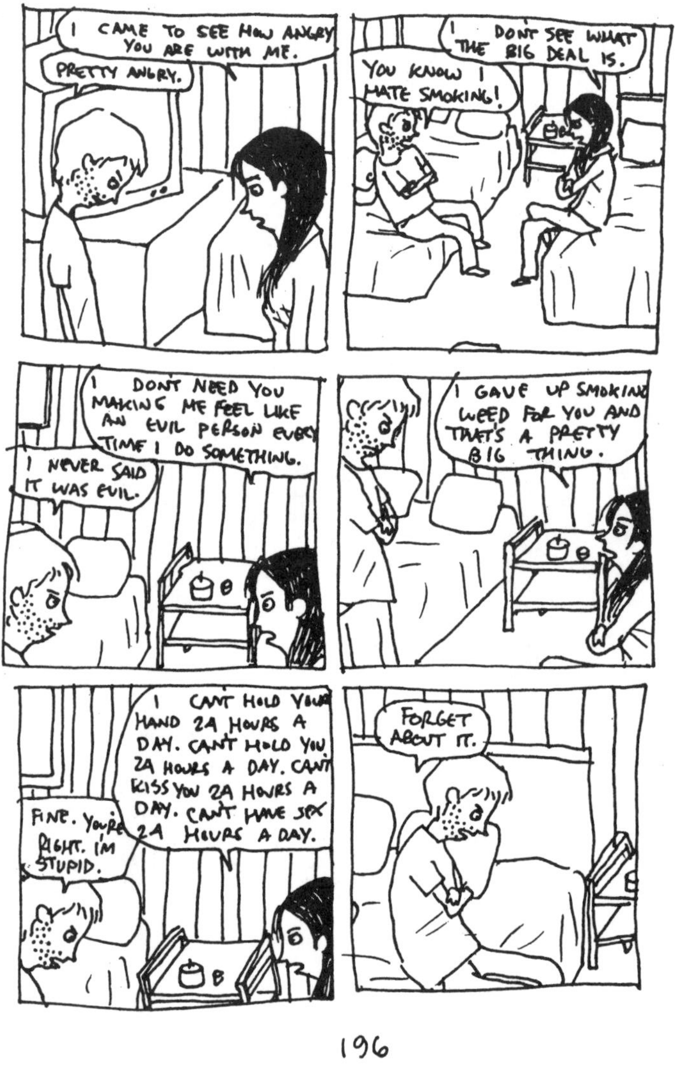
I CAME TO SEE HOW ANGRY YOU ARE WITH ME.
PRETTY ANGRY.
I DON'T SEE WHAT THE BIG DEAL IS.
YOU KNOW I HATE SMOKING!
I DON'T NEED YOU MAKING ME FEEL LIKE AN EVIL PERSON EVERY TIME I DO SOMETHING.
I NEVER SAID IT WAS EVIL.
I GAVE UP SMOKING WEED FOR YOU AND THAT'S A PRETTY BIG THING.
I CAN'T HOLD YOUR HAND 24 HOURS A DAY. CAN'T HOLD YOU 24 HOURS A DAY. CAN'T KISS YOU 24 HOURS A DAY. CAN'T HAVE SEX 24 HOURS A DAY.
FINE. YOU'RE RIGHT. I'M STUPID.
FORGET ABOUT IT.

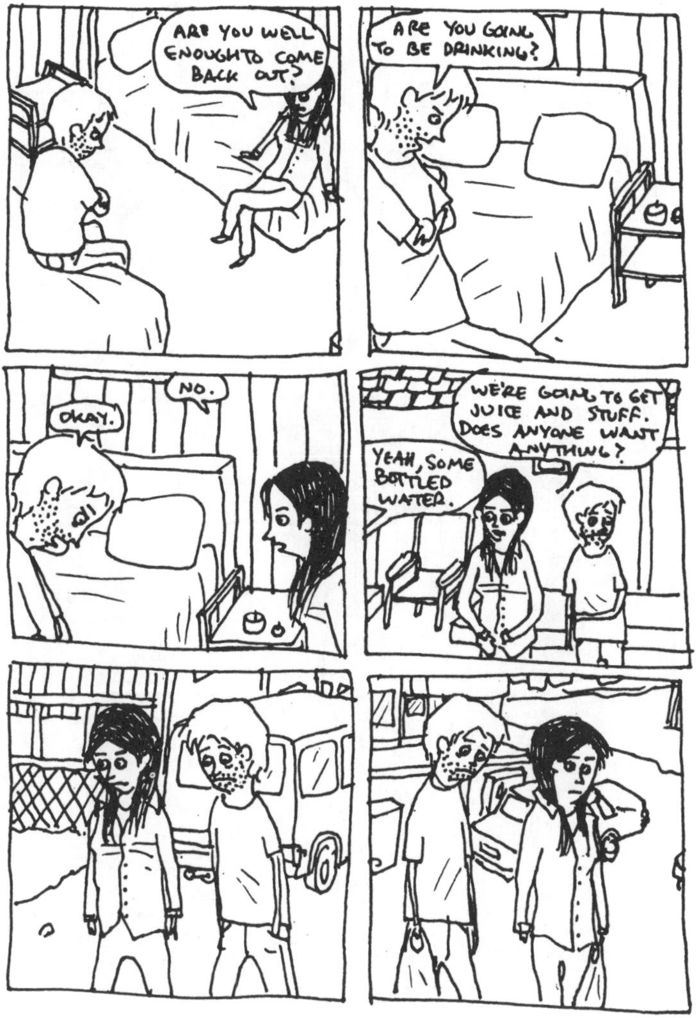
ARE YOU WELL ENOUGH TO COME BACK OUT?
ARE YOU GOING TO BE DRINKING?
NO.
OKAY.
WE'RE GOING TO GET JUICE AND STUFF. DOES ANYONE WANT ANYTHING?
YEAH, SOME BOTTLED WATER.

FALLS

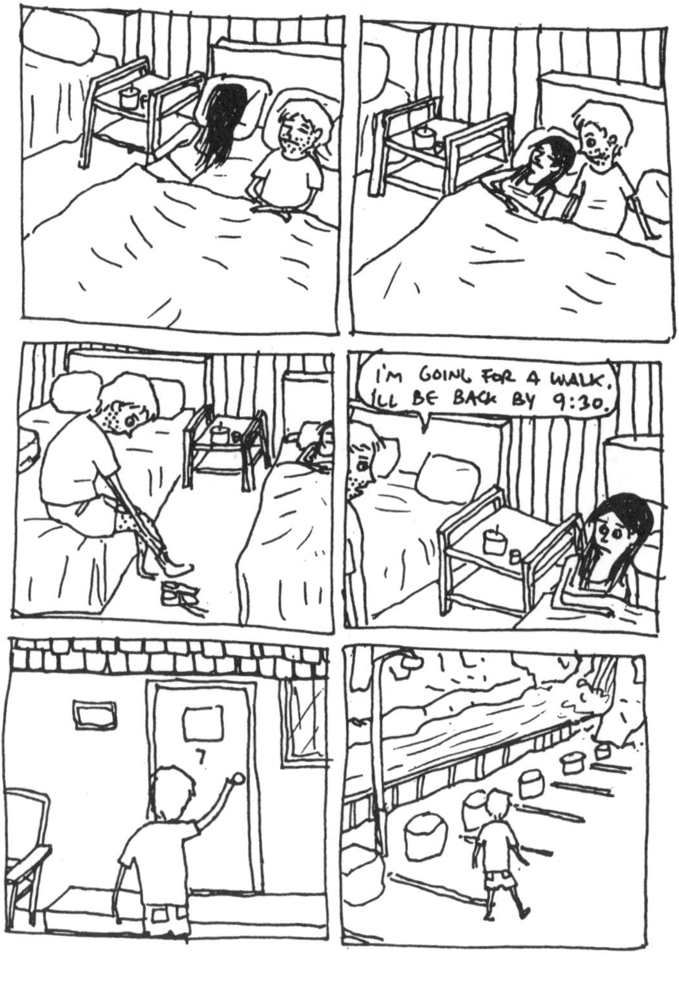
I'M GOING FOR A WALK. I'LL BE BACK BY 9:30.

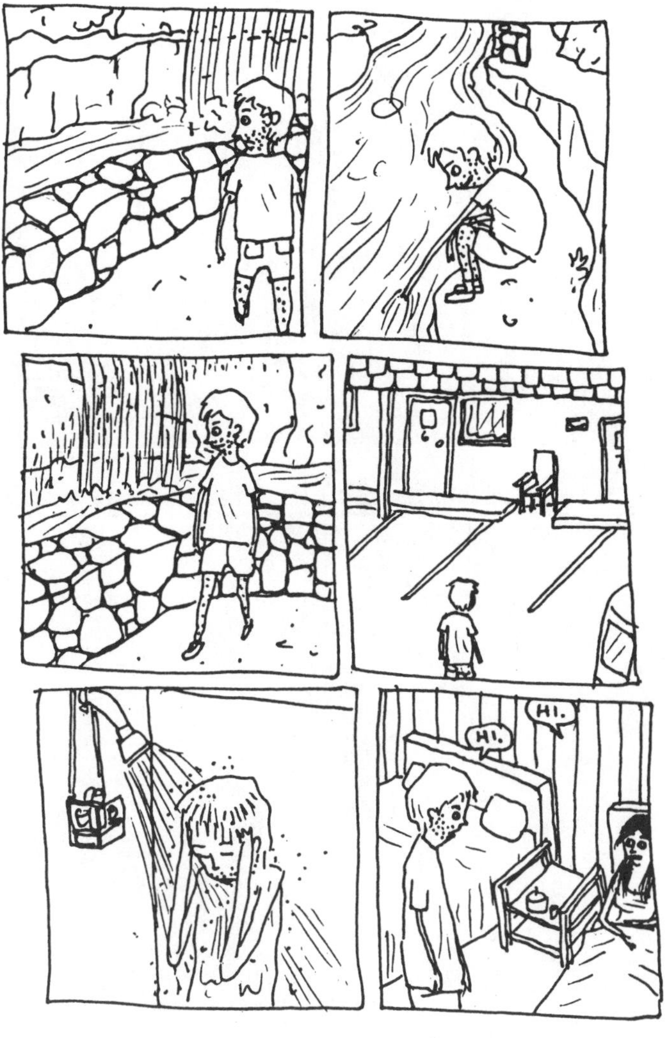
HI.
HI.

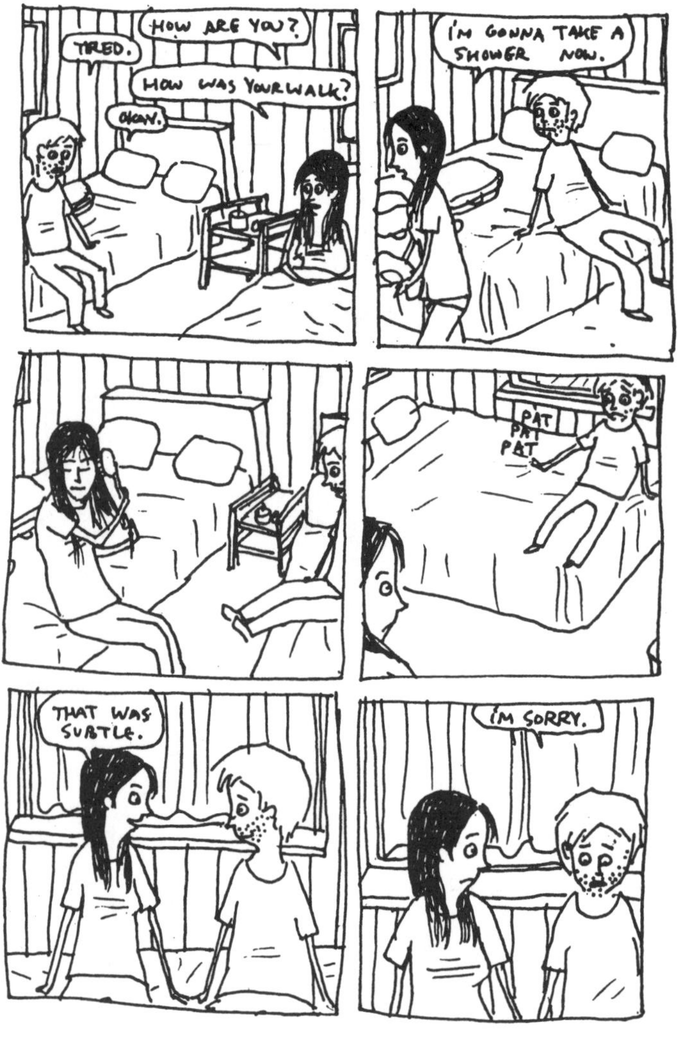
HOW ARE YOU?
TIRED.
HOW WAS YOUR WALK?
OKAY.
I'M GONNA TAKE A SHOWER NOW.
PAT
PAT
PAT
THAT WAS SUBTLE.
I'M SORRY.

NEW YORK MORNING

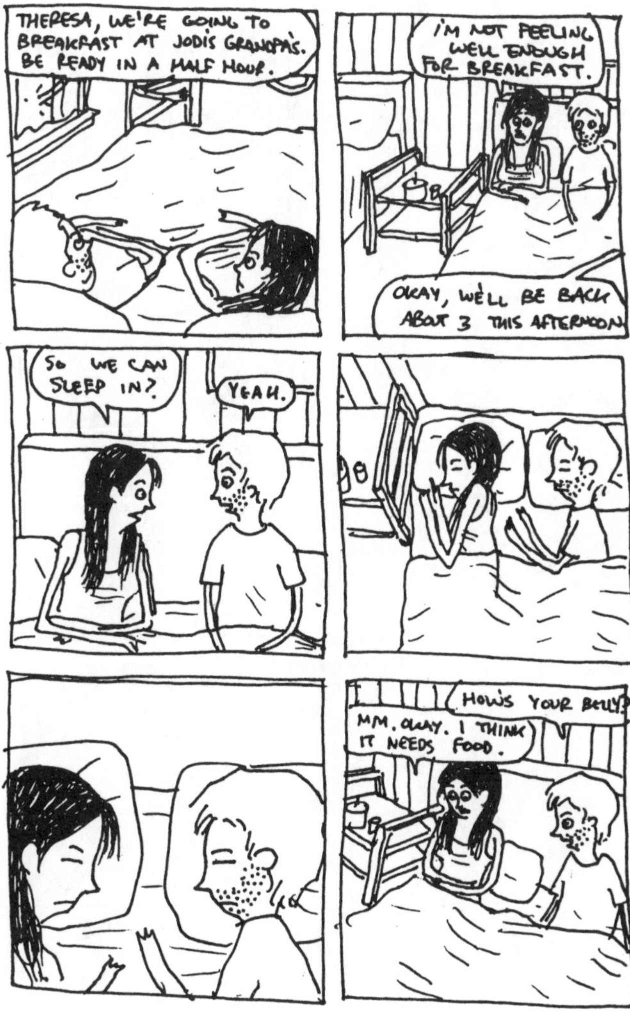
THERESA, WE'RE GOING TO BREAKFAST AT JODI'S GRANDPA'S. BE READY IN A HALF HOUR.
I'M NOT FEELING WELL ENOUGH FOR BREAKFAST.
OKAY, WE'LL BE BACK ABOUT 3 THIS AFTERNOON.
SO WE CAN SLEEP IN?
YEAH.
HOW'S YOUR BELLY?
MM. OKAY. I THINK IT NEEDS FOOD.

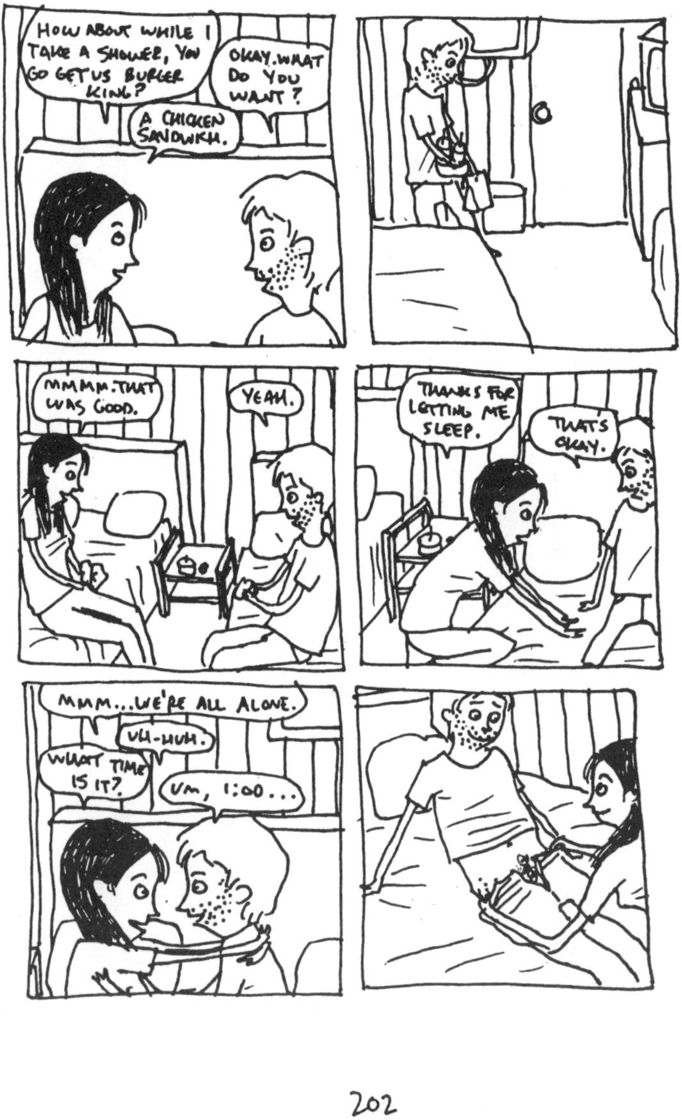
HOW ABOUT WHILE I TAKE A SHOWER, YOU GO GET US BURGER KING?
OKAY. WHAT DO YOU WANT?
A CHICKEN SANDWICH.
MMMM. THAT WAS GOOD.
YEAH.
THANKS FOR LETTING ME SLEEP.
THAT'S OKAY.
MMM... WE'RE ALL ALONE.
UH-HUH.
WHAT TIME IS IT?
UM, 1:00...

112

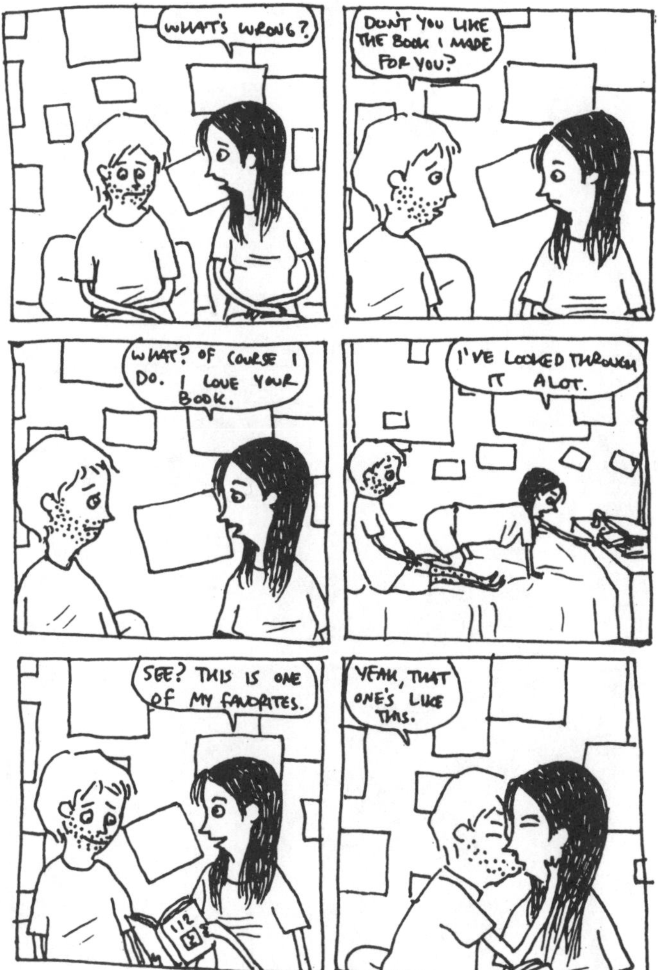
WHAT'S WRONG?
DON'T YOU LIKE THE BOOK I MADE FOR YOU?
WHAT? OF COURSE I DO. I LOVE YOUR BOOK.
I'VE LOOKED THROUGH IT ALOT.
SEE? THIS IS ONE OF MY FAVORITES.
YEAH, THAT ONE'S LIKE THIS.

BLUEBERRY

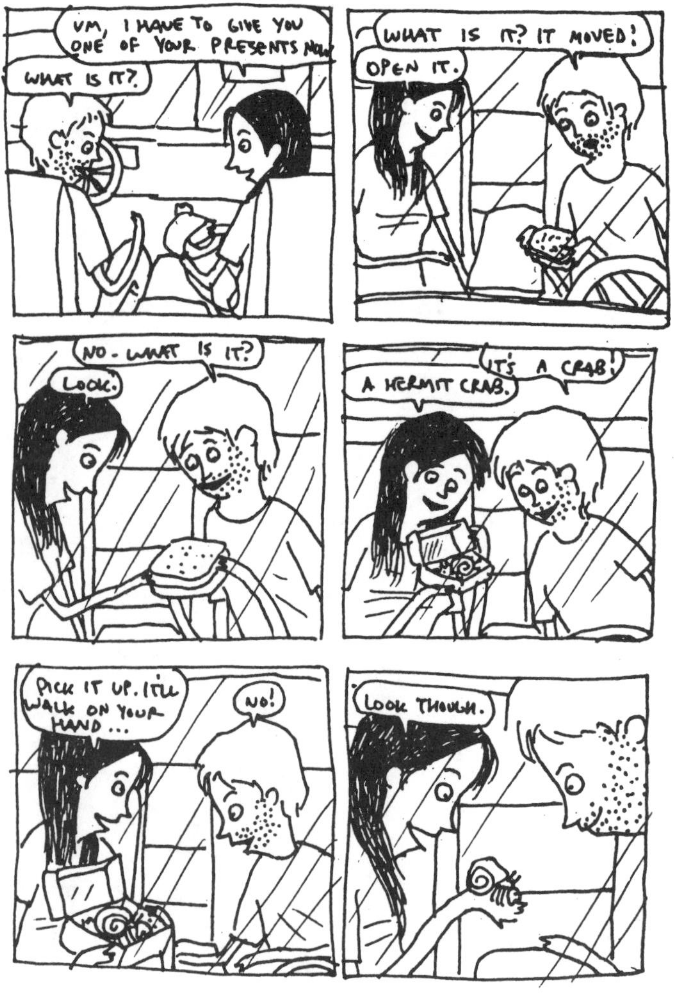
UM, I HAVE TO GIVE YOU ONE OF YOUR PRESENTS NOW
WHAT IS IT?
WHAT IS IT? IT MOVED!
OPEN IT.
NO - WHAT IS IT?
LOOK.
IT'S A CRAB!
A HERMIT CRAB.
PICK IT UP. IT'LL WALK ON YOUR HAND...
NO!
LOOK THOUGH.

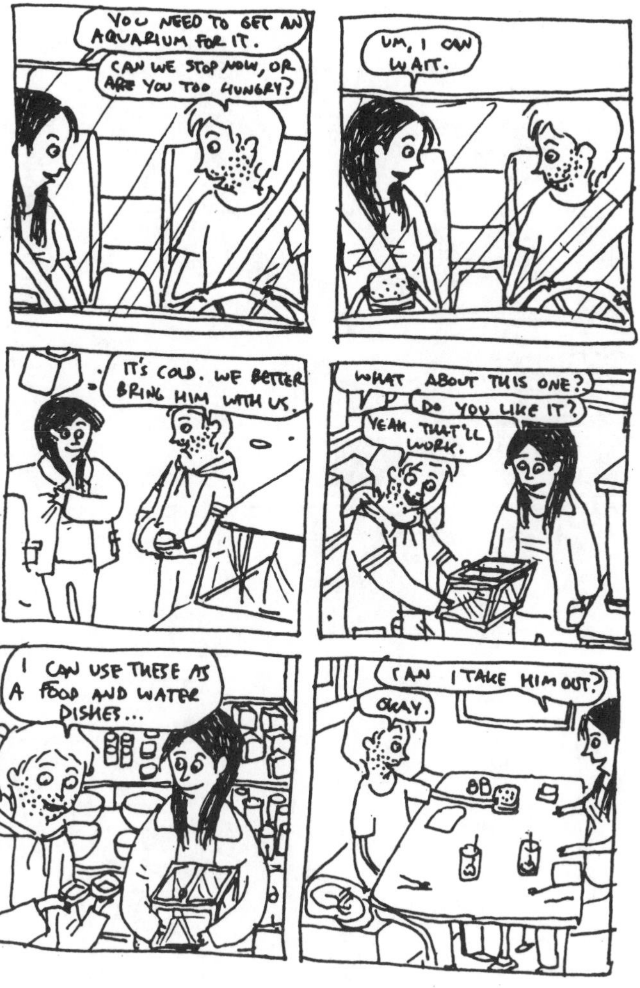

YOU NEED TO GET AN AQUARIUM FOR IT.
CAN WE STOP NOW, OR ARE YOU TOO HUNGRY?
UM, I CAN WAIT.
IT'S COLD. WE BETTER BRING HIM WITH US.
WHAT ABOUT THIS ONE?
DO YOU LIKE IT?
YEAH. THAT'LL WORK.
I CAN USE THESE AS A FOOD AND WATER DISHES...
CAN I TAKE HIM OUT?
OKAY.

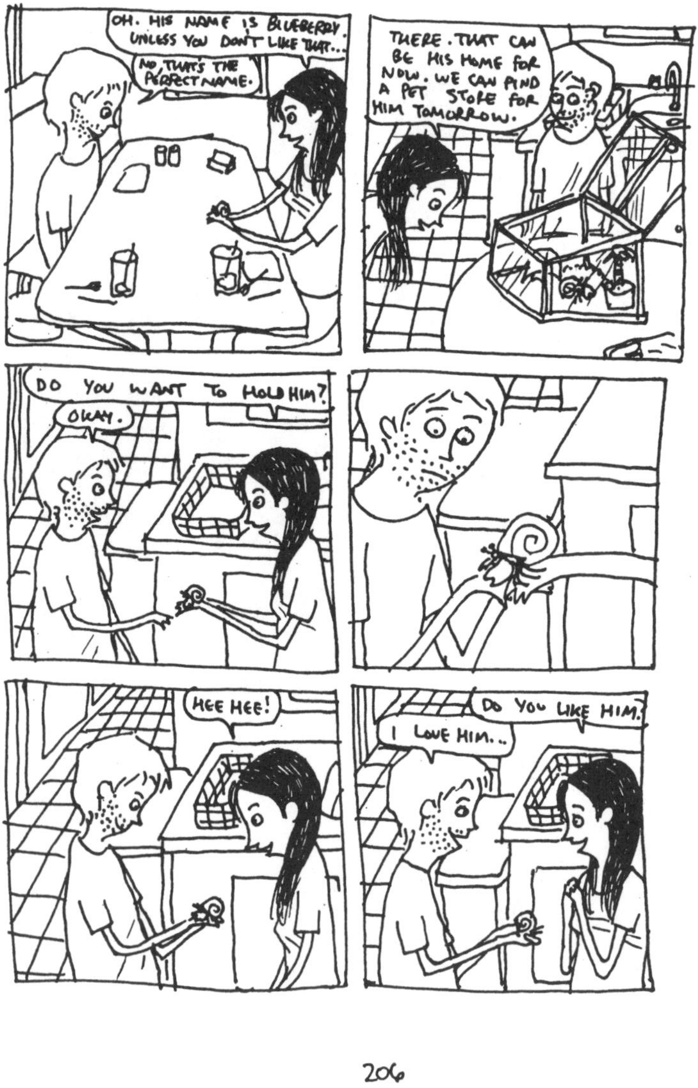
OH. HIS NAME IS BLUEBERRY. UNLESS YOU DON'T LIKE THAT...
NO, THAT'S THE PERFECT NAME.
THERE. THAT CAN BE HIS HOME FOR NOW. WE CAN FIND A PET STORE FOR HIM TOMORROW.
DO YOU WANT TO HOLD HIM?
OKAY.
HEE HEE!
DO YOU LIKE HIM?
I LOVE HIM...

NO KITTIES

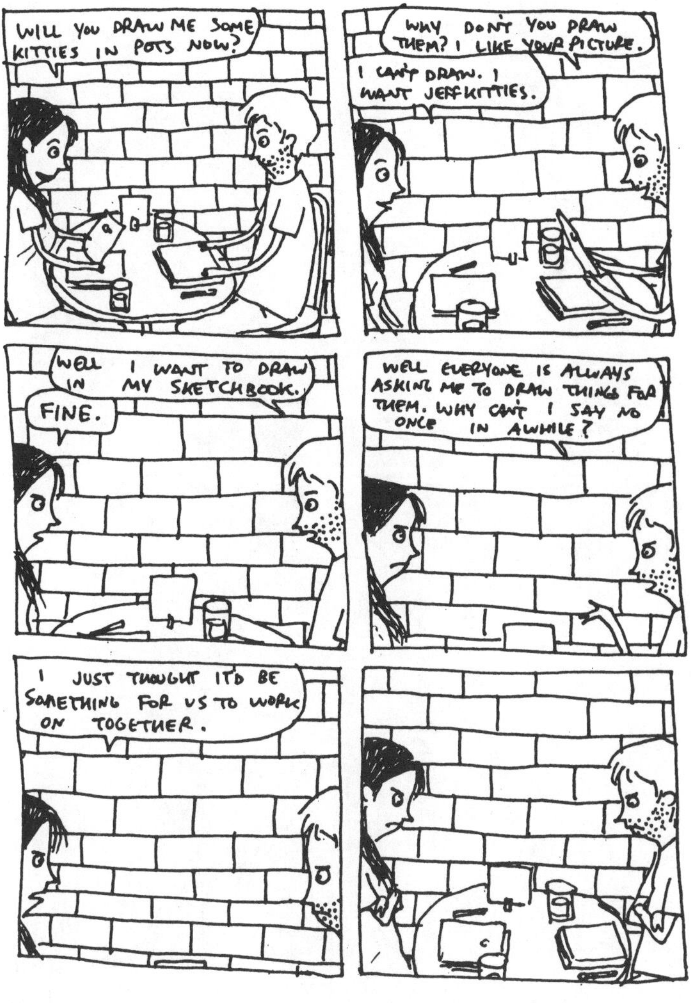

WILL YOU DRAW ME SOME KITTIES IN POTS NOW?
WHY DON'T YOU DRAW THEM? I LIKE YOUR PICTURE.
I CAN'T DRAW. I WANT JEFF KITTIES.
WELL I WANT TO DRAW IN MY SKETCHBOOK.
FINE.
WELL EVERYONE IS ALWAYS ASKING ME TO DRAW THINGS FOR THEM. WHY CAN'T I SAY NO ONCE IN AWHILE?
I JUST THOUGHT IT'D BE SOMETHING FOR US TO WORK ON TOGETHER.

CAR SICK

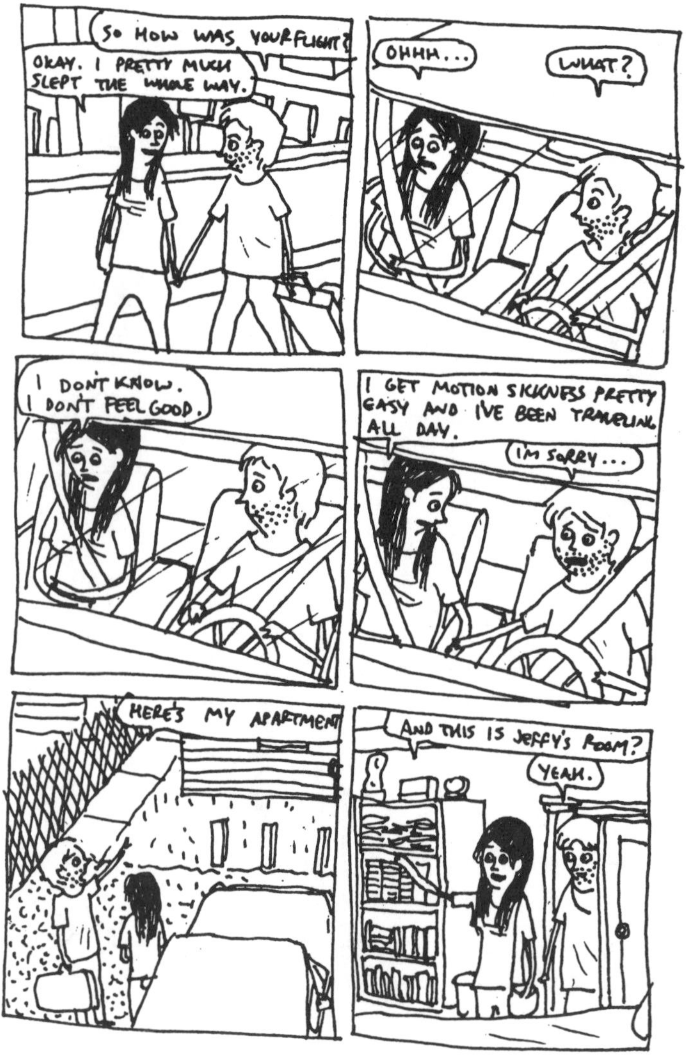
SO HOW WAS YOUR FLIGHT?
OKAY. I PRETTY MUCH SLEPT THE WHOLE WAY.
OHHH...
WHAT?
I DON'T KNOW. I DON'T FEEL GOOD.
I GET MOTION SICKNESS PRETTY EASY AND I'VE BEEN TRAVELING ALL DAY.
I'M SORRY...
HERE'S MY APARTMENT
AND THIS IS JEFFY'S ROOM?
YEAH.

HAPPY BIRTHDAY JEFF

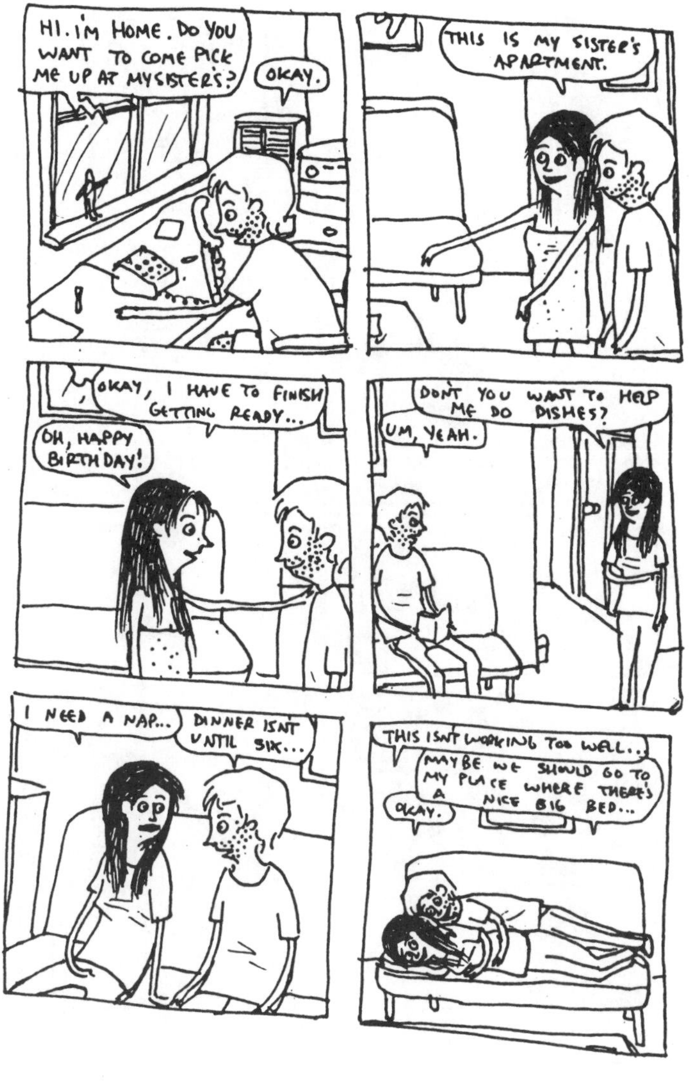
HI. I'M HOME. DO YOU WANT TO COME PICK ME UP AT MY SISTER'S?
OKAY.
THIS IS MY SISTER'S APARTMENT.
OKAY, I HAVE TO FINISH GETTING READY...
OH, HAPPY BIRTHDAY!
DON'T YOU WANT TO HELP ME DO DISHES?
UM, YEAH.
I NEED A NAP...
DINNER ISN'T UNTIL SIX...
THIS ISN'T WORKING TOO WELL...
MAYBE WE SHOULD GO TO MY PLACE WHERE THERE'S A NICE BIG BED...
OKAY.

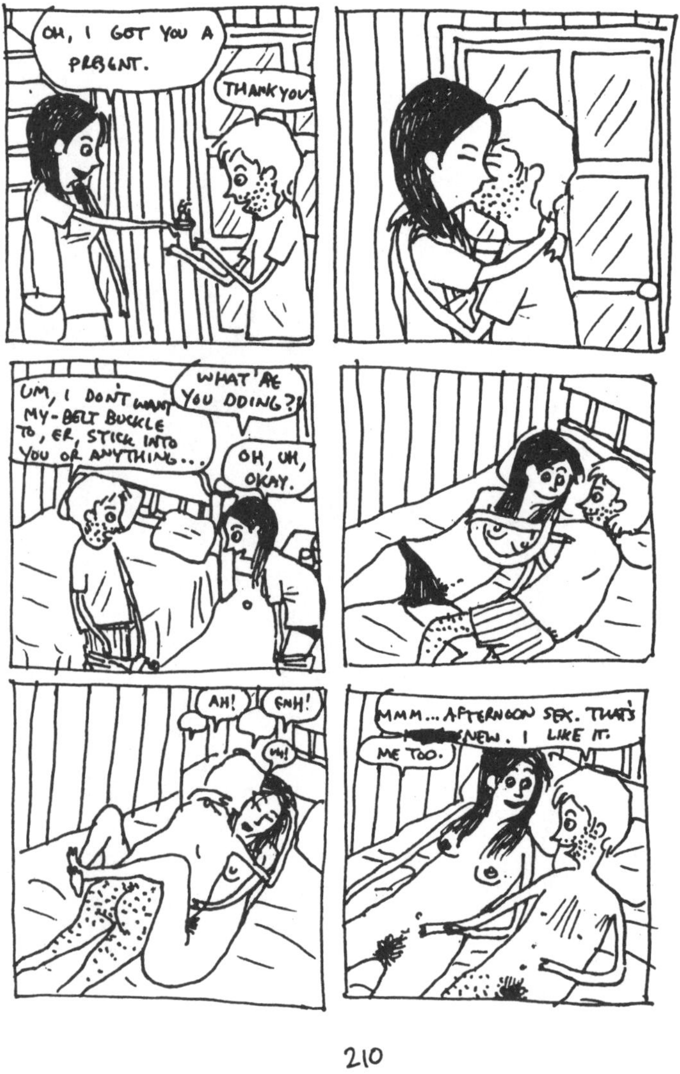
OH, I GOT YOU A PRESENT.
THANK YOU!
WHAT ARE YOU DOING?!
UM, I DON'T WANT MY-BELT BUCKLE TO, ER, STICK INTO YOU OR ANYTHING...
OH, UH, OKAY.
AH!
ENH!
UH!
MMM... AFTERNOON SEX. THAT'S [redacted] NEW. I LIKE IT.
ME TOO.

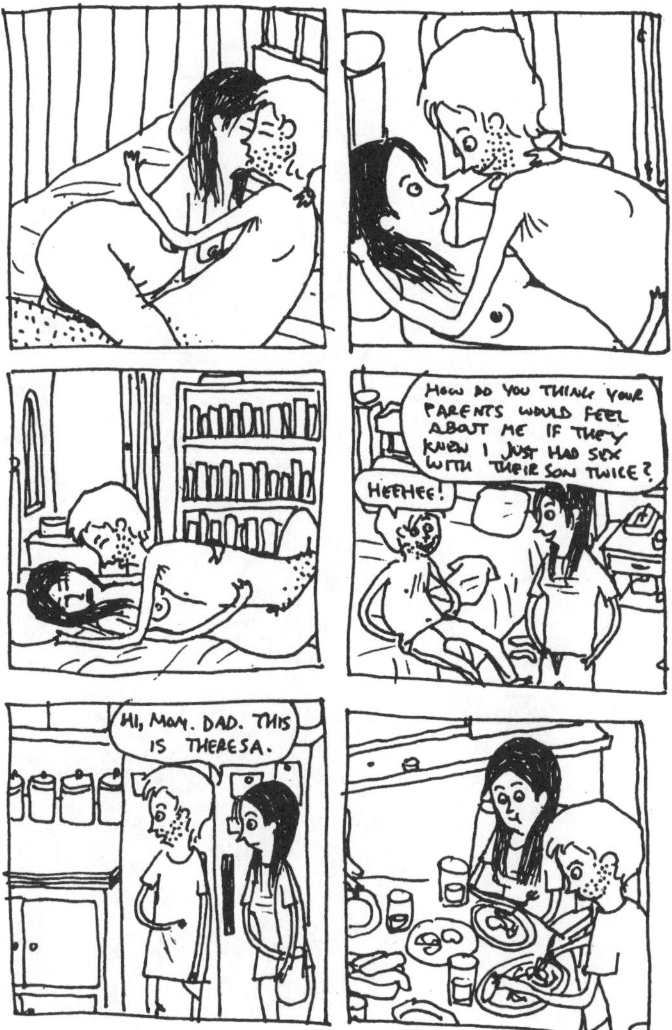
HOW DO YOU THINK YOUR PARENTS WOULD FEEL ABOUT ME IF THEY KNEW I JUST HAD SEX WITH THEIR SON TWICE?
HEEHEE!
HI, MOM. DAD. THIS IS THERESA.

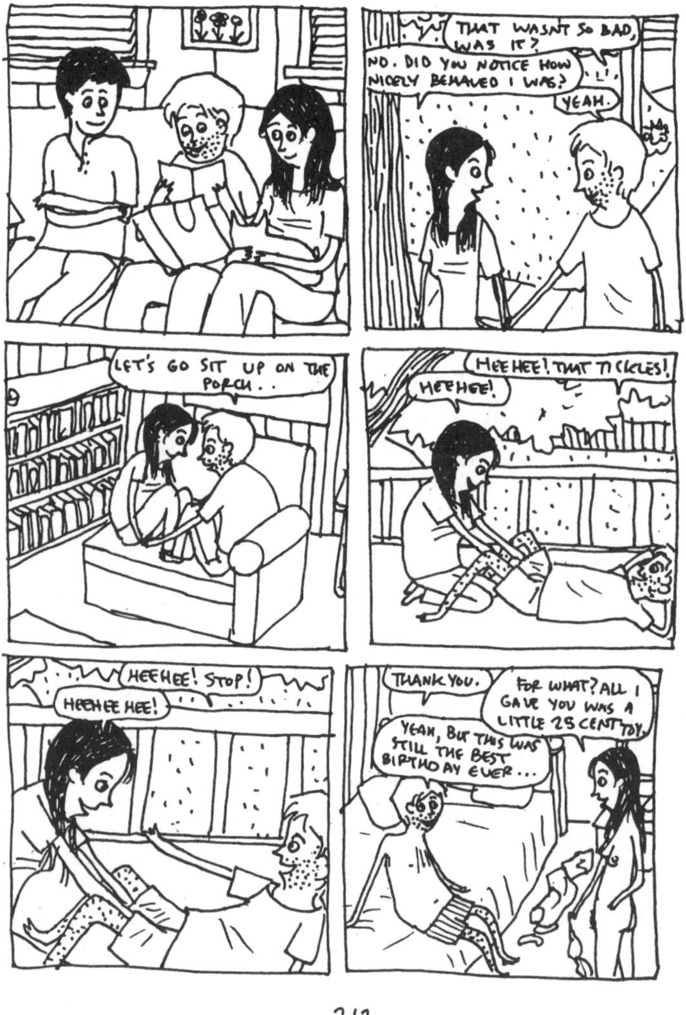
THAT WASN'T SO BAD, WAS IT?
NO. DID YOU NOTICE HOW NICELY BEHAVED I WAS?
YEAH.
LET'S GO SIT UP ON THE PORCH..
HEEHEE! THAT TICKLES!
HEEHEE!
HEEHEE! STOP!
HEEHEE HEE!
THANK YOU.
FOR WHAT? ALL I GAVE YOU WAS A LITTLE 25 CENT TOY.
YEAH, BUT THIS WAS STILL THE BEST BIRTHDAY EVER...

TELL ME A STORY

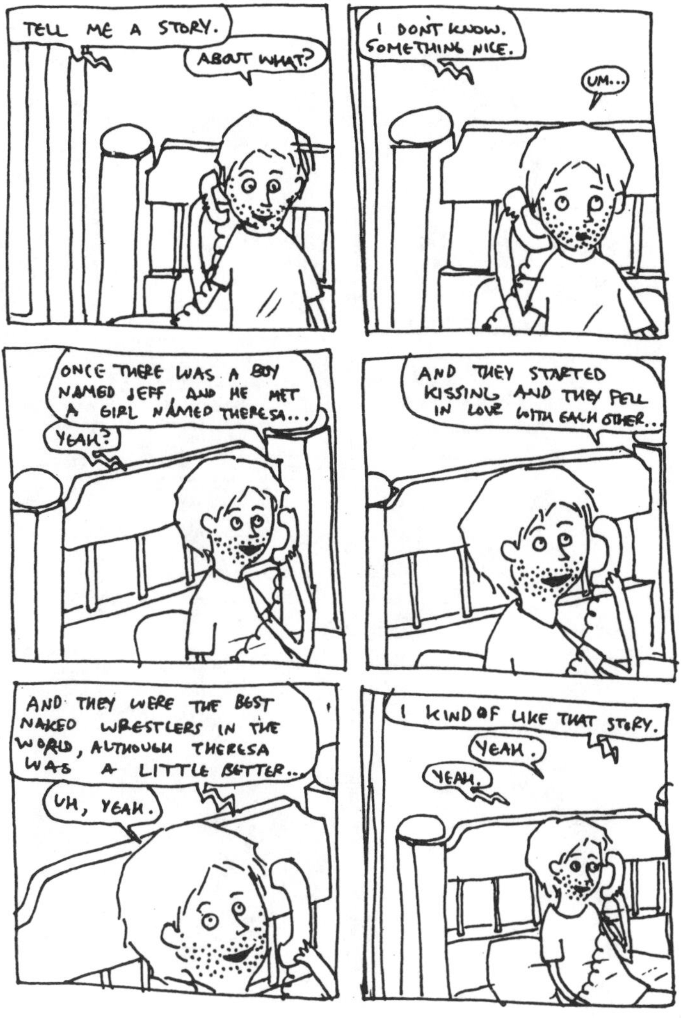

TELL ME A STORY.
ABOUT WHAT?
I DON'T KNOW. SOMETHING NICE.
UM...
ONCE THERE WAS A BOY NAMED JEFF AND HE MET A GIRL NAMED THERESA...
YEAH?
AND THEY STARTED KISSING AND THEY FELL IN LOVE WITH EACH OTHER...
AND THEY WERE THE BEST NAKED WRESTLERS IN THE WORLD, ALTHOUGH THERESA WAS A LITTLE BETTER...
UH, YEAH.
I KIND OF LIKE THAT STORY.
YEAH.
YEAH.

STAY UP FOREVER

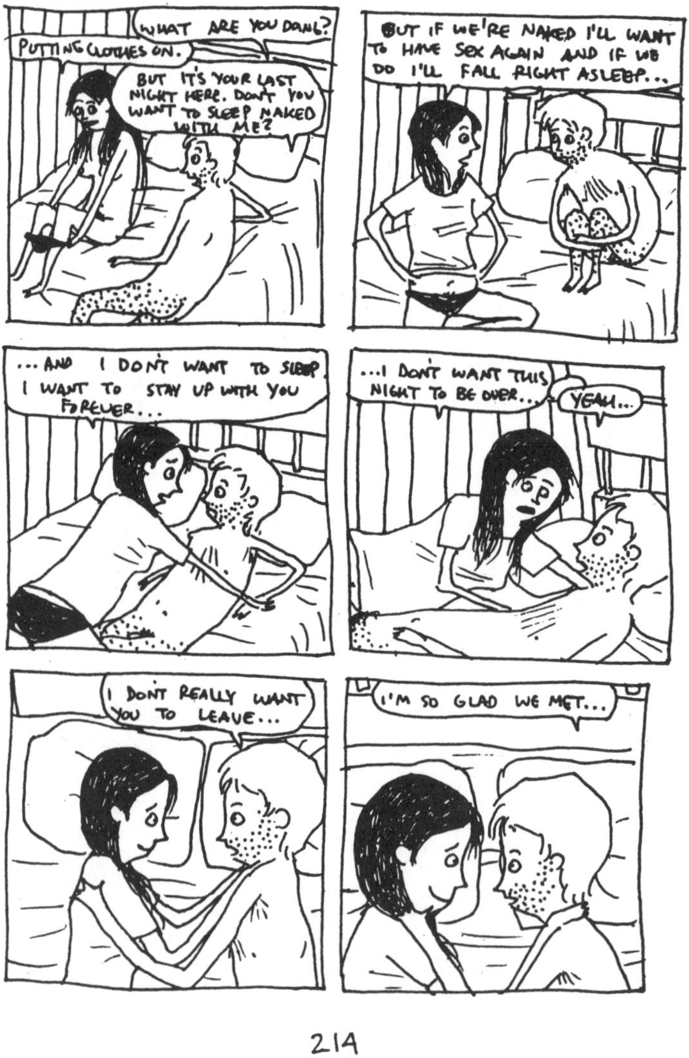
WHAT ARE YOU DOING?
PUTTING CLOTHES ON.
BUT IT'S YOUR LAST NIGHT HERE. DON'T YOU WANT TO SLEEP NAKED WITH ME?
BUT IF WE'RE NAKED I'LL WANT TO HAVE SEX AGAIN AND IF WE DO I'LL FALL RIGHT ASLEEP...
...AND I DON'T WANT TO SLEEP I WANT TO STAY UP WITH YOU FOREVER...
...I DON'T WANT THIS NIGHT TO BE OVER...
YEAH...
I DON'T REALLY WANT YOU TO LEAVE...
I'M SO GLAD WE MET...

THE END

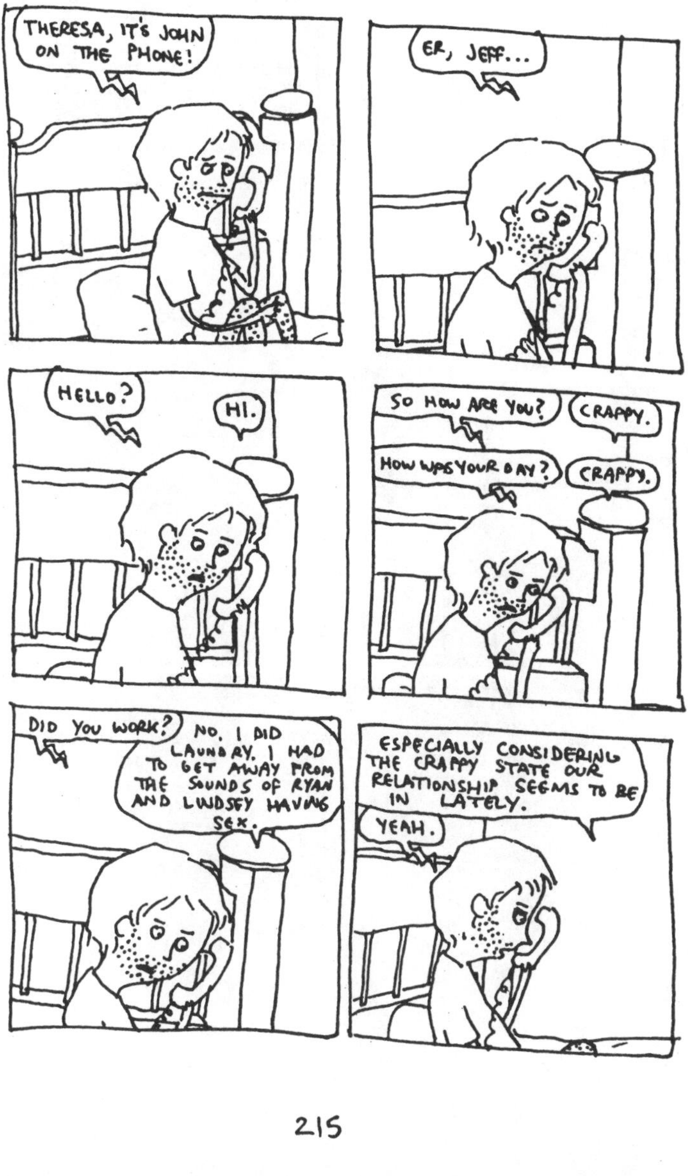
THERESA, IT'S JOHN ON THE PHONE!
ER, JEFF...
HELLO?
HI.
SO HOW ARE YOU?
CRAPPY.
HOW WAS YOUR DAY?
CRAPPY.
DID YOU WORK?
NO. I DID LAUNDRY. I HAD TO GET AWAY FROM THE SOUNDS OF RYAN AND LINDSEY HAVING SEX.
ESPECIALLY CONSIDERING THE CRAPPY STATE OUR RELATIONSHIP SEEMS TO BE IN LATELY.
YEAH.

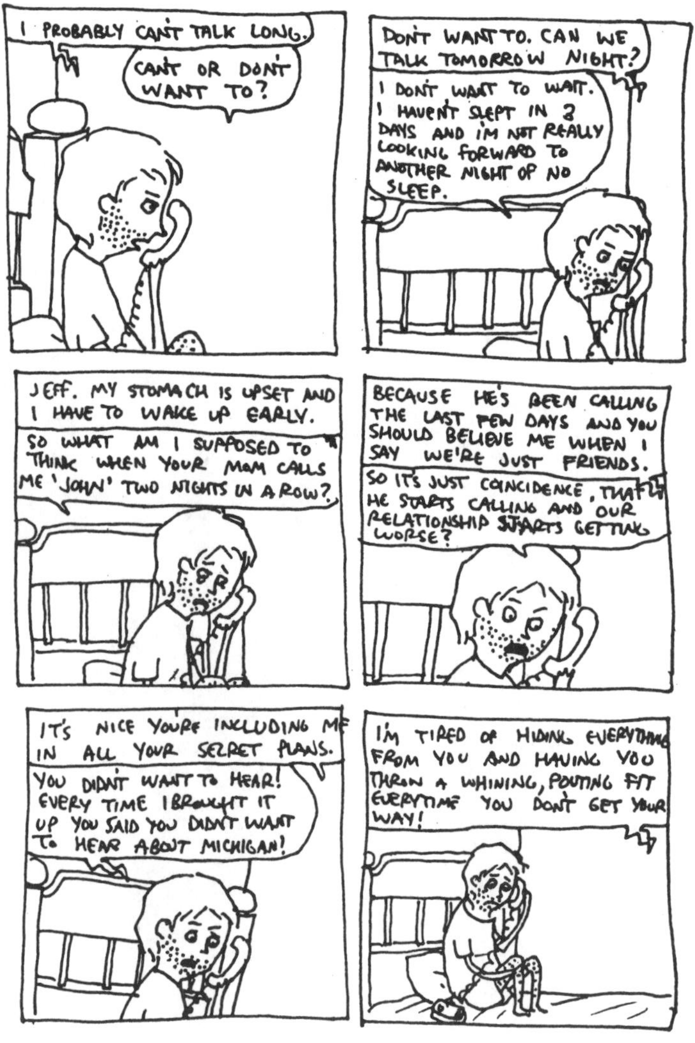

I PROBABLY CAN'T TALK LONG.
CAN'T OR DON'T WANT TO?
DON'T WANT TO. CAN WE TALK TOMORROW NIGHT?
I DON'T WANT TO WAIT. I HAVEN'T SLEPT IN 3 DAYS AND I'M NOT REALLY LOOKING FORWARD TO ANOTHER NIGHT OF NO SLEEP.
JEFF. MY STOMACH IS UPSET AND I HAVE TO WAKE UP EARLY.
SO WHAT AM I SUPPOSED TO THINK WHEN YOUR MOM CALLS ME 'JOHN' TWO NIGHTS IN A ROW?
BECAUSE HE'S BEEN CALLING THE LAST FEW DAYS AND YOU SHOULD BELIEVE ME WHEN I SAY WE'RE JUST FRIENDS.
SO IT'S JUST COINCIDENCE, THAT HE STARTS CALLING AND OUR RELATIONSHIP STARTS GETTING WORSE?
IT'S NICE YOU'RE INCLUDING ME IN ALL YOUR SECRET PLANS.
YOU DIDN'T WANT TO HEAR! EVERY TIME I BROUGHT IT UP YOU SAID YOU DIDN'T WANT TO HEAR ABOUT MICHIGAN!
I'M TIRED OF HIDING EVERYTHING FROM YOU AND HAVING YOU THROW A WHINING, POUTING FIT EVERYTIME YOU DON'T GET YOUR WAY!

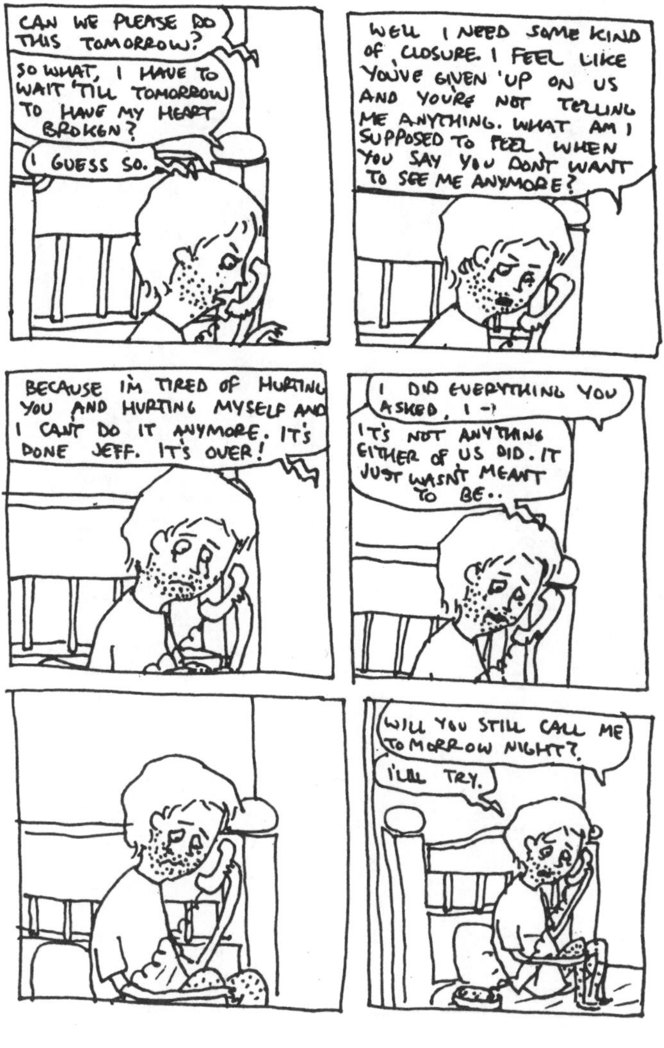
CAN WE PLEASE DO THIS TOMORROW?
SO WHAT, I HAVE TO WAIT 'TILL TOMORROW TO HAVE MY HEART BROKEN?
I GUESS SO.
WELL I NEED SOME KIND OF CLOSURE. I FEEL LIKE YOU'VE GIVEN UP ON US AND YOU'RE NOT TELLING ME ANYTHING. WHAT AM I SUPPOSED TO FEEL WHEN YOU SAY YOU DON'T WANT TO SEE ME ANYMORE?
BECAUSE I'M TIRED OF HURTING YOU AND HURTING MYSELF AND I CAN'T DO IT ANYMORE. IT'S DONE JEFF. IT'S OVER!
I DID EVERYTHING YOU ASKED, I -?
IT'S NOT ANYTHING EITHER OF US DID. IT JUST WASN'T MEANT TO BE..
WILL YOU STILL CALL ME TOMORROW NIGHT?
I'LL TRY.

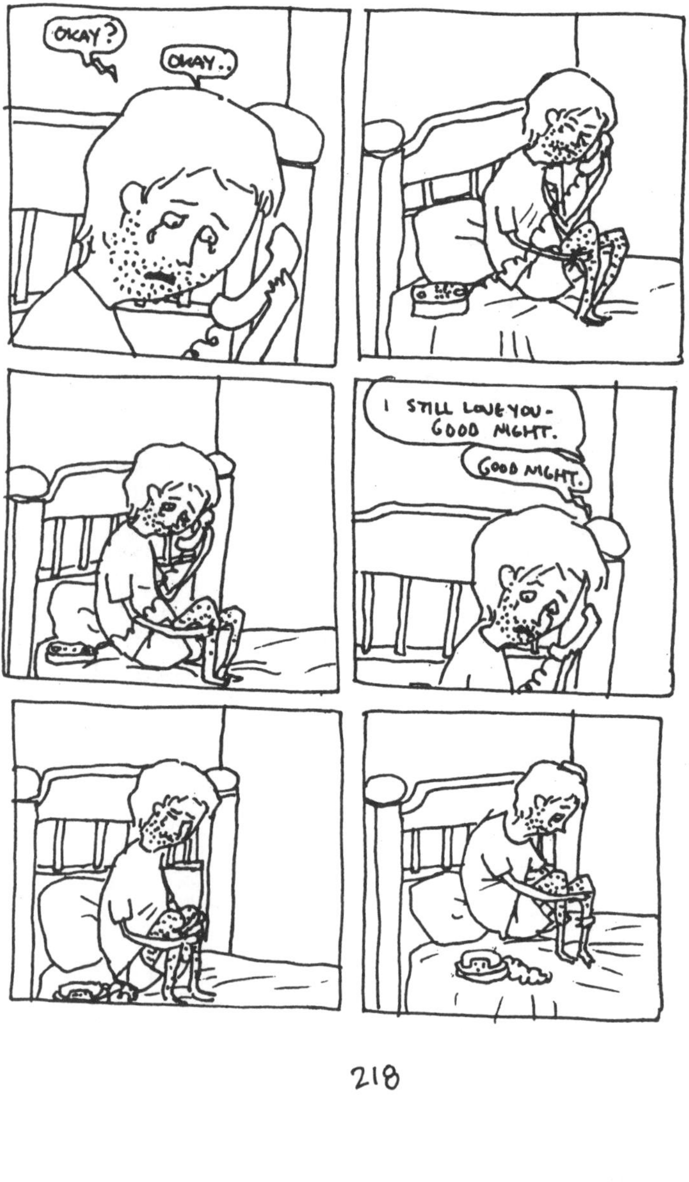
OKAY?
OKAY..
I STILL LOVE YOU-
GOOD NIGHT.
GOOD NIGHT.

FIRST TIME

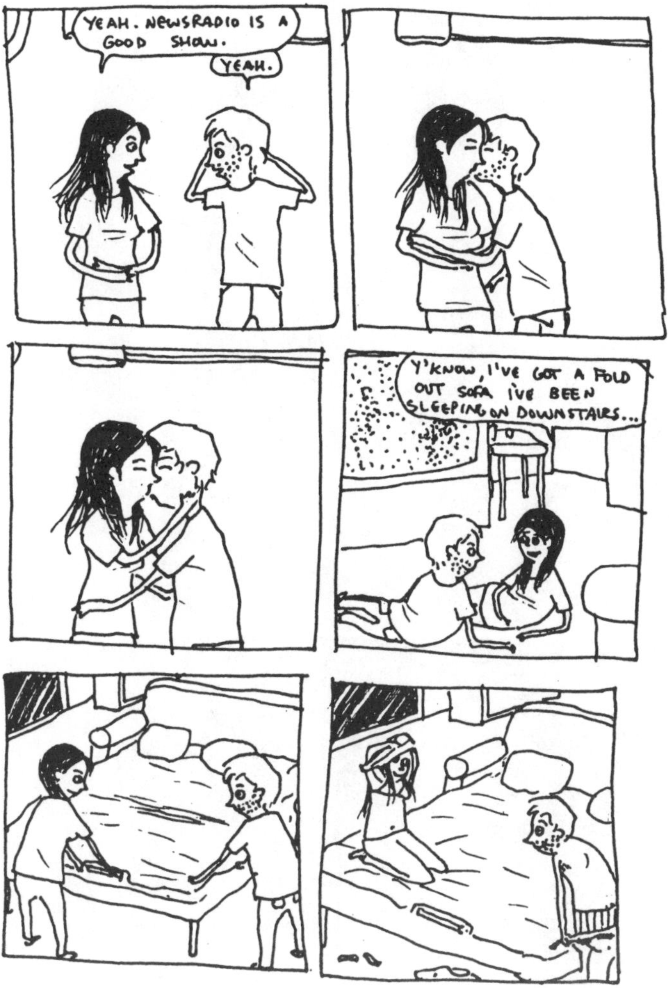
YEAH. NEWSRADIO IS A GOOD SHOW.
YEAH.
Y'KNOW, I'VE GOT A FOLD OUT SOFA I'VE BEEN SLEEPING ON DOWNSTAIRS...

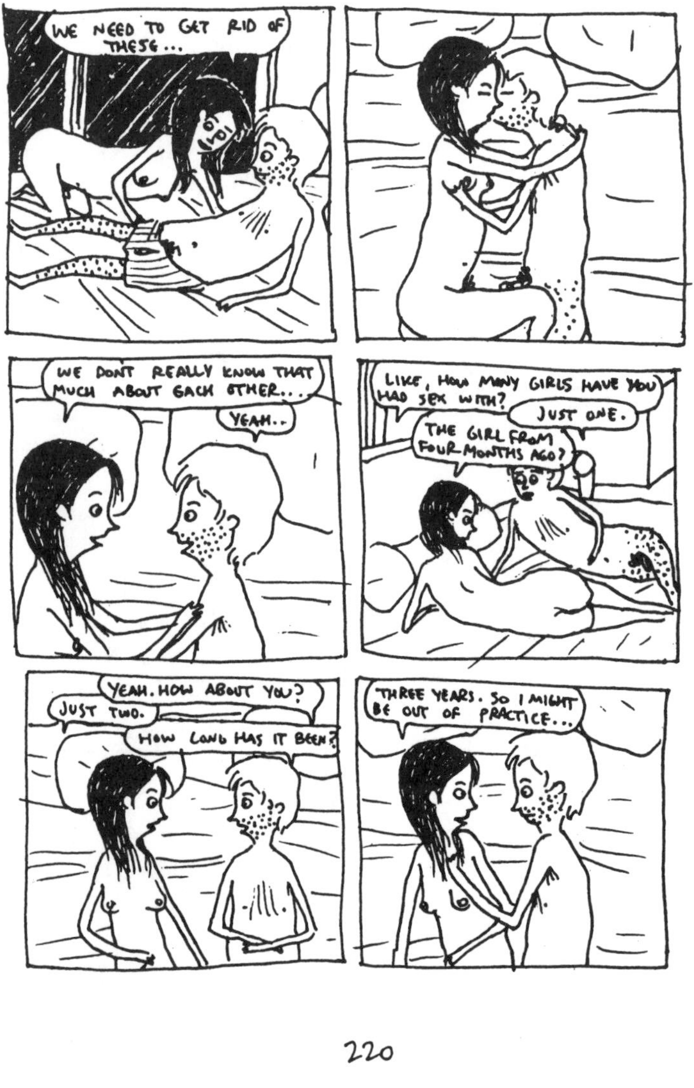
WE NEED TO GET RID OF THESE...
WE DONT REALLY KNOW THAT MUCH ABOUT EACH OTHER...
YEAH..
LIKE, HOW MANY GIRLS HAVE YOU HAD SEX WITH?
JUST ONE.
THE GIRL FROM FOUR MONTHS AGO?
YEAH. HOW ABOUT YOU?
JUST TWO.
HOW LONG HAS IT BEEN?
THREE YEARS. SO I MIGHT BE OUT OF PRACTICE...

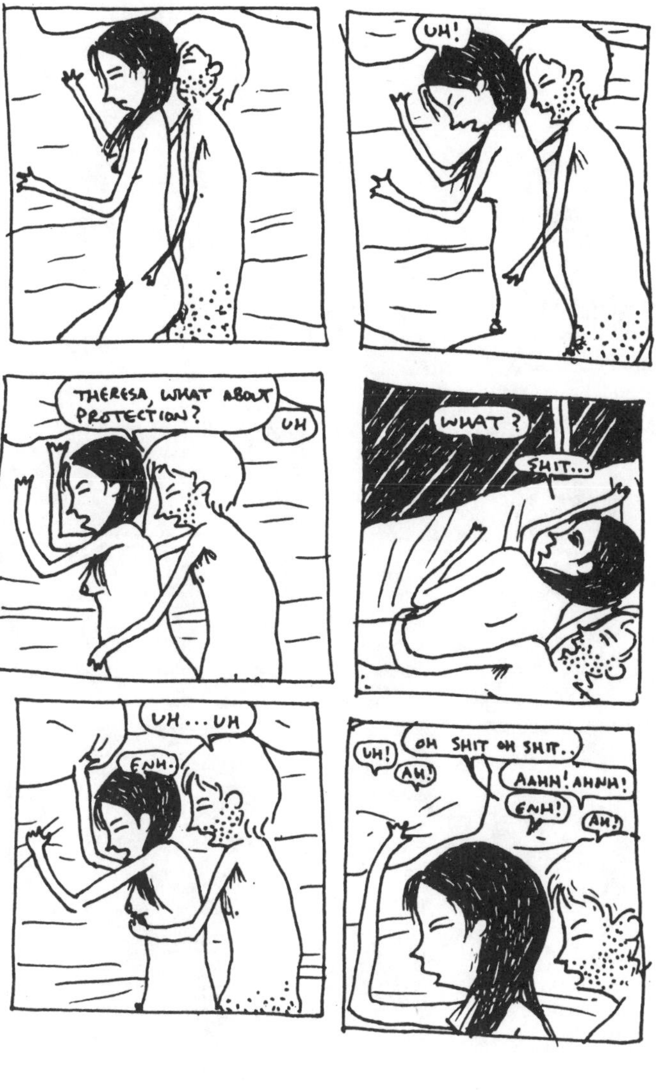
UH!
THERESA, WHAT ABOUT PROTECTION?
UH
WHAT?
SHIT...
UH...UH
ENH.
OH SHIT OH SHIT..
UH!
AH!
AAHH! AHNH!
ENH!
AH!

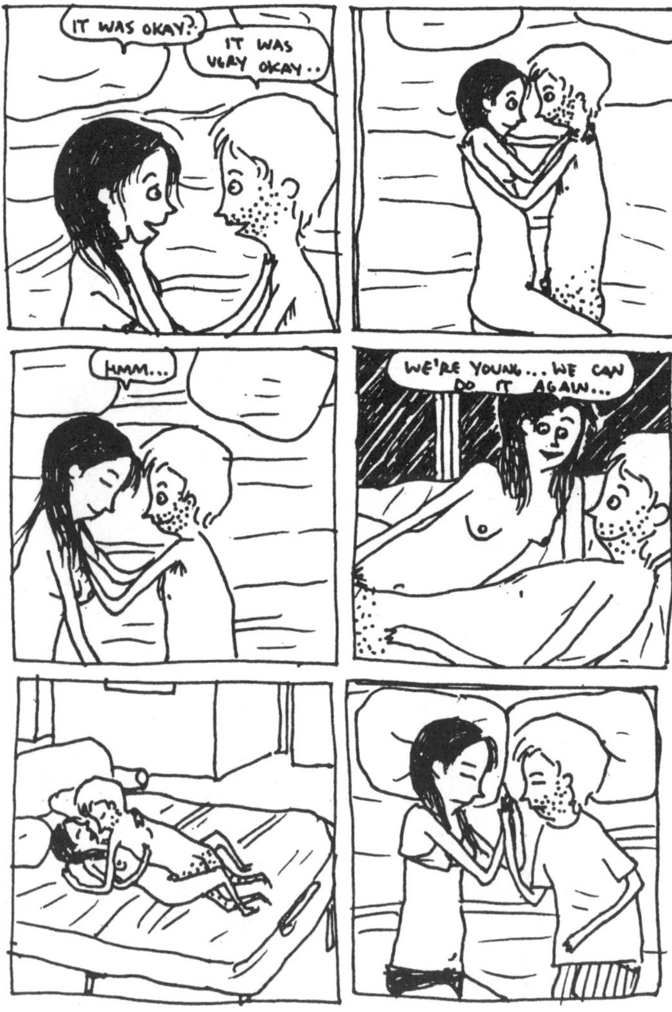
IT WAS OKAY?
IT WAS VERY OKAY..
HMM...
WE'RE YOUNG... WE CAN DO IT AGAIN...

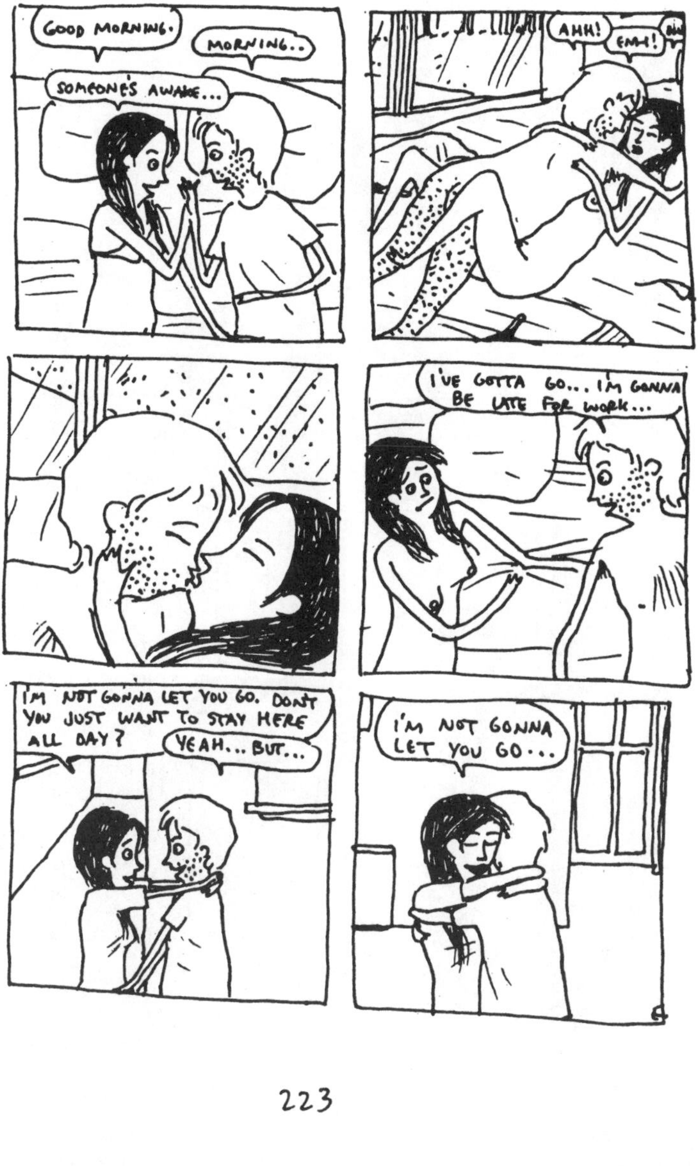
GOOD MORNING.
MORNING..
SOMEONE'S AWAKE...
AHH!
EMM!
I'VE GOTTA GO... I'M GONNA BE LATE FOR WORK...
I'M NOT GONNA LET YOU GO. DON'T YOU JUST WANT TO STAY HERE ALL DAY?
YEAH... BUT...
I'M NOT GONNA LET YOU GO...

YOU CAN ASK ME

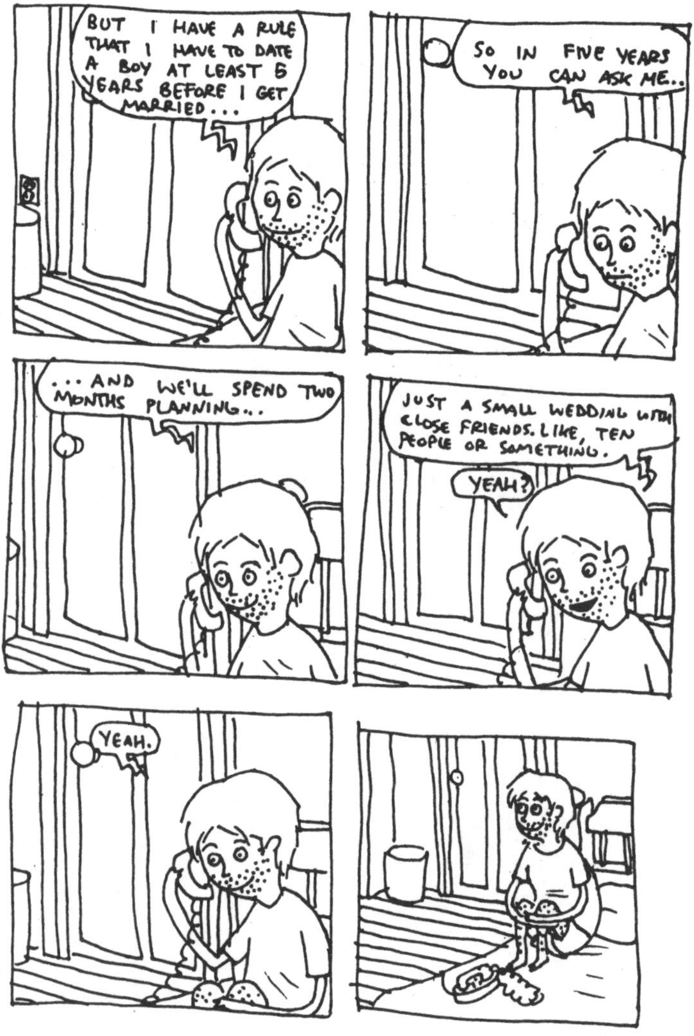
BUT I HAVE A RULE THAT I HAVE TO DATE A BOY AT LEAST 5 YEARS BEFORE I GET MARRIED...
SO IN FIVE YEARS YOU CAN ASK ME..
...AND WE'LL SPEND TWO MONTHS PLANNING..
JUST A SMALL WEDDING WITH CLOSE FRIENDS. LIKE, TEN PEOPLE OR SOMETHING.
YEAH?
YEAH.